£4.99
6.8

CW01630963

WIT & HUMOUR IN ANCIENT EGYPT

By the same author:

The Birds of Ancient Egypt
The Animal World of the Pharaohs

WIT & HUMOUR IN ANCIENT EGYPT

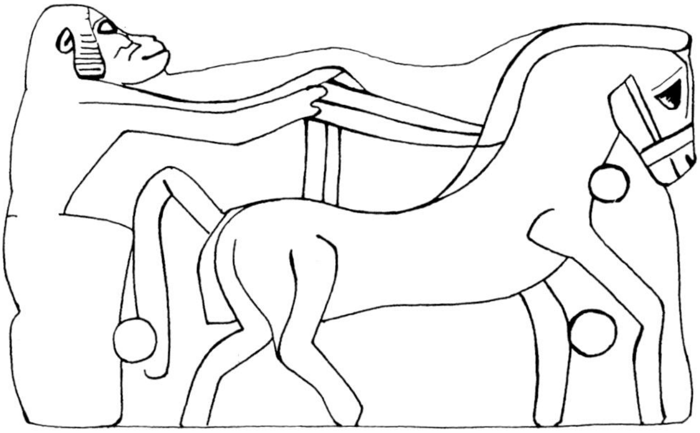

Patrick F. Houlihan

The Rubicon Press

The Rubicon Press
57 Cornwall Gardens
London SW7 4BE

British Library Cataloguing-in-Publication Data

A catalogue record for this book is available from the British Library.

ISBN 0-948695-69-2 (hardback edition)
ISBN 0-948695-68-4 (paperback edition)

Designed by Peartree Design, Manchester
Printed and bound in Great Britain by Biddles Limited of
Guildford and King's Lynn

To my son Sean,
thanks for the laughs.

"Those who see the Nile when it surges tremble, the meadows laugh, and the river-banks are inundated. The god's offerings descend, the faces of men are bright, and the hearts of the gods rejoice."

Pyramid Texts (Utterance 581)

"For the rest of time it would symbolize the human race. The psychologists of Venus would analyze its actions and watch its every movement until they could reconstruct its mind. Thousands of books would be written about it. Intricate philosophies would be contrived to account for its behavior. But all this labor, all this research, would be utterly in vain. Perhaps the proud and lonely figure on the screen was smiling sardonically at the scientists who were starting on their age-long fruitless quest. Its secret would be safe as long as the universe endured, for no one now would ever read the lost language of Earth. Millions of times in the ages to come those last few words would flash across the screen, and none could ever guess their meaning: A Walt Disney Production."

Sir Arthur C. Clarke, *History Lesson* (1949)

Table of Contents

Preface

In his 1942 essay covering writing and literature in ancient Egypt for the first edition of *The Legacy of Egypt*, (Sir) Alan H. Gardiner remarked that "It will be news to some readers that the Egyptians had a sense of humour, but such is a fact, as much evidence could be brought to show." Fifty-eight years later, this apt observation will still be news to a great many, even to some readers who already possess a fairly extensive background in the study of pharaonic civilisation. Ancient Egypt's place in the "history of laughter" has received comparatively little attention. In fact, the role of humour in their culture has consistently been undervalued and, occasionally, some serious-minded scholars have even maintained that the Egyptians were devoid of it altogether. Despite this extreme assessment, it must be pointed out that humour is such a fundamental characteristic of human nature, there can be no doubting that the ancient inhabitants of the Nile Valley found certain things funny and delighted in laughing, just like people of other times and places the world over. What's more, the ancient Egyptians were clearly not adverse to expressing what struck them as humorous in their literature and representational art. As Gardiner correctly pointed out above, a wealth of evidence can be brought to bear on this subject. The trick is, of course, being able to identify their light-heartedness after the passing of more than three thousand years, which is not always an easy task. It is complex enough to recognize humour in a culture other than one's own, let alone a distant ancient one.

An aim of this book is to help dispel the view among some in the general public that the ancient Egyptians were a weird lot, a brooding and pessimistic people, obsessed with death and the hereafter, preoccupied with such things as mummy-making and tomb and temple-building. On the contrary, they were ordinary men and women, not gloomy, but cheerful people who loved to laugh and were blessed with a keen sense of humour. As we shall see, traces of their humorous side is pervasive and manifested itself in a considerable range of media. A selection of this material, drawn from an assortment of textual and pictorial sources, is presented in the following pages. For the purposes of this book, humour is here defined in hugely broad terms. It is seen as anything that was intended by its creator in antiquity to produce a smile or a laugh, whether for one's own private pleasure or for a viewing audience. It is very much hoped that by giving some consideration to wit and humour, having a glimpse at some of the ancient Egyptians' jokes and chuckles, and discussing how they enjoyed a hearty laugh, will help in making them seem less remote, perhaps a bit less stoical, acknowledging what they definitely were: human beings.

Patrick F. Houlihan
Santa Rosa, California

April, 2000

Acknowledgments

I should like to express my heartfelt gratitude to all the people who, in any number of ways, have helped me in the preparation of this small volume. Its imperfections are due solely to myself and not in anyway a reflection on those individuals who so kindly answered my numerous queries pertaining to wit and humour in ancient Egypt. Many thanks are also due to various institutions and individuals for generously furnishing information and good photographs, and then granting permission to publish. A more explicit acknowledgment of their courtesy is given in each case in the List of Illustrations. In addition, I would like to express appreciation of special help provided by the following. At an early stage of my study, Dr. Waltraud Guglielmi graciously provided me with off-prints of her important articles dealing with aspects of humour and laughter in ancient Egypt. My indebtedness to her valuable work on these subjects, taken up in diverse publications, will immediately be evident from even a cursory glance through the accompanying notes. Mr Arpag Mekhitarian not only very kindly provided me with a selection of his excellent photographs, but also drew my attention to additional touches of humour in Theban tomb-chapels. My sister, Mrs. Mary Beth Wheeler, read the entire manuscript and provided many useful remarks for its improvement. I gratefully acknowledge the assistance of the Wilbour Library of Egyptology in helping me obtain a number of obscure articles and for doing so in a most timely manner. Further, I would like to offer my thanks to all the comedians at Ridgway, past and present, for helping me keep in excellent humour. My former student, Ms. Kim McInerney, kindly contributed two beautiful line-drawings of figured ostraca. Thanks to Ms. Anthea Page and all the others at The Rubicon Press for including this book in their publishing program. Above all, I thank my wife Susan, for her unfailing encouragement, forbearance, and assistance at every step of this writing project, even if she didn't find much of the material even remotely humorous! And last but not least, it is a pleasure to dedicate this book to my son, a constant source of laughter in my life.

List of Illustrations

91. Figured limestone ostracon. Reproduced from Brunner-Traut 1984a, fig. 25. By courtesy of the author. *Staatliche Sammlung Ägyptischer Kunst, Munich* (ÄS 1540).
92. Figured limestone ostracon. *Museum of Art and Archaeology, University of Missouri – Columbia*, gift of Mr. and Mrs. Donald N. Wilber, Acc. No. 63.6.3, drawing by John Huffstot.
93. Figured limestone ostracon. Reproduced from Brunner-Traut 1984a, fig. 26. By courtesy of the author. *Institut Français D'Archéologie Orientale, Cairo* (IFAO 4010).
94. Figured limestone ostracon. Photograph courtesy of the Medelhavsmuseet, Stockholm. *Medelhavsmuseet, Stockholm* (MM 14 047).
95. Figured limestone ostracon. Photograph © Maurice et Pierre Chuzeville/Musée du Louvre, Paris. *Musée du Louvre, Paris* (E 14368).
96. Figured limestone ostracon. Photograph is copyright IRPA-KIK, Brussels. *Musées Royaux d'Art et d'Histoire, Brussels* (E 6765).
97. Figured limestone ostracon. Photograph is copyright IRPA-KIK, Brussels. *Musées Royaux d'Art et d'Histoire, Brussels* (E 6836).
98. Glazed steatite frog-backed scaraboid with musical donkey on the underside. Photograph © Maurice et Pierre Chuzeville/Musée du Louvre, Paris. *Musée du Louvre, Paris* (AF 6950).
99. Figured limestone ostracon. Reproduced from Curto 1965, fig. 5. By courtesy of the author and the Museo Egizio, Turin. *Museo Egizio, Turin* (N. Suppl. 6299).
100. Figured limestone ostracon. Photograph © Maurice et Pierre Chuzeville/Musée du Louvre, Paris. *Musée du Louvre, Paris* (E 25309).
101. Figured ostracon. Reproduced from Page 1983, no. 48. By courtesy of the author. *Petrie Museum of Egyptian Archaeology, University College London* (UC 15946).
102. Figured limestone ostracon. Photograph © Christian Larrieu/Musée du Louvre, Paris. *Musée du Louvre, Paris* (E 27666).
103. Figured limestone ostracon. Reproduced from Vandier d'Abbadie 1936, pl. 2 no. 2004. © Institut Français d'Archéologie Orientale, Cairo. This piece was at one time in a private collection. Its current whereabouts is not known to me.
104. Figured limestone ostracon. Photograph courtesy of the Ashmolean Museum, Oxford. *Ashmolean Museum, Oxford* (1938.914).
105. Figured limestone ostracon. Reproduced from Vandier d'Abbadie 1936, pl. 4 no. 2036. © Institut Français d'Archéologie Orientale, Cairo. *Musée du Louvre, Paris* (E 14308).
106. Figured limestone ostracon. Photograph is copyright IRPA-KIK, Brussels. *Musées Royaux d'Art et d'Histoire, Brussels* (E 6380).
107. Figured limestone ostracon. Photograph courtesy of the Medelhavsmuseet, Stockholm. *Medelhavsmuseet, Stockholm* (MM 14 052).
108. Figured limestone ostracon. Reproduced from Brunner-Traut 1984a, fig. 14. By courtesy of the author. *Museo Egizio, Turin* (N. Suppl. 6333).
109. Figured limestone ostracon. *Museum of Art and Archaeology, University of Missouri – Columbia*, gift of Mr. and Mrs. Donald N. Wilber, Acc. No. 63.6.7, drawing by John Huffstot.
110. Figured limestone ostracon. Photograph courtesy of the Medelhavsmuseet, Stockholm. *Medelhavsmuseet, Stockholm* (MM 14 059).
111. Figured limestone ostracon. Reproduced from Vandier d'Abbadie 1937, pl. 48 no. 2317. © Institut Français d'Archéologie Orientale, Cairo. *Institut Français d'Archéologie Orientale, Cairo* (IFAO 3508).
112. Figured limestone ostracon. Reproduced from Vandier d'Abbadie 1937, pl. 48 no. 2316. © Institut Français d'Archéologie Orientale, Cairo. *Institut Français d'Archéologie*

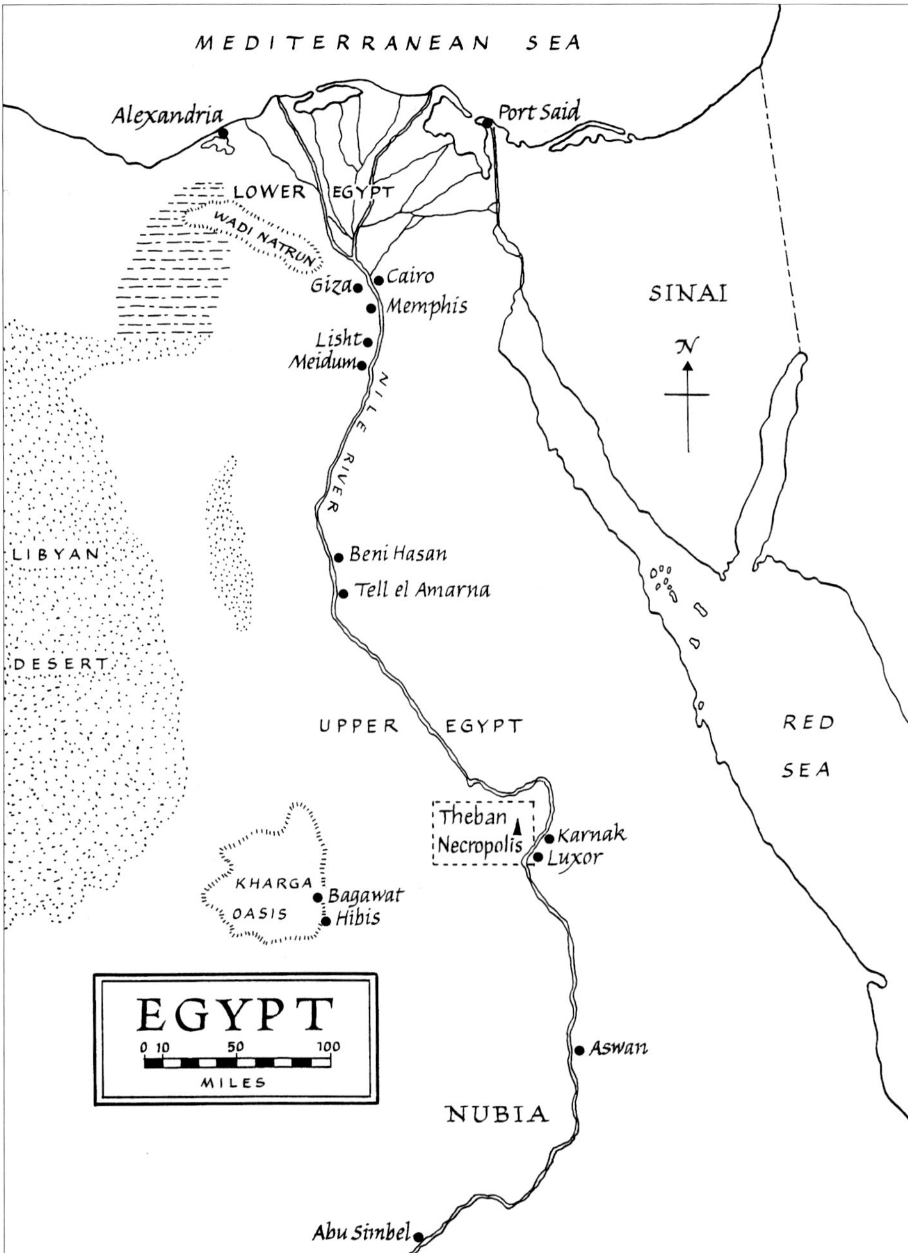

Fig. 1. Map of Egypt.

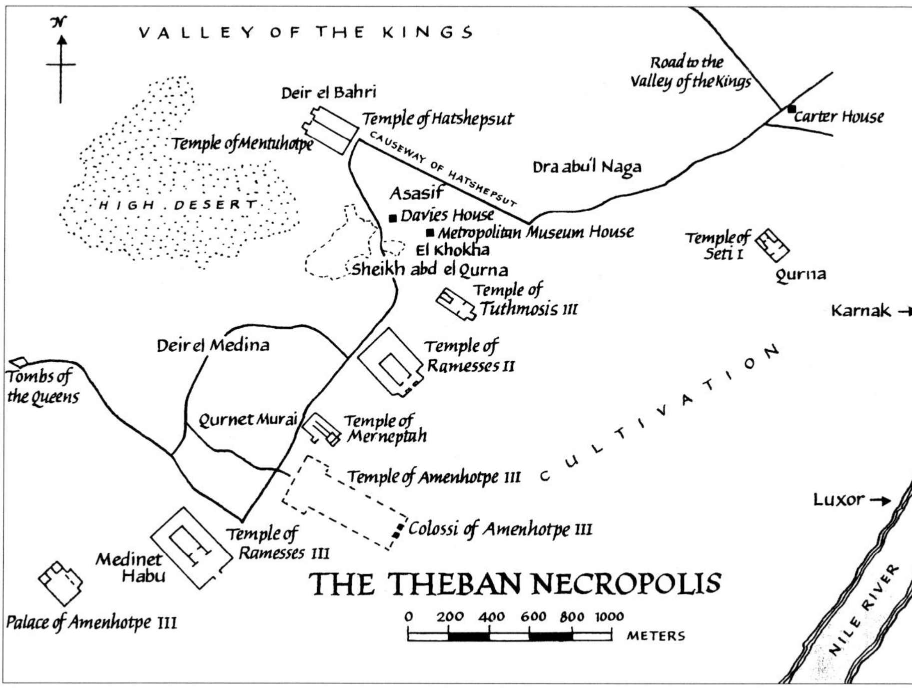

Fig. 2. Map of the Theban Necropolis.

Chronology of Egypt

The ancient dates utilised in this volume generally adhere to the chronological scheme proposed by John Baines and Jaromír Málek in their widely known reference work *Atlas of Ancient Egypt* (Oxford, 1980), pp. 36-37. All dates are BCE (Before Common Era) except where indicated by CE (Common Era), and correspond exactly to the same times in the older tradition of using BC and AD, respectively. Dates before the emergence of Dynasty XXVI (664 BCE) are not necessarily exact and should be considered only approximate. In general, the earlier the date, the less certain it is. The individual monarchs listed below are only those who are mentioned in the pages of this book.

PALEOLITHIC PERIOD	500,000-5500
PREDYNASTIC PERIOD	5500-2920
Badarian	5500-4000
Amratian (Naqada I)	4000-3500
Gerzean (Naqada II)	3500-3000
Dynasty "0" (Naqada III)	3000-2920
EARLY DYNASTIC PERIOD	2920-2649
Dynasty I	2920-2770
Dynasty II	2770-2649
OLD KINGDOM	2649-2134
Dynasty III	2649-2575
Dynasty IV	2575-2465
Snofru	2575-2551
Cheops (Khufu)	2551-2528
Dynasty V	2465-2323
Dynasty VI	2323-2150
Pepy II	2246-2152
Dynasty VII/Dynasty VIII	2150-2134

FIRST INTERMEDIATE PERIOD	2134-2040
Dynasty IX/Dynasty X	2134-2040
Merykare	
Dynasty XI (Theban)	2134-2040
Mentuhotpe	2061-2010
MIDDLE KINGDOM	2040-1640
Dynasty XI (all Egypt)	2040-1991
Mentuhotpe	2061-2010
Dynasty XII	1991-1783
Senwosret (Sesostris) I	1971-1926
Senwosret (Sesostris) II	1897-1878
Dynasty XIII	1783-after 1640
Dynasty XIV	?1675-after 1640
SECOND INTERMEDIATE PERIOD	1640-1532
Dynasty XV (Hyksos)	1640-1532
Apophis	1585-1542
Dynasty XVI (Lesser Hyksos)	1640-1532
Dynasty XVII	1640-1550
Seqenenre Tao II	?1560
NEW KINGDOM	1550-1070
Dynasty XVIII	1550-1307
Amenhotpe I	1525-1504
Tuthmosis III	1479-1425
Hatshepsut (Queen)	1473-1458
Amenhotpe III	1391-1353
Akhenaten (Amenhotpe IV)	1353-1335
Tutankhamen	1333-1323
Horemhab	1319-1307
RAMESSIDE PERIOD	1307-1070
Dynasty XIX	1307-1196
Seti I	1306-1290
Ramesses II	1290-1224
Merneptah	1224-1214
Dynasty XX	1196-1070
Ramesses III	1194-1163
Ramesses V	1156-1151
Ramesses VI	1151-1143

THIRD INTERMEDIATE PERIOD	1070-712
Dynasty XXI	1070-945
Dynasty XXII	945-712
Dynasty XXIII	828-712
Dynasty XXIV (Sais)	724-712
Dynasty XXV (Nubia and Theban area)	770-712
LATE DYNASTIC PERIOD	712-332
Dynasty XXV (Nubia and all Egypt)	712-657
Dynasty XXVI	664-525
Amasis	570-526
Dynasty XXVII (Persian)	525-404
Dynasty XXVIII	404-399
Dynasty XXIX	399-380
Dynasty XXX	380-343
Second Persian Period (Dynasty XXXI)	343-332
GRAECO-ROMAN PERIOD	332 BCE-CE 395
Macedonian Dynasty	332-304
Ptolemaic Period	304-30
Roman Period	30 BCE-CE 395
COPTIC OR BYZANTINE PERIOD	CE 395-640
ARAB PERIOD	CE 640-1517
OTTOMAN PERIOD	CE 1517-1805
REPUBLIC OF EGYPT	CE 1953-present

1 The Egyptian Wit: A Literary Sense of Humour

The ancient Egyptians' sense of humour was manifested in a wide range of media. Some of what made them laugh is clearly evident, as we shall see later in this book, in private tomb-chapel decoration and illustrations on papyri and figured ostraca. It is perhaps less well-known that written materials were also a vehicle to entertain and evoke laughter. This chapter briefly surveys the highlights of wit and humour in Egyptian texts, primarily from their literature. It is not always possible, however, to be altogether certain what it was in Egyptian tales that induced smiles in ancient audiences. Aspects of these works that may seem light-hearted today may not have been intended as amusement, thus we must be on guard not to read humour into them. It is likewise true that passages that were meant to be uproarious in nature might now be missed and thought of as quite serious. Visual pharaonic humour is frequently more immediately grasped than are the subtleties of its textual counterpart. Humour is often quite difficult to recognise in a language that remains imperfectly known and is as remote from ourselves as the ancient Egyptians. Mindful of this basic problem, and even when exercising the appropriate caution, there are a considerable number of examples that can be confidently described as having deliberately been composed for comic effect. A few pieces of Egyptian literature, such as the burlesqued episodes in the New Kingdom mythological *The Contendings of Horus and Seth*, plainly exhibit a rich vein of humour. The ancient Egyptians undoubtedly chuckled at writing that employed wit, satire, word-plays, irony, puns, metaphors, similes, and other sophisticated literary devices.[1] Humour played a variety of roles in ancient Egyptian texts.

It seems only befitting to begin our discussion of humour with a rare instance of an actual joke to have survived from ancient Egypt. It appears in a Dynasty XX letter penned by Dhutmose (nicknamed Tjaroy), a scribe from the community of royal tomb-builders at Deir el Medina, situated on the western bank of Thebes near the Valley of the Kings, a village we will have occasion to say much more about later (see Chapter 3). In his letter, Dhutmose reveals himself to be a bit of a waggish character. He laments having told a joke to the chief tax master that apparently went over quite wrongly, but then proceeds to relate another:

"I've heard that you are angry and that you have caused me to be maligned through slander on account of that joke which I told the chief taxing master in that letter, although it was Henuttowy (his wife) who had urged me to tell him some jokes in my letter. You are just like the wife blind in one eye who had been married to a man for twenty years, and when he found another woman he said to her, 'I shall divorce you because you are said to be blind in one eye.' And she answered him, 'Have you just discovered that after twenty years of our marriage?' Such am I and such is my joking with you..."[2]

Other humorous turns are occasionally encountered in letters penned by the inhabitants of Deir el Medina.[3] In Dynasty XIX, the draughtsman Prehotpe wrote to his superior a very harsh message that also appears to contain, at least to the modern eye, an appreciable element of joking:

"The draughtsman Prehotpe communicates to his superior, the scribe Kenhikhopeshef: In life, prosperity and health! What's the meaning of this negative attitude that you are adopting toward me? I'm like a donkey to you. If there is work, bring the donkey! And if there is fodder, bring the ox! If there is beer, you never ask for me. Only if there is work (to be done), will you ask for me!"[4]

Going back to a curious Middle Kingdom epistolary work from El Lahun, an author has acidly written to a minor official by the name of Pepy concerning the news of his safe return. It is also accompanied by the correspondent's scathingly sarcastic reply to it. The polite standard letter-writing formulae have been deliberately altered in both so that the entire composition has taken on an amusing offbeat tone of an angry exchange between the writers. For instance, the appropriate closing of a conventional letter would be, "May your hearing be good," but it is parodied as "Bad be your hearing." Here is the entire document:

"A communication of the effect that I, your humble servant, have been told that the lord, life, prosperity and health, reached the mortuary temple 'Powerful is Senwosret (II), the deceased,' in the fourth month of the third season, day 10. How bad it is that you arrived safe and sound! *(Reply)*: It is only all manner of evil that you utter. In the favour of Sobek, lord of Rosehwy, who shall put you into the caldron, and in the favour of his Ka! May action be taken for the benefit of the dean of the temple of Heket, Pepy, against you so as to be lasting and enduring forever and ever. Bad be your hearing – a plague upon you! *(Postscript)*: Come that I may see you. See, we will have a bad time."[5]

The most renowned of such letters was one not actually intended to ever be sent, but takes the form of a popular Dynasty XIX epistolary schoolboy exercise, entitled *The Satirical Letter*, from Papyrus Anastasi I, which was also admired as a literary composition.[6] In this lengthy work of fiction, the scribe Hori mockingly interrogates his colleague, the unskilful scribe Amenemope, on his knowledge of various specific topics, such as Syro-Canaanite geography, mathematical problems, and military matters. While this model letter was designed to teach, for instance, to familiarise apprentice scribes with a wide range of technical terms and many foreign words, its light-hearted passages and mordant wit must have brightened up many a student struggling with this challenging, but entertaining lesson.[7]

One section of this polemical letter includes several laughable descriptions of scribes and minor officials, clearly written in the spirit of comical exaggeration and caricature.[8] The audience is introduced to Roy:

> "Come, let me describe to you the way of the scribe Roy, dubbed the firebrand of the granary. He neither budged nor stirred since his birth. Strenuous work was an abomination to him, and he never became acquainted with it… Let me tell you about Paherypedjet, who used to live in Heliopolis. He is a veteran of the Palace. He is smaller than a cat but bigger than a monkey, yet he is well-off in his home having his property in his possession… Have you heard the name of Kyky, the dust ball? It is unnoticed that he moves over the ground, dishevelled in attire and tightly girt. If you were to see him at evening in the dark, you would think that he was a bird passing by. Put him on the scales and see how heavy he is! He will weigh for you twenty *deben* (not quite 4 pounds), excluding rags. If you should exhale close to him as he passes by, like a leaf of foliage he will drop down far away."[9]

Elsewhere in *The Satirical Letter* is a greatly exaggerated account of the hardships and risks suffered by an army scribe, cast in the role of a would-be soldier or charioteer, on an incredibly bungled military mission in western Asia. At the Canaanite city of Joppa (modern Jaffa), he has a sexual encounter with a local woman, but even with this there are problems:

> "You are a Maher-warrior who is experienced in heroic deeds!... The narrow pass is dangerous having Shasu-Beduin concealed beneath the bushes, some of whom are four cubits or five cubits from their nose to foot (giants, around 7 to 9 feet tall!) and have fierce faces. They are unfriendly and do not take to cajolery while you are alone having no aide with you nor soldiery backing you up. You find no scout to prepare safe passage for you. You reach a decision by forging ahead ignorant of the road. Such bristling fright grips you that the hair of your head is ruffled. Your *Ba* lies in your hands. Your path is filled with boulders and small stones without a toe hold for passage, as it is overgrown with reeds and thorns, brambles, and 'wolf's-paw'. The declivities lie to one side of you, and the mountain rises on the other side of you. With your chariot lying on its side, you move along swerving to and fro afraid to pursue your horses.... You are disgusted and get set to trot off. The sky is now clear, but you imagine that the enemy is behind you, and trembling grips you. If only you had a hedge of shrubbery to put on the other side! The team is exhausted by the time you locate a camping spot. You have undergone a miserable experience. You have now entered Joppa and find the meadowland verdant in its season. You force your way in because of appetite and encounter the beautiful maiden who is tending the vineyards. She allures you to herself to be a partner in love and surrenders to you the flesh of her bosom. You are recognised as soon as you have uttered advice.[10] So judgement is rendered against a Maher-warrior, and you must sell your tunic of fine thin linen. Tell me how you can go to sleep each evening with only a piece of sackcloth over you. You slumber only because you are so exhausted. A poltroon takes away your bow, your girdle-dagger, and your pair of quivers. Your reins have been severed in the darkness, and your team goes off picking up speed over the slippery terrain as the road extends ahead of it. It smashes your chariot and makes your leather canteens fall to the ground and (they) are buried in the sand. They become part of the dry earth. Your aide begs for bread for your mouth, 'Now that I have safely arrived, you people should give a bit of food and water.' But they play deaf and do not hearken. They take no notice of your accounts."[11]

In the conclusion of the letter, during the course of a sarcastic assault on his correspondent's scribal abilities, Hori comically compares the lack of clarity in Amenemope's writing with the evidently marked dialectical differences that existed in ancient Egypt between its northern and southern boundaries. The humorist writes:

> "Your discourses are collected on my tongue and remain fixed on my lips, for they are so confused when heard that no interpreter can unravel them. They are like a Delta man's conversation with a man of Elephantine."[12]

In quite another vein altogether is the royal letter written by the boy-king Pepy II of Dynasty VI to the expedition leader Harkhuf concerning his eager anticipation to view the dancing pygmy that was being brought to him as a gift from the subtropical southern lands. Harkhuf proudly had a copy of this now famous letter incorporated into his funerary autobiography on the façade of his tomb-chapel (A 8) at Qubbet el Hawa (Aswan). It is full of picturesque charm and may well have been relished by passers-by for its pleasing good-natured humour about the young monarch's excitement for seeing this exotic wonder:

> "Come north to the residence at once! Hurry and bring with you this pygmy who you brought from the land of the horizon-dwellers live, hale, and healthy, for the dances of the god, to gladden the heart... When he goes down with you into the ship, get worthy men to be around him on deck, lest he fall into the water! When he lies down at night, get worthy men to lie around him in his tent. Inspect ten times at night! My majesty desires to see this pygmy more than the gifts of the mine-land (Sinai) and of Punt! When you arrive at the residence and this pygmy is with you live, hale, and healthy, my majesty will do great things for you..."[13]

Flashes of humour in Egyptian texts are also detectable in unexpected sources. Take, for example, during the construction the Dynasty XVIII tomb of the famed courtier Senenmut (TT 71) at Thebes, when a passing scribe or a workman on the job jotted down on an ostracon (a flake of limestone) a brief satirical poem about the work underway. It wryly notes that "more numerous are those who are in charge (of it) than the fruits of the persea tree!"[14] It was then tossed into the rubble after the amusement had passed. Again, in the Rhind Mathematical Papyrus of the Middle Kingdom, in the British Museum, London, there is a droll nursery rhyme problem for students to solve involving "7 houses, 49 cats, 343 mice, 2401 ears of spelt, and 16807 *hekat* of grain", which is based on a progression of (7x7x7x7x7)[15], while in another example, an apparently overly servile Dynasty XI official ironically praises himself on a stela in the following manner: "I was like a dog, which sleeps in the tent, a hound of the bed, beloved by his mistress."[16] Although this description may strike us moderns as rather playfully put, it is impossible to say with certainty

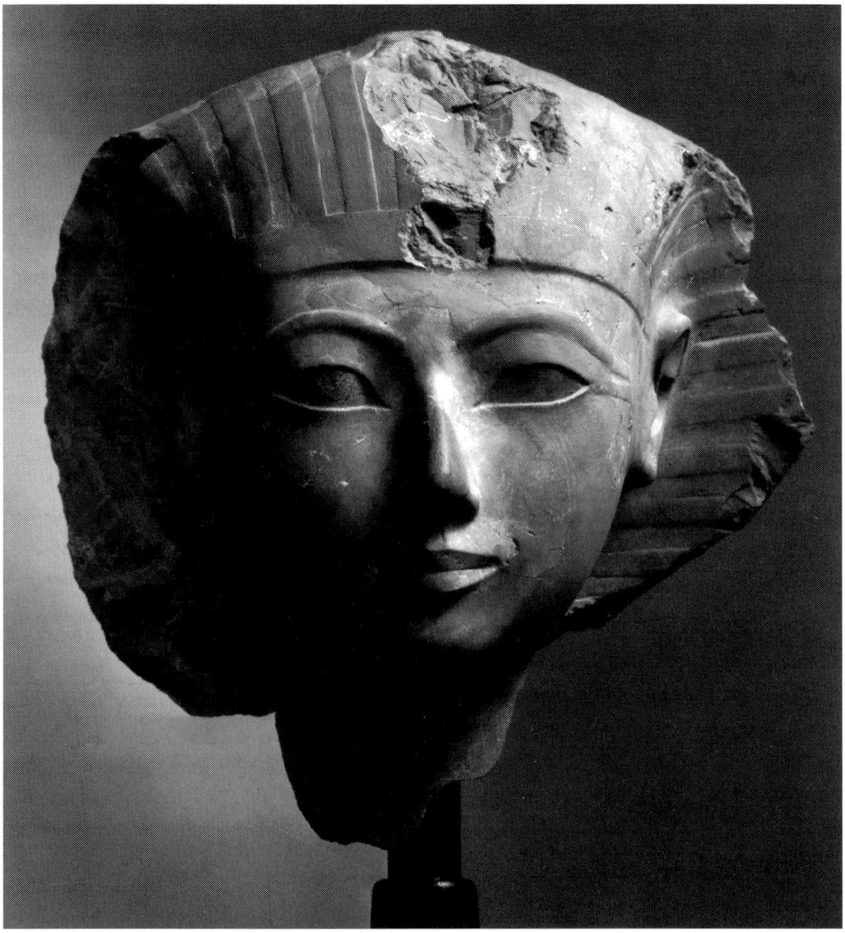

Fig. 3. Indurated limestone head of Queen Hatshepsut; detail from a seated statue of the female pharaoh from her mortuary temple at Deir el Bahri. She is portrayed with youthful feminine features. Her lips are drawn up in a pleasant, gentle smile. Dynasty XVIII.

whether pharaonic Egyptians would have shared this amusing perception of it or not. Visual puns, sometimes elegantly witty, were composed by scribes in otherwise formulaic inscriptions with figurative hieroglyphs or cryptography: the intentional writing of words, such as kings' and gods' names, in a very creative or puzzling form. The purpose of these writings was to attract the interest of the viewer into reading the text in which they appeared.[17] This practice reached its enigmatic height on the walls of certain temples in the Graeco-Roman Period. In the temple of the ram-headed god Khnum at Esna, there are official hymns written to him almost entirely executed with hieroglyphs of rams, another with crocodiles. It is also possible that the Egyptians may have derived an element of comedic enjoyment from the contemptuous characterisations heaped upon their foreign enemies.[18] For instance, in *The Teaching for King Merykare*, dating from the time of the turbulent First Intermediate Period, Asiatics are derogatorily described:

> "Lo, the miserable Asiatic, he is wretched because of the place he's in: short of water, bare of wood, its paths are many and painful because of mountains. He does not dwell in one place, food propels his legs, he fights since the time of Horus, not conquering nor being conquered, he does not announce the day of combat, like a thief who darts about a group... The Asiatic is a crocodile on its shore, it snatches from a lonely road, it cannot seize from a populous town."[19]

Beyond the evidence in letters, another genre of Egyptian prose exhibiting humour is the narrative. We start with the classic story entitled *The Tale of Sinuhe*, widely considered to be the masterpiece among the numerous compositions to have come down to us from the golden age of literature during the Middle Kingdom.[20] Many centuries afterwards, it was still frequently copied by boys preparing for the scribal profession and remains appealing even today. This wonderfully-told and adventure-packed autobiographical-like story contains several scenes which were likely to have been adored by audiences for their beguiling charm. During the course of his long, self-imposed exile in western Asia, the protagonist Sinuhe is provoked into an armed combat with a great Canaanite strong man, reminiscent of the Biblical account of David and Goliath, whom he ironically slays with his own axe. Upon doing so, the Egyptian hero wittily, but laconically, states that: "What he had meant to do to me, I did to him."[21] After many years, a letter from King Senwosret I pardons him, which allows him to return to his beloved Egypt. Still clad in his outlandish Asiatic garb and bearded, Sinuhe's reception before the disbelieving royal family in the great hall of the palace is full of cheerful humour.[22] It could very well have been the most popular point of this captivating narrative:

> "Then the royal daughters were brought in, and his majesty said to the queen, 'Here is Sinuhe, come as an Asiatic, a product of nomads!' She uttered a very great cry, and the royal daughters shrieked all together. They said to his majesty, 'Is it really he, O king, our lord?' Said his majesty, 'It is really he!'"[23]

In a subsequent passage, Sinuhe's delightful description of the transforming effects of his toilet may have brought grins to the faces of generations of ancient Egyptians.[24] He observes that:

> "I was shaved; my hair was combed. Thus was my squalor returned to the foreign land, my dress to the Sand-farers. I was clothed in fine linen; I was anointed with fine oil. I slept on a bed. I had returned the sand to those who dwell in it, the tree-oil to those who grease themselves with it."[25]

Moments of a quieter humour are evident in the delightful Middle Kingdom narrative *The Tale of King Cheops' Court.*[26] Its cycle of stories about marvels, which are set in various Old Kingdom courts, are told to King Cheops by his sons. In one of them, we meet a legendary magician by the name of Djedi. This venerable long-lived character possessed an extraordinarily voracious appetite and was capable of truly miraculous deeds. We learn that:

> "He is a commoner, a hundred and ten years old. He eats five hundred loaves of bread, a shoulder of an ox for meat, and also drinks a hundred jars of beer, up to this day. He knows how to rejoin a severed head. He knows how to make a lion walk behind him with its leash on the ground."

When Cheops' son, prince Hordedef, ventured out to seek the sage,

> "He found him lying on a mat, on the threshold of his (porch), with a servant holding his head, rubbing it for him, and another massaging his feet. Then prince Hordedef said, 'Your condition is like living before old age – though age is the time of death, the time of burial, the time of joining the earth – sleeping until dawn, free from illness, without the hacking of a cough. Here are greetings for a blessed one!"[27]

These passages not only serve to introduce Djedi, but provide an amusing image of an extremely old man, who has reached the Egyptians' ideal lifetime of one hundred and ten years, but who is still vigorous and in good heath, and is capable of enjoying a massage. Nor has his advanced age seem to have effected his remarkable daily caloric intake ![28]

The real chuckles in *The Tale of King Cheops' Court* may have come from the erotic episodes, one involving an adulterous wife and her lover, a second involving a group of young women rowing King Snofru's boat. Another Middle Kingdom story entitled *The Tale of King Neferkare and General Sasenet*, has an intriguing plot revolving around a king's clandestine homosexual affair with one of his generals. This shockingly irreverent narrative may have evoked laughter through the loss of royal dignity. These and other humorous sexual incidents encountered in Egyptian literature are discussed elsewhere in this book (see Chapter 4).

The final line of the Dynasty XII marvellous adventure story, *The Tale of the Shipwrecked Sailor*, takes the form of a proverbial question, bringing the work to an abrupt end: "Who gives water at dawn to a goose that will be slaughtered in the morning?"[29] This use of grim or "gallows" humour to conclude the story seems to be a device of ironical intent.[30]

Turning to the New Kingdom narratives, in the unfortunately fragmentary work *The Tale of Apopis and Seqenenre*, there seems to be a decided element of humour in the preposterous and insulting complaint of Apopis, the Hyksos ruler residing at Avaris in the eastern Nile Delta.[31] He sent a message to his rival King Seqenenre at Thebes, far to the south, that the bellowing of hippopotamuses there was disturbing his sleep: "They don't let sleep come to me either in the daytime or at night." His hearing must have been nothing less than divinely acute, of course, since this is a distance of some four hundred miles away! At this point, the text breaks away, but we may imagine it continuing to include Seqenenre's sharply worded reply, couched in terms of a similarly absurd riposte.[32] This tall story appears to be the stuff of a popular folk-tale, rather than an accurate historical reflection of the causes leading to the war to expel the Hyksos from Egyptian soil.

Set against the Syrian wars of the great Dynasty XVIII warrior-pharaoh Tuthmosis III, the fantastic tale *The Capture of Joppa* concerns the taking of the rebellious Canaanite city of Joppa by Egyptian military forces under the hero general Djehuty.[33] The narrative includes a splendid ruse, not unlike the Trojan Horse in the *Iliad* or the jars of Ali Baba and the Forty Thieves in *One Thousand and One Arabian Nights*. In this yarn, 200 well-armed Egyptian soldiers, hidden in enormous baskets, which supposedly contain tribute, are secretly smuggled into the strategic port-city in order to seize it. While not humorous *per se*, this rousing piece of historical fiction of war abroad, and featuring a bold and clever stratagem, was likely to have been told and retold, continually entertaining and lighting up smiles on audiences.[34]

The misadventures of a lone official from the temple of Amen at Thebes, travelling to far-off Byblos in Phoenicia to purchase timber for the processional barque of the god, are described in an amusing and lively manner in the story *The Report of Wenamun*.[35] This gem of pharaonic literature takes the shape of an official report, written in a factual style, but the account contains numerous elements of dark humour, especially evident in its rich use of irony.[36] Set in the closing years of Dynasty XX, the protagonist Wenamun's mission is rife with bad luck and failures right from the start. He is robbed while *en route* to Byblos, and even on his journey home upon procuring the cedar logs, only after protracted haggling with the local prince, the poor hero is nearly killed by a mob at Alasiya, probably in Cyprus. At one point, after he gets to Byblos, he sits on the shore for twenty-nine days without being allowed even an audience with the prince, who humiliatingly orders him daily to "Leave my harbour!" Whereas *The Tale of Sinuhe* is a story of personal triumphs in western Asia, against a backdrop of Egyptian power and prestige, *The Report of Wenamun* is one of haplessness and ridicules the loss of Egypt's might and influence abroad.[37]

Other literary examples of humour are afforded in mythological tales from the New Kingdom. A burlesque characterisation of the divine actors is revealed in *The Story of Isis and Re.*[38] In this tale, the goddess Isis cunningly plotted to learn the secret name of the aged and feeble sun-god Re, in order to obtain this power for herself. To this end, she made a snake that bit the highest of the gods, and in order to be alleviated from the fiery pain, he told her what she sought to know. While it may be easy for us to see such behaviours as a bit comical, it is much less certain that the ancient Egyptians did, particularly since this tale is preserved in a magical text.[39] The truth is we just do not know.

We are on considerably firmer ground seeing conspicuous humorous intent behind the delightful farce *The Contendings of Horus and Seth*, which dates from Dynasty XIX.[40] Its comedic sexual escapades are dealt with later on (see Chapter 4), but this, the bawdiest of ancient Egyptian tales, includes other mythological material that was meant to encourage laughter.[41] Set in the world of the gods, the narrative revolves around the struggle of Horus and Seth for the succession to the throne of Osiris and the right to rule Egypt. It takes the form of a court trial, with the two rival gods as the litigants, who state their arguments and engage in combat, and Re-Harakhty, the sun-god, as the presiding judge. The cast of divine characters is treated in a rather caricatured fashion. There is little of the majestic dignity in the Egyptian pantheon that we are accustomed to seeing from traditional sources. One of the episodic adventures is devoted to a ludicrous nautical contest, when Seth proposed that he and Horus race one another in "ships of stone" to settle their feud. However, Horus proved to be a trickster of sorts.[42] Under the cover of darkness, so as to ensure secrecy, he built himself a ship of wood and then plastered it over with gypsum. Seth saw Horus' vessel and thought it was, of course, made of solid stone and then:

> "He went to the mountain, cut off a mountain peak, and built himself a ship of stone of 138 cubits (over 230 feet). Then they went into their ships in the presence of the Ennead. Thereupon the ship of Seth sank in the water."[43]

Seth is made to look thoroughly foolish.

Earlier in the story, the goddess Isis also uses trickery against Seth on two occasions. In one ruse, she disguises herself as a sexually desirable girl and, by using a clever play on words, is able to deceive Seth into proclaiming judgement on himself and validating the claim of his nephew, Horus.[44] Later, during Horus and Seth's battle as hippopotami, Isis comes off as rather fickle, when she inadvertently harpoons her son Horus, whom she is attempting to assist, only then to have second thoughts about attacking her brother Seth on behalf of Horus. Needless to say, Horus is furious with his mother for this and proceeds to lop her head off and carries it away. Such are the subtle ways of the gods conveyed here! The concluding scenes of *The Contendings of Horus and Seth* have a pronounced satirical tone to them and feature two of Egypt's most important and powerful deities penning highly insulting letters to each other. Re-Harakhty writes to Osiris, who is associated with the resurgence of vegetation, that: "If you had not existed, if you had not been born, barley and emmer would yet exist!" Osiris responds to the sun-god with caustic derision, accusing him that he has allowed justice to be neglected in his court: "Maat has been made to sink into the netherworld!"[45] But in the end, Horus is rightfully awarded the throne of his father, Osiris.

Turning for a moment to Egyptian narratives of demotic literature, the everyday script of the Late Dynastic and Graeco-Roman Periods, we draw attention to the story of *Setne Khamwas and Naneferkaptah (Setne I)*, from the Ptolemaic Period.[46] There is an amusing incident where the princess Ahwere declares that she wants to marry her elder brother, prince Naneferaptah, with whom she is in love. However, her father, the king of Egypt, wants his only two children to be wed into the families of his generals, so his family may increase in size. Her humorous reply to her father, in which she pertly mimics the king's wishes for his children's marital plans, wins him over to her desire: "I laughed and pharaoh laughed." She was then allowed to marry her brother.

There is also a fragment of a demotic tale of Ptolemaic date, only the beginning of which has been preserved, entitled *King Amasis and the Skipper*. It portrays Amasis of Dynasty XXVI as a drunkard and a debaucher. While we cannot be absolutely certain, there seems to have been a measure of comedic intent behind this yarn, even if it took a more serious turn later on.[47] The famous Greek traveller and historian Herodotus, who visited Egypt round 450 BCE, a century after the time of Amasis, recounts similar folk-stories regarding this monarch's alleged unsavoury personal characteristics.[48]

In addition to epistolary exercises for training schoolboys in the art of letter-writing, teachers in ancient Egypt introduced into their scribal curriculums an assortment of didactic material that addressed the development of personal character and correct social behaviour. The literary "satire" is amply attested within these wisdom (instructional) texts. By utilising elements of humour, parody and caricature, a favourite theme of the authors who made up these varied writings was the glorification of the scribal profession, by wittily pouring scorn on all other vocations.[49] The Middle Kingdom schoolroom classic, *The Teaching of Khety*, also widely known as *The Satire on the Trades*, was an exceedingly popular school-text for scribes learning to write during the late New Kingdom.[50] This work treats a considerable variety of menial occupations in disparaging and exaggerated terms, almost to the point of being grotesque, producing grim humour and mischievous wit. It is set within the frame of advice and precepts from a wise father to his young son, who is being taken to the capital to begin his scribal training, about the proper ways of the world. Some of the vignettes are as follows:

> "But I have seen the metalworker at his labour at the mouth of his furnace, with his fingers like a crocodile's, and stinking more than fish roe... The reed-cutter goes north to the Delta, to carry off arrows for himself; he has done more than his arms can do, the mosquitoes have killed him, and the sandflies have butchered him, so that he is cut to pieces... And the maker of pots is under earth, though standing up with the living. He grubs in the meadows more than pigs do, to fire his pottery, and his clothes are stiff with mud, and his loincloth in rags... The sandal-maker is very badly off, under his vats for eternity. He's well – as well as a corpse, chewing on hides!... And the washerman washes on the riverbank, and he is near to the crocodile. 'Father, come out of the flowing water!' say his son and daughter. This is no profession that anyone can be content in, more so than any other profession; his food is mixed with shit, and no part of him is clean. He puts himself to the underskirts of a woman who is in her period; he weeps, spending the day at the washing board. The washing stone is by him; he is told, 'Here's dirty clothes! Get over here!' and the edge sinks under their weight."[51]

While one might be able to envision scribal pupils chuckling their way through these copying lessons, at the very same time, these hyperbolic characterisations of the hardships of the uneducated and illiterate probably had a cold sobering effect on students too. It was only through their studies, leading to jobs as professional scribes and bureaucrats, that such miseries in their own lives would be prevented. There is an iconographic counterpart to these mocking literary images in the depiction of lowly labourers in the reliefs and paintings of daily life decorating the walls of tomb-chapels belonging to the élite from early times (see Chapter 2).

During the New Kingdom, *The Teaching of Khety* was the model for many scholastic imitators along these same lines. One of the characteristic features of these miscellany texts is the theme of unstinting praise for the scribal craft, to the ridicule of other careers.[52] Perhaps not surprisingly, the dreams of young men for an adventurous life as a soldier resulted in this profession coming under particular fire from schoolmasters' pens. Some of these compositions are not without a trace of over-the-top hilarity in their sneering condemnation:

> "What is this that you say, so it is reported, 'The soldier's calling is pleasanter than the scribe's'? Come, let me describe to you the condition of the soldier, that much tormented one. He is taken when yet a child to be imprisoned in a barrack. A searing blow is dealt his body, a rending blow is dealt his eyebrows. His head is spilt open with a wound. He is laid down and beaten like papyrus and battered with castigation. Come, let me describe to you his going to Khor, and concerning his marching upon the hills. His bread and his water are upon his shoulder like the load of an ass, his neck having formed a ridge like that of an ass. The vertebrae of his back are broken whilst he drinks of smelly water and halts only to keep watch. He reaches the battle: he is like a plucked bird. He proceeds to return to Egypt: he is like a stick which the worm has eaten. He is ill, prostration takes hold of him: he is brought back upon the ass, his clothes removed through theft, his attendant run away. Scribe Inena, turn back from the proposition that the soldier's calling is pleasanter than the scribe's."[53]

Budding apprentice scribes would be required to tediously copy out short exercises like this one, which decries all employment save, naturally, that of the scribe:

> "Be a scribe. It saves you from toil and protects you from all manner of work. It spares you bearing hoe and mattock, so that you do not carry a basket. It sunders you from plying the oar and spares you torment, as you are not under many lords and numerous masters. Man comes forth from his mother's womb and runs to his master: the child is in the service of a soldier, the stripling is a skirmisher. The old man is put to be a cultivator, and the grown man to be a soldier. The lame is put to be a doorkeeper, and the blind to be a fattener of cattle. The bird-catcher goes onto the threshing platform, and the

> fisherman sinks into the water. The prophet stands as a tenant-farmer. The priest performs the service, and spends the time – there being three services daily – soaking himself in the river: he does not distinguish between winter and summer, nor whether the sky be windy and rainy. No sooner the stable-master stands still in the toil than his horse-team is abandoned in the field; and whilst barley is doled out to the wife, his daughter is in the dyke, maid-servant being in the hired gang and his retainer in Troia. The baker regularly bakes and puts bread onto the fire, his head being inside the oven and his son holding fast his feet. In the event of slipping from his son's hand he thereby falls down into the oven's bottom. But the scribe, he is ahead of all manner of work in this world."[54]

Demotic wisdom (instructional) literature contains a fair amount that is humorous in tone.[55] In compositions such as *The Teaching of Ankhsheshonq* and *The Teaching of Papyrus Insinger*, the sayings are expounded in the form of brief, easily-remembered maxims and proverbs. Some of these "one-liners" are quite amusing and this feeling may well have been accentuated by a rapid, one-right-after-another, style of oral presentation to audiences. Among the diverse topics touched upon are witty sayings pertaining to human sexual relationships (see Chapter 4). A flavour of the popular light-hearted wisdom in *The Teaching of Ankhsheshonq* can be had from the sage's advice on such areas as: "He who sends spittle up to the sky will have it fall on him"; "When a man smells of myrrh his wife is a cat before him"; "When a man is suffering his wife is a lioness before him"; "Do not speak of pharaoh's business when drinking beer"; "A slip of the tongue in the royal palace is a slip of the helm at sea"; and finally, the very practical "Yesterday's drunkenness does not quench today's thirst."[56]

2 Smiling for Eternity: Humour in Tomb-chapel and Temple Decoration

Much of the evidence that the pharaonic Egyptians have left us comes from funerary and religious contexts, especially the iconography of tomb-chapel decoration, where conspicuous instances of humour may seem inappropriate or strangely out of place to those in modern Westernised societies. The ancient Egyptians, however, had different attitudes toward death and the afterlife, which allowed the inclusion of a range of comical and light-hearted details on the walls of these monuments. Such vignettes were presumably represented with the approval and satisfaction of the tomb-owners who, quite likely, would have taken delight in them. They also probably had the effect of raising broad grins across the faces of keen-witted visitors to the tomb-chapel to say a prayer or leave an offering on behalf of the deceased. Some can still coax smiles from visitors even today. These artistic expressions were drawn from the joys and pleasures of life on this earth and, through the magical power that lies dormant in picture and word, it was hoped that these fleeting moments of comedy would be perpetuated for all eternity. For this reason, laughter in tomb-chapels was not incongruous or impiously offensive, but was a much-appreciated, if not an integral, addition.

These elements of hilarity are usually found in the painted carved reliefs and wall-paintings depicting aspects of everyday life along the Nile, a common theme recorded in private tombs of the élite during most periods. The scenes provide glimpses of the ideal world in which the blessed dead wished to dwell. While they may have been dimly-lit places, the ambience of an ancient Egyptian tomb-chapel was not a gloomy or lifeless one.[1] Well-to-do citizens can be seen attending lavish banquets, really more like drinking parties, with scantily clad dancing girls and orchestras filling the air with music. There are compositions of desert hunting and fowling in the swamplands. The pursuits and activities of the peasantry and lower orders abound. Labourers with their distinguishing rough, unkempt appearances sing and cheerfully banter with each other in fields and vineyards, on the river, and in the dense papyrus swamps. Skilled craftsmen do the same in their various workshops. Herdsmen and field hands must often contend with stubborn or defiant beasts and shout exhortations at them. Wild and domestic creatures are pictured gambolling

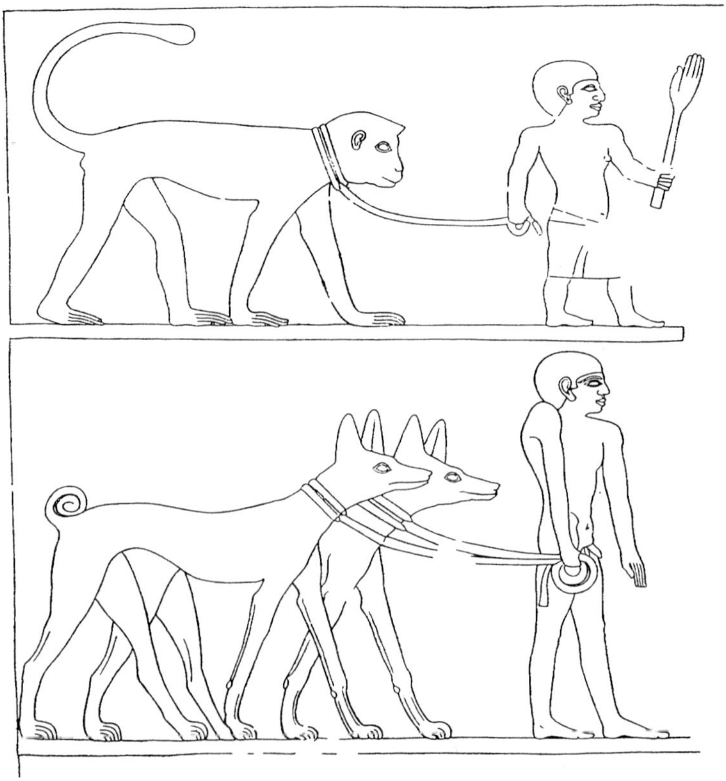

Fig. 4. Drawing of a painted relief from the tomb-chapel of Ti (D 22) at Saqqara, portraying the deceased's retainers bringing his pets. In the upper register, an achondroplastic dwarf, carrying a small truncheon, leads Ti's monkey. Below, a hunchbacked man is walking a pair of dogs on leashes. Dynasty V.

about or engaging in all manner of puckish horseplay. Retainers can unexpectedly express quips or complaints as they prepare food and drink for the funerary feasts of their masters. In this chapter, we will examine a selection of this charming and endearing human material and, to a lesser degree, a few of the humorous touches that occasionally can be observed depicted on the walls of grand state temples.[2]

The Egyptians were tremendous pet-fanciers and tomb-chapels of the élite contain a rich pictorial record of their varied pet-keeping practices. Scenes on these sepulchres routinely contain images of beloved household creatures close to their masters' sides. They are usually to be found sitting beneath the tomb-owners' chair or kept on leashes being tended by their minders who, during the Old and Middle Kingdoms, were often men suffering from physical abnormalities (figs. 4 and 12). People fervently hoped that they would be able to continue to enjoy the companionship and warmth of their close favourites in the Beyond. From Dynasty IV onwards, pet animals are also repeatedly portrayed, chiefly monkeys, hilariously cavorting in mischievous shenanigans and aping human behaviour (figs. 5-12). These were very likely regarded as just as delightful and entertaining in antiquity as they strike us nowadays. It is in playful images such as these that we find the earliest and some of the most striking evidence for the ancient Egyptians' sense of humour.[3] However, in the past Egyptologists have sometimes mistakenly interpreted these intelligent simians as actually having been trained to assist humans with all kinds of hard work, instead of accepting them for what they appear to be, merely amusements.[4] This recurring motif developed fairly early on and became a highly convenient vehicle for expressing a bit of comic relief within the constraints of religious guidelines and the strict limits of canonical representation in the decoration of tomb-chapels. It is a forerunner of the genre of humorous animals executed on figured ostraca and satirical papyri much later during the Ramesside Period (see Chapter 3). These whimsical creations attest to the

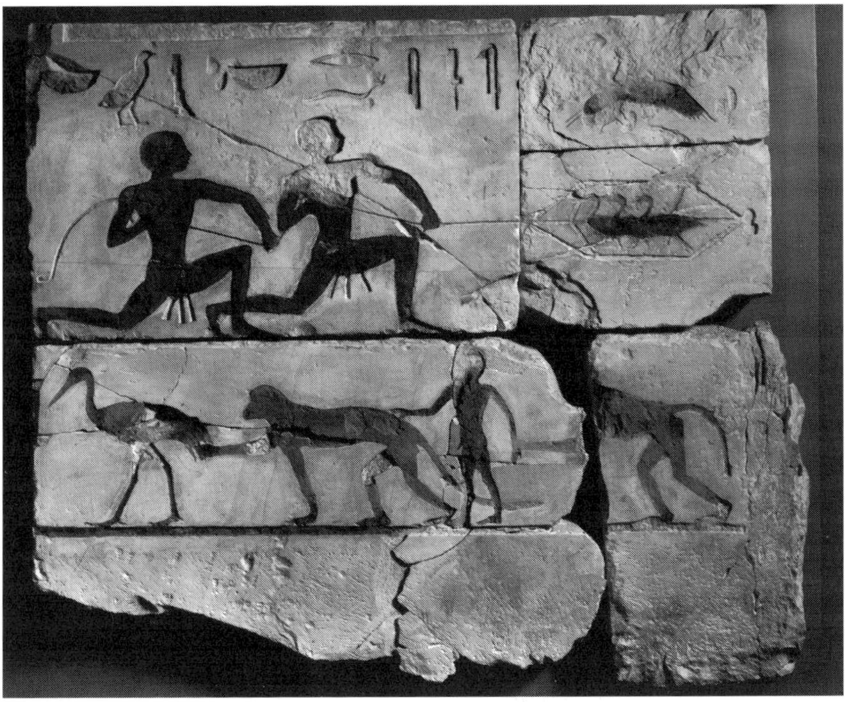

Fig. 5. Fragment of limestone inlaid with coloured paste, from the tomb of Nefermaat and Atet (mastaba 16) at Meidum. In the top register, the couple's sons are shown fowling with a clap-net. Below, a boy is playing with his pet monkeys. One is grasping the child's hand, the other naughtily pulls the tail feathers of a passing crane. Dynasty IV.

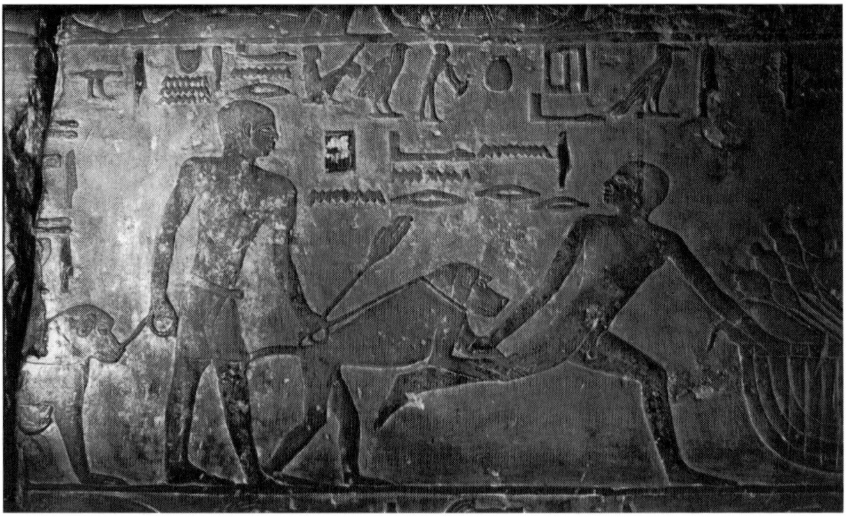

Fig. 6. This limestone relief depicts a detail of a marketing-scene, showing a man holding two pet baboons on leashes, one of whom has apprehended a shoplifter. The startled thief turns and appeals to the keeper to restrain the baboon! From the tomb-chapel of Tepemankh (D 11) at Saqqara. Dynasty V.

ancient Egyptian artisans' acute sense of observation and bespeak of their own enjoyment, if not for that of the viewers.

The first conspicuous instance of this brand of humour is preserved on a fragment of limestone relief from the early Dynasty IV tomb of Nefermaat and his wife Atet at Meidum (fig. 5). In the top register, the couple's sons are shown trapping fowl with a clap-net, while below, a young boy is playing with his pet monkeys. One of these is grasping the child's hand; the other appears to be pulling on the long tail feathers of a passing crane. There is clearly more than a hint of merriment in this procession of characters.[5] This rather sedate example is followed by far more zany incidents of monkey business.[6] The real fun starts during Dynasty V with, for instance, an escapade appearing on a block of relief from the tomb-chapel of Tepemankh at Saqqara (fig. 6). It depicts a vignette from an open-air market composition, illustrating a man brandishing a short stick or truncheon terminating in an open hand and holding two pet baboons on leashes, walking them through the marketplace. The female monkey is realistically shown with her baby clinging beneath her underside, while the male has firmly seized the leg of a young boy, probably a shop-lifter, who has approached a large basket of produce and is apparently about to pinch some of it. The startled thief turns his head and cries out to the baboon-keeper: "Hey! Help! Strike to restrain this baboon!"[7] This humorous episode is paralleled in the decoration of a few other Dynasty V monuments, both royal and private.

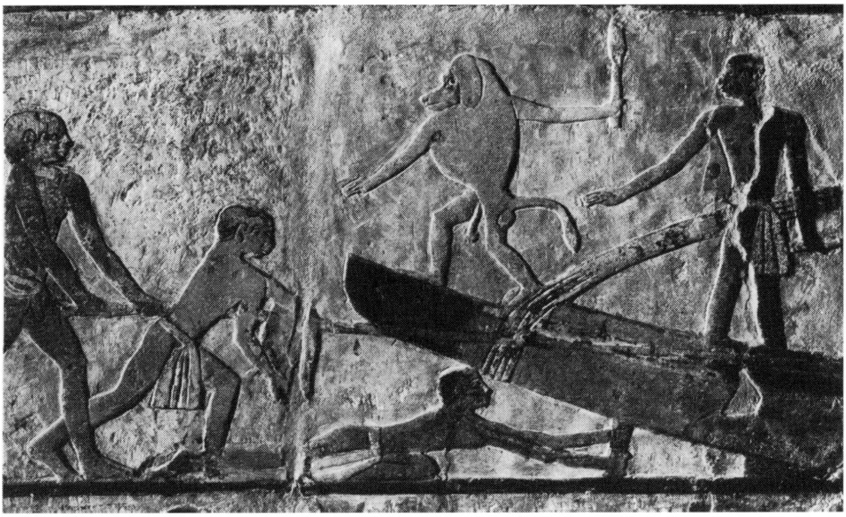

Fig. 7. Painted limestone relief portraying men engaged in shipbuilding. A large male baboon is shown standing at the stern, hilariously aping the gestures of an overseer. From the tomb-chapel of Nefer at Saqqara. Dynasty V.

On one of these, in the well-preserved tomb-chapel of the two senior officials, the brothers Niankhkhnum and Khnumhotpe at Saqqara, the baboon is rendered sinking his long, very pointed teeth into the culprit's leg![8] Such unconventional policing of the marketplace, enlisting tame baboons for the apprehension of common criminals, serves as a welcome introduction of levity into an otherwise formal scene. In certain respects, it may actually reflect some of the clamour and gaiety of everyday life in a pharaonic Egyptian market.

Even greater laughs along just these same lines are to be found in the Dynasty V tomb-chapel of Nefer at Saqqara, a courtier who seems to have had an exceptionally well-developed sense of the ludicrous! The carved wall-reliefs of Nefer's modestly-sized tomb-chapel display a pair of outstanding incidents of boisterous comedy involving pet baboons imitating human occupations. The first of these occurs within the contexts of a standard theme in tomb-chapel decoration, men engaged in shipbuilding. But here, the viewer is surprisingly confronted with a huge male baboon standing near the stern of the vessel, hilariously mimicking the gestures of the overseer in charge and wielding a sceptre-like baton of authority (fig. 7). The boss appears to be giving the orders for the shipwrights to pull away the wooden wedge so the craft can be dragged to the river and launched. In the second detail, equally clever, a group of men is represented undertaking the arduous process of twisting and pulling on poles attached to both sides of a must-sack, filled with juicy crushed grapes,

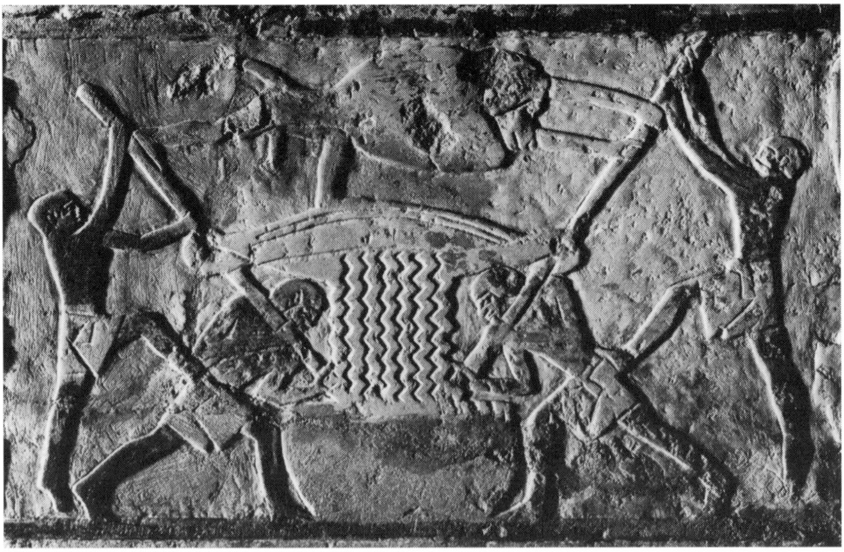

Fig. 8. Painted limestone relief illustrating men twisting the must-sack during wine-making. They are assisted by the prankish intervention of a talented male baboon. From the tomb-chapel of Nefer at Saqqara. Dynasty V.

during wine-making. Replacing the usual fifth man on top is a large, acrobatic male baboon that is clownishly assisting with the pressing operation (fig. 8). These wonderful gems of comedy were likely to have been included in the decoration of the tomb-chapel entirely for their uplifting laughs, bringing additional life to this rosy world.

In Old Kingdom tomb-chapels, monkeys can occasionally be observed participating in a range of other vivacious endeavours: carrying a heavy load using a shoulder yoke (fig. 9), burlesquing the gestures of a woman dancing (fig. 10), waggishly donning woman's apparel, wielding the long steer-oar of a Nile vessel (fig. 11), assisting with the rigging of a ship under full sail, catching a ride on the back of a pet dog, perching on the head of their dwarf guardians (fig. 12), singing to the accompaniment of a musician (fig. 13), among other delightful amusements.

These types of pleasurable diversions continue to appear in tomb-chapel iconography during the Middle and New Kingdoms, though with somewhat less frequency than in earlier epochs (figs. 14 and 16). Surely one of the most celebrated examples in this long-lived tradition is to be found in a vignette from a wall-painting in the rock-cut tomb of Khnumhotpe II at Beni Hasan. Here, two men are portrayed gathering figs from a sycamore tree, with three baboons laughably competing with them for a portion of the delicious crop (fig. 15). The naughty monkey on the left appears to be reaching for the same piece of fruit as one of the harvesters,

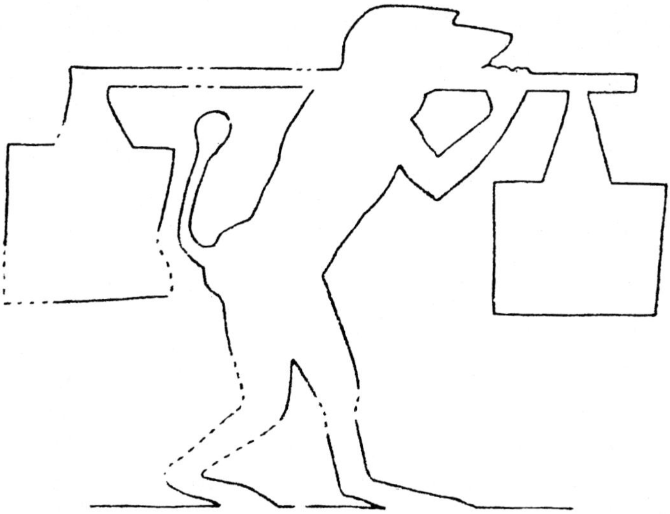

Fig. 9. Drawing of a relief depicting a monkey humorously carrying a load on either end of a yoke in human fashion. From the tomb-chapel of Niankhpepy at Zawiyet el Maiyitin. Dynasty VI.

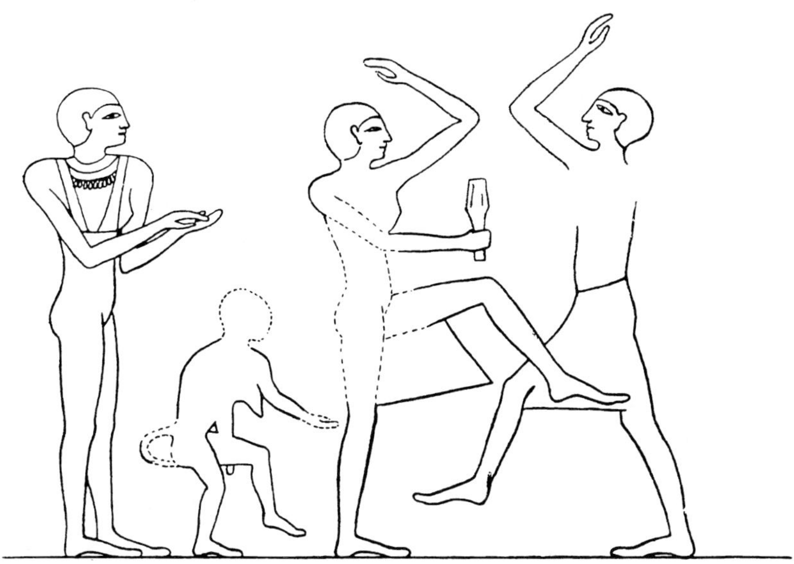

Fig. 10. Drawing of a damaged relief showing a female monkey burlesquing the gestures of a woman dancing. From the tomb-chapel of Serfka (no. 24) at El Sheikh Said. Dynasty V.

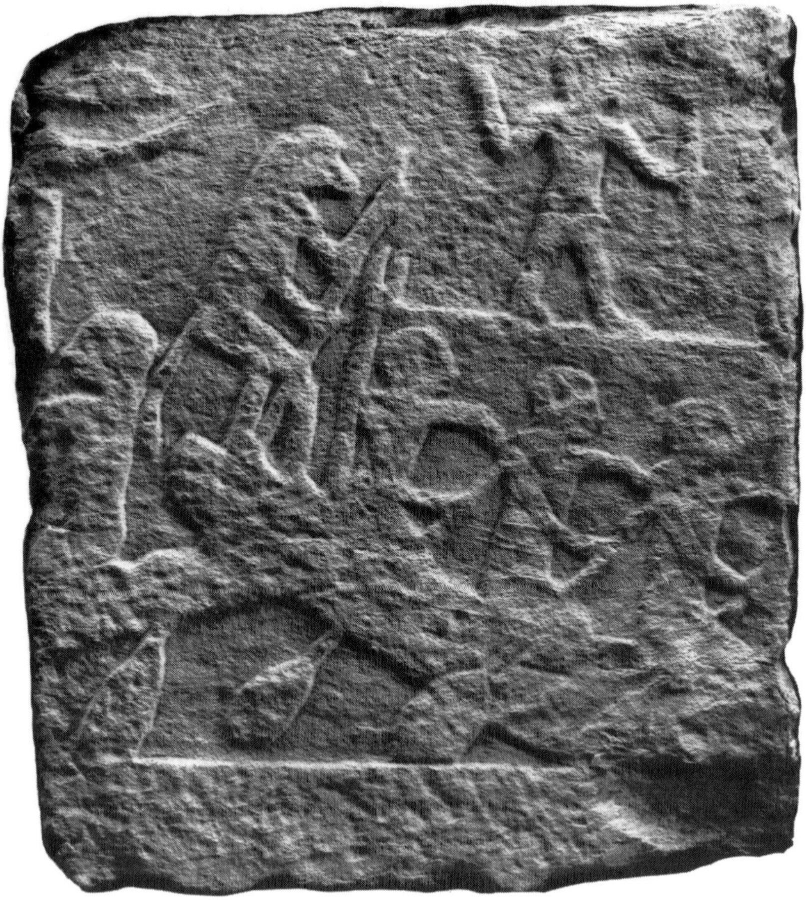

Fig. 11. Fragment of limestone relief showing a baboon comically imitating a human occupation, that of a river boat navigator. The monkey is standing high at the stern of the vessel, wielding the long steering-oar. Dynasty V or VI.

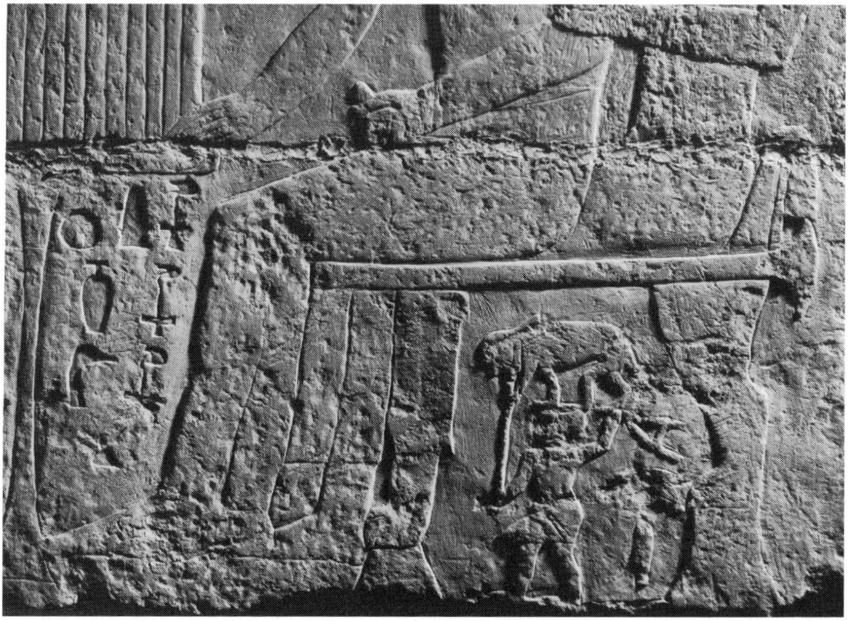

Fig. 12. Detail of relief portraying a leashed monkey and its minder, named Mereri, beneath the chair of the tomb-owner and his wife, the pet amusingly perched on the dwarf's head. From the tomb-chapel of Nefer (G 5550) at Giza. Dynasty VI.

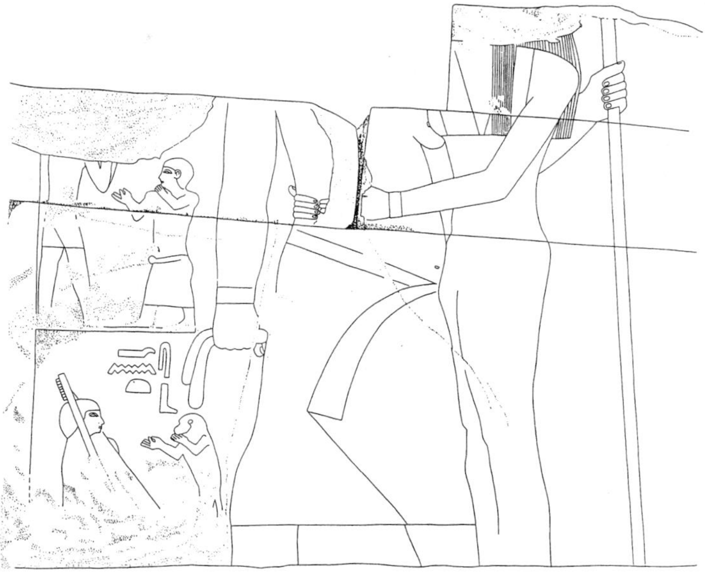

Fig. 13. Drawing of a partially preserved wall-relief from the tomb-chapel of Kaaper at Saqqara, depicting the corpulent tomb-owner being embraced by his slender wife. Behind them are small musical scenes. In the lower register, a monkey is shown as though singing to the accompaniment of a human harpist. Dynasty V.

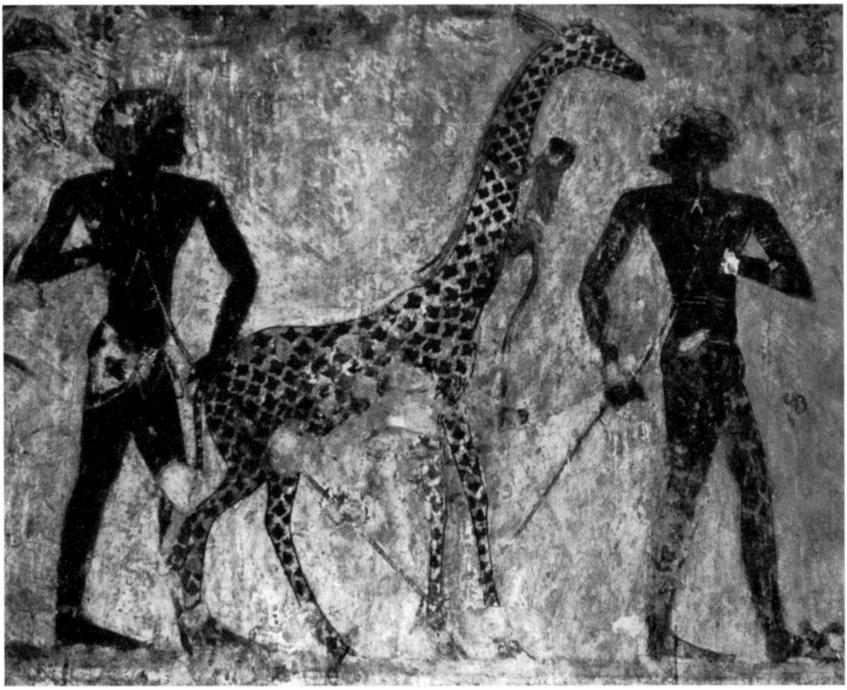

Fig. 14. This detail is from a wall-painting in the tomb-chapel of the Rekhmire (TT 100) at Thebes, where it is part of a scene featuring the arrival of trade or tribute from various foreign lands. Two Nubian men are pictured bringing a live giraffe, which is restrained by ropes tied to its forelegs, with a perky monkey whimsically scampering up its long neck. Dynasty XVIII.

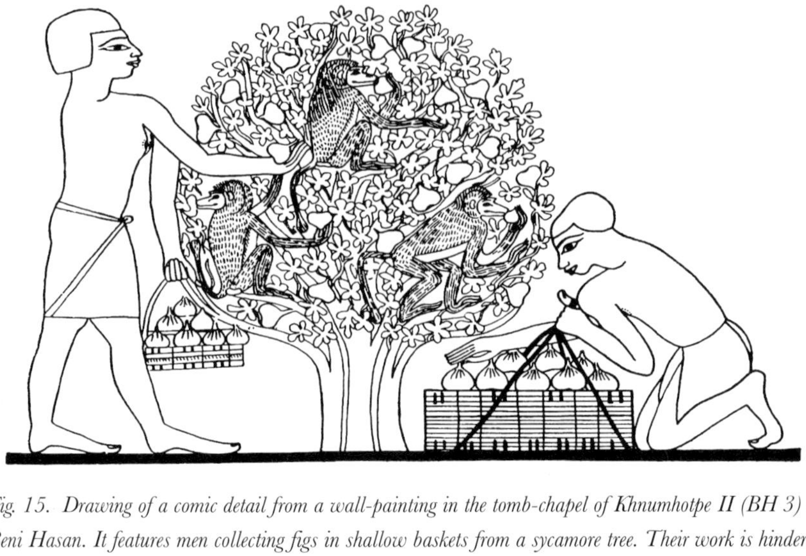

Fig. 15. Drawing of a comic detail from a wall-painting in the tomb-chapel of Khnumhotpe II (BH 3) at Beni Hasan. It features men collecting figs in shallow baskets from a sycamore tree. Their work is hindered by three tame baboons hungrily helping themselves to the delicious crop. Dynasty XII.

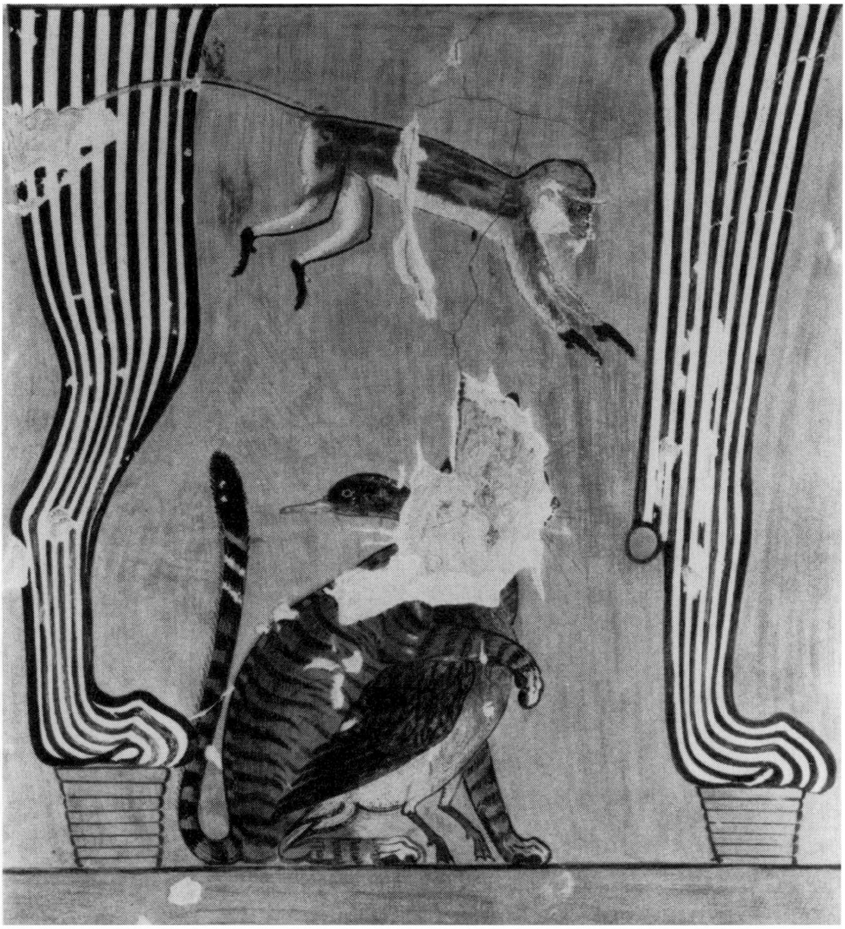

Fig. 16. Detail of wall-painting showing Queen Tiye's pets cavorting beneath her throne: a monkey, a cat, and a pintail duck. From the tomb-chapel of Anen (TT 120) at Thebes. Dynasty XVIII.

and turns its head as if to say to him, with a measure of light-hearted imagination: "Hey! This one belongs to me!" Just as well-known is a marvellous detail in the Dynasty XVIII tomb-chapel of Anen at Thebes. A wall-painting of an enthroned Queen Tiye, the illustrious wife of Amenhotpe III, portrays her perky pets frolicking beneath her arm-chair: a monkey, a cat, and a pintail duck (fig. 16). The painter has added a touch of frivolity to this already charming little group by portraying the cat with its leg mischievously wrapped around the back of the duck, while the excited monkey had been caught in mid-flight bounding over them. There is no need to see any political symbolism in the antics of these royal favourites, as some have proposed. Such an overly serious reading of it would stretch credulity.

In the decoration of Theban tomb-chapels during Dynasties XVIII and XIX, the familiar cat, to some degree, supersedes exotic monkeys as being the preferred element of affectionate, comical domestic situations.[9] While these details can be every bit as appealing as those of their monkey predecessors, the cats lack the prominence and anthropomorphic characteristics that made the earlier instances of this animal motif so immediately noticeable. The cats provide quiet chuckles rather than loud laughs, which, some might say, befits the dignity of these natural jokesters.

Most of the situational comedies revolving around cherished pet animals mentioned thus far were executed without explanatory inscriptions. The humour of the episodes is timeless, and wholly self-evident, even to the modern eye. In concluding our look at pets, we note at least one occasion where what seems to have been regarded as amusing about them relies on accompanying texts, giving their bizarre names (fig. 17). On a block of Middle Kingdom relief, a man is shown holding six household pets on leashes: three baboons, two monkeys (damaged), and a dog. The individual names of the baboons are carved beside them, and are extraordinarily complex: "When the foreign country is pacified, the land is happy", "His father awaits him" and "The followers of Tiye (?)". The label identifying the animals' minder is also peculiar and likely had humorous intent; he is called an "overseer of lions".[10] Perhaps looking after this ferocious pack of domestic beasts required the talents of a lion-keeper!

The scenes of daily life on private tomb-chapel walls are an invaluable source of information on ancient Egyptian arts and crafts, agriculture, animal husbandry, brewing and baking, games, dances, sports, and various manners and customs (figs. 18-20). Beginning in Dynasty V onwards, these subjects are sometimes enlivened with short snatches of texts reproducing the conversations, shouts, and songs of the various workers involved, which even turn to witticisms and insults.[11] They function very much like the "speech balloons" of a contemporary cartoon strip (fig. 21). It is frequently the candid dialogue between the men and women that is the source of the laughter in tomb-chapel scenes. The illustrations often give little or no hint whatever to the caustic utterances and gibes among the squabbling parties described by the captions. The human figures appear to be nonchalantly carrying out their tasks for the eternal benefit of the deceased tomb-owner. This is especially true during the Old and Middle Kingdoms. In Theban tomb-chapel paintings of the New Kingdom, on the other hand, there is a tendency for a number of these humorous asides to be less reliant on the accompanying hieroglyphic texts recording the speeches of the characters, the comedy being more visually oriented. We shall begin our look at a number of these vignettes starting with a few good examples in the famed tomb-chapel of Ti at Saqqara, a high-ranking Dynasty V court official.

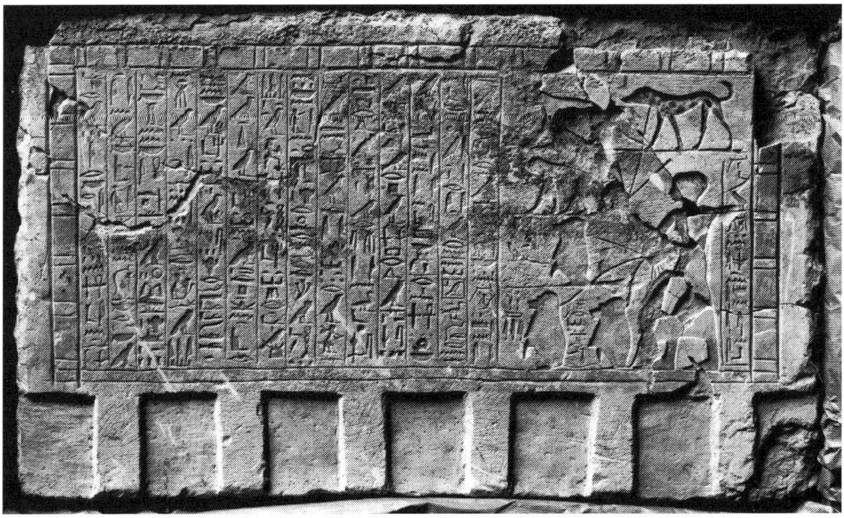

Fig. 17. A block of limestone from a curious monument depicting, in sunk relief, a man holding six household pets on leashes. The names of the baboons, inscribed beside them, are humorously bizarre, as is the label identifying their minder. Reportedly from the Faiyum. Dynasty XII-XIII.

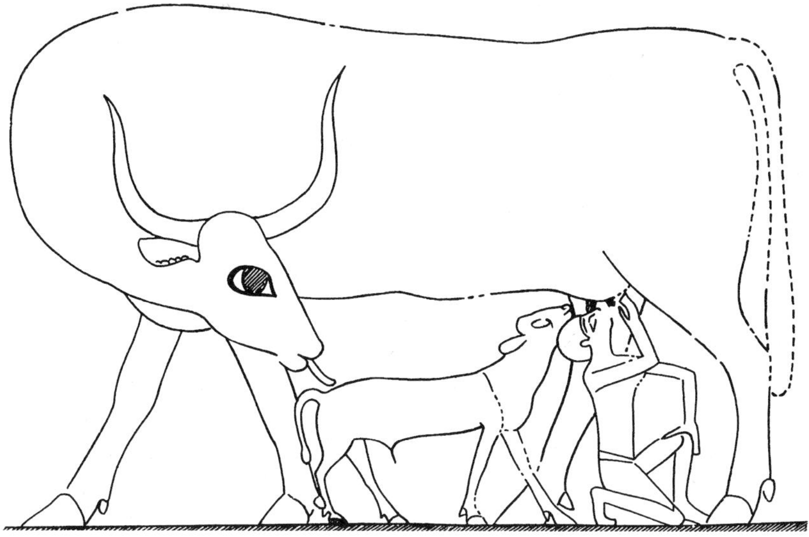

Fig. 18. Drawing of a humorous detail of country life from a wall-painting in the tomb-chapel of Baket III (BH 15) at Beni Hasan. It represents a boy usurping the place of a calf at the udder its mother, whom she affectionately consoles. Dynasty XI.

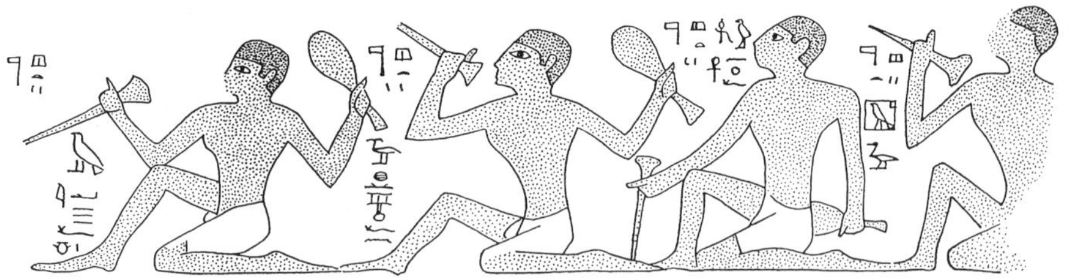

Fig. 19. Drawing of an amusing and unusual tomb-relief which cleverly pictures a gang of stone-masons, equipped with mallets and chisels, busily chipping away at the very wall on which they are represented. From the tomb-chapel of Sobeknakht (EK 10) at El Kab. Dynasty XIII.

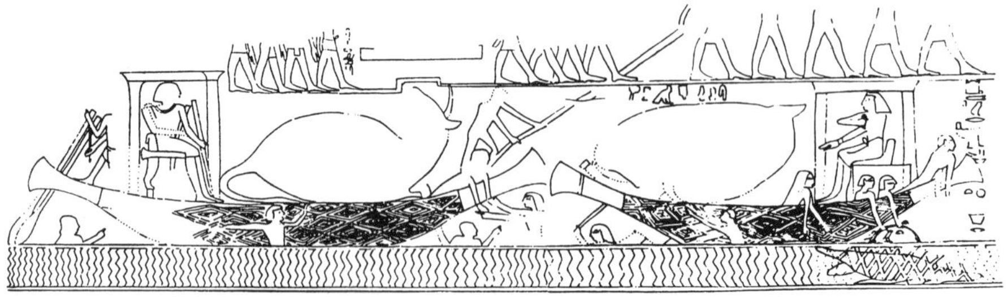

Fig. 20. Drawing of an original and entertaining subject from the tomb-chapel of Niankhpepy at Kom el Ahmar (Hierakonpolis). Navigation on the River Nile has always been a rather tricky business. Here, boats in a funeral scene have run aground on a hidden sandbank, and the tomb-owner's distressed men have jumped into the water to help push the boats free, trying to get him out of this seemingly embarrassing situation. Middle Kingdom or later.

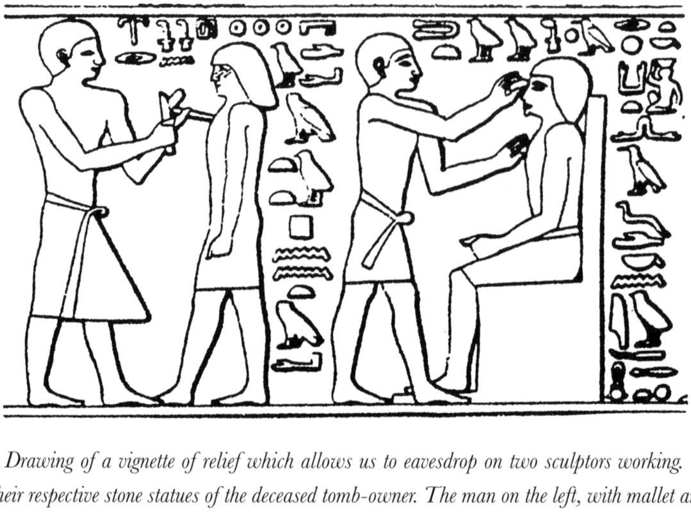

Fig. 21. Drawing of a vignette of relief which allows us to eavesdrop on two sculptors working. They are busy on their respective stone statues of the deceased tomb-owner. The man on the left, with mallet and chisel, complains to the other how long the piece is taking to complete. His colleague replies to him with derision that the material is stone, not wood! From the tomb-chapel of Wepemnofret at Giza. Dynasty V.

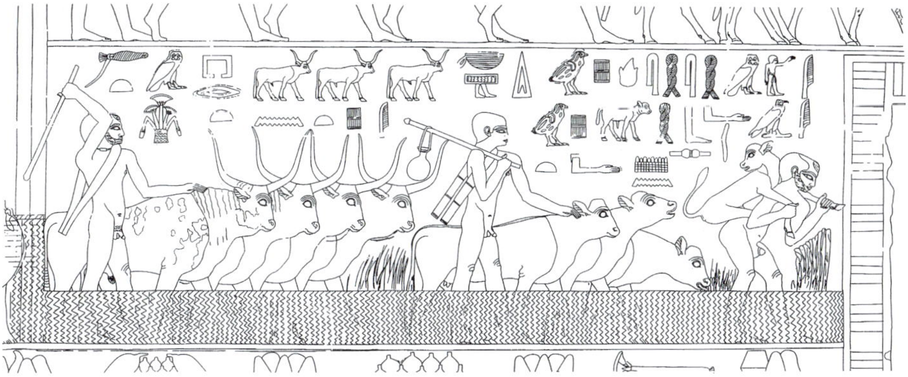

Fig. 22. Drawing of a painted relief scene from the tomb-chapel of Ti (D 22) at Saqqara, showing a cowherd carrying a new-born calf on his shoulders. The tranquillity of this idyllic pastoral scene is broken by the coarse speech of the second herdsman, who uses an ugly swear-word. Dynasty V.

The use of ribald language in Old Kingdom tomb-chapel inscriptions is rare and confined to the vulgar remarks of those of humble station. It seems the foul exclamations of lowly peasants, along with their toil-worn physiques, paunches, nakedness, baldness and unshaven faces, amused the wealthy and socially superior tomb-owners. It was a manner of speaking that they themselves claim to have avoided.[12] A classic example of swearing occurs in an appealing pastoral episode in the tomb-chapel of Ti that appears to be intentionally funny in more than one respect (fig. 22). It represents a herdsman carrying a newborn calf on his shoulders as he fords a canal. The terrified young animal looks back and cries out anxiously to its worried mother, which is following close behind. The herdsman's gentle words spoken to the cow are intended to give her reassurance: "Your calf will not come to harm, mother!" The tranquillity of this idyllic tableau is broken by the crude wisecrack of the second herdsman, who hollers an order to his companion with the raised stick taking-up the rear: "Come on, you shit, drive the cattle forward!"[13] Use of this strong expletive is surprising and was likely to have been recorded for comic effect. Nevertheless, it probably also realistically reflects the rich vocabulary of the average worker; some things don't change much! Other injurious terms are put to use by bickering workmen in Old Kingdom tomb-chapel scenes which have a nasty sexual edge to them, as in "you copulator", its modern equivalent is well-known.[14] Elsewhere, in a scene depicting a heated boatmen's jousting tournament, we read the obscene assertion "you whoremonger."[15] A commonly used pejorative expression among these simple country folks, certainly akin to swearing, was for someone to call or describe another as being "bald-headed" (see below).[16]

Elsewhere in Ti's tomb-chapel, a pair of field labourers is up to some real mischief, apparently engaged in an act of petty thievery. The small vignette pictures a long-horned cow, its hind legs restrained by means of a rope, being secretly milked by two naked peasants on Ti's estates (fig. 23). The fellow who is standing and holding a vase nervously remarks to his mate: "Milk quickly, hurry up, before our master (the overseer) comes back!"[17] This group is made all the more delightful by the inkling of a grin on the face of the cow, who seems to be well aware of the peasants' wrongdoing. Moreover, this comic escapade unfolds only a short distance from the tomb-owner, who is probably smiling knowingly at the surreptitious actions of his underlings. As with the shoplifting scene we recounted above (fig. 6), the foibles, predicaments and weaknesses of the peasantry and other menial workers seem to have tickled the dignified tomb-owners' fancies.

The panoramic scenes of ancient country life revealed in Ti's spectacular tomb-chapel contain other light-hearted snippets, ranging from recalcitrant farm beasts (fig. 24) to the dishevelled appearances and physical deformities of peasants and servants (fig. 4). The Egyptians seem to have had a strange fascination with freaks, humans suffering deformities caused by disease or hunger.[18] This is especially apparent in Old and Middle Kingdom tomb-chapel iconography. Images of hunchbacks and achondroplastic dwarfs, people with clubfeet, abnormalities of the genitalia, emaciation, turricephalic skulls, *genu recurvatum* (a deformity resulting possibly from a kick on the knee-joint) and protruding navels, among a range of others, were unsympathetically displayed on the walls of private tomb-chapels and elsewhere for humorous effect. Some may have been conscious attempts to show caricature. A literary counterpart, of sorts, for the visual mockery labourers in private tomb-chapel scenes, can be found in scathingly satiric descriptions of the lower orders of Egyptian society in *The Teaching of Khety* and other instructional texts used for training schoolboys in the scribal profession (see Chapter 1).

Above all, the prosperous élite had a predilection for laughing at bustling diminutive dwarfs. These short-statured persons were routinely depicted as happy-go-lucky household retainers, and were frequently placed in charge of the family's dogs, monkeys or occasionally even a tamed leopard (figs. 4 and 12); these human curiosities were, for all intents and purposes, kept as pets themselves.[19] Their status may additionally have been linked with functions as the ancient Egyptian counterpart of a medieval European court jester, serving as clever entertainers and foils for the aristocracy. This brand of comedy, just as with the antics of pet animals, was presented on a purely visual level; only rarely do texts accompany them. In the Dynasty XVIII tombs of notables at Tell el Amarna, the site

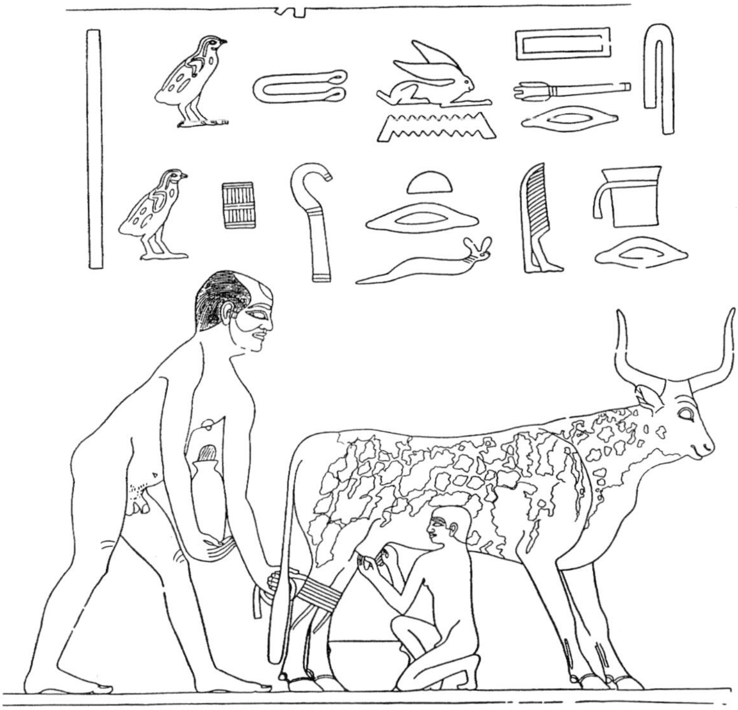

Fig. 23. Drawing of a detail of painted relief depicting a long-horned cow, its hind legs restrained with a rope, being surreptitiously milked by two naked peasants. From the tomb-chapel of Ti (D 22) at Saqqara. Dynasty V.

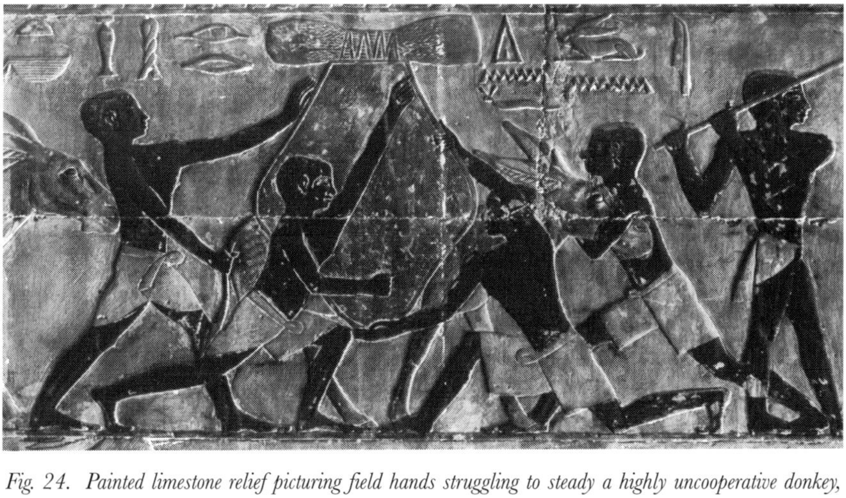

Fig. 24. Painted limestone relief picturing field hands struggling to steady a highly uncooperative donkey, one forcefully applying a headlock to the poor beast, another yanking on its tail, as they attempt to load it with sacks of cut grain. From the tomb-chapel of Ti (D 22) at Saqqara. Dynasty V.

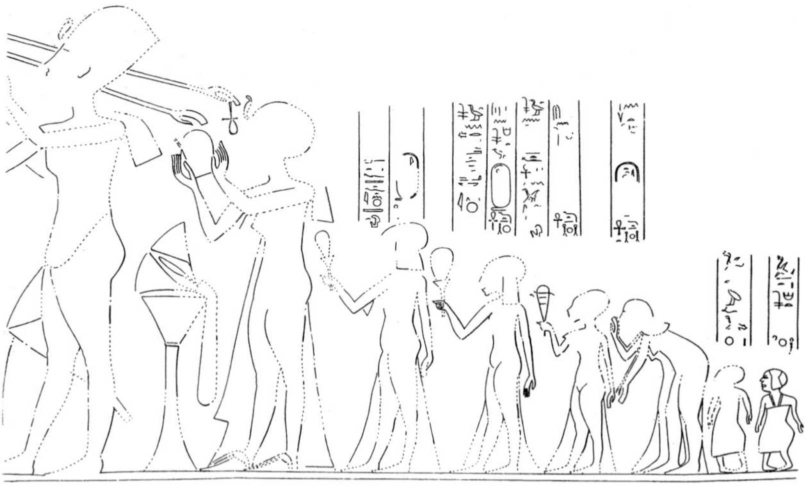

Fig. 25. Drawing of a tomb relief portraying the royal family, Akhenaten and Nefertiti, and their three eldest daughters, worshipping the Aten. The group is joined by the queen's sister, Mutnodjmet, who is accompanied by her cruelly deformed dwarf retainers. From tomb-chapel of Panehsy (EA 6) at Tell el Amarna. Dynasty XVIII.

Akhenaten's brief capital city, a pair of dwarfs was repeatedly represented, one female, the other male, and both severely crippled with limb disfigurements (fig. 25). The two dwarfs are invariably depicted accompanying Mutnodjmet, younger sister of the renowned Queen Nefertiti and future wife of King Horemhab. These privileged dwarfs are further encumbered with funny names and titles. One is called: "the vizier of the Queen, Forever," the other is "the vizier of his mother, the Sun."[20] They are quite odd indeed. There is no mistaking the merciless satire shown these two misshapen individuals. This in spite of the teachings of a well-known New Kingdom sage, who advises: "Do not laugh at a blind man, nor tease a dwarf, nor cause hardship for the lame."[21]

Of all the varied repertoire of artistic themes depicting daily life on the river and backwaters, that of the traditional boatmen's jousting tournament, is clearly among the most vivid and high-spirited (fig. 26). The ancient Egyptians appear to have appreciated a good brawl, and this rough-and-tumble game, found in private tomb-chapel decoration of the Old and Middle Kingdoms, provided an excellent opportunity for busy sportive battles. It was usually performed in the presence of the tomb-owner and his family. Although it was quite violent, there was plenty of horseplay and humour.[22] These scenes sometimes include brief captions recording the sharp cries and taunts of the combatants. The men yell from one boat to another as they clobber and wrestle their opponents, trying to

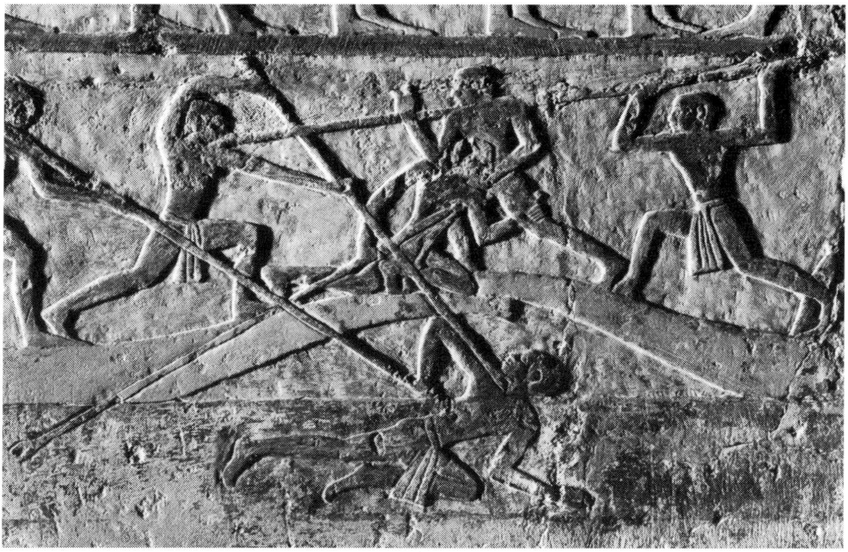

Fig. 26. Detail of painted limestone relief picturing a highly animated boatmen's jousting match. The crews have long poles to knock their opponents into the water. From the tomb-chapel of Nefer at Saqqara. Dynasty V.

topple them into the water, using long punt poles with forked ends. During one heated exchange, for instance, a fisherman or fowler encourages his mate to strike an opponent hard: "Open him in his noggin!" or, not to put too fine a point on it: "Break his skull open!"[23] It is in such a composition in the Dynasty V tomb-chapel Ptahhotpe II at Saqqara that a fascinating detail appears. Off to the side of a standard scene featuring the crews of three boats engaged in a jousting tournament, a fourth vessel peacefully floats with a sole passenger on board (fig. 27). He is calmly watching the boatmen's fight, while taking a meal and drinking beer from a tall jar offered by a server. This is the "overseer of sculptors" Niankhptah, who had the distinct privilege of including an image of himself in the very decoration he executed. Not only is this unusual, since as a rule ancient Egyptian artisans remained anonymous (also see below), but he has managed to devise a clever and amusing artistic signature, befitting the creator of Ptahhotpe's astonishingly lively series of wall-reliefs.[24]

Several Old Kingdom tomb-chapels are decorated with lively episodes depicting the tomb-owners travelling on official tours of inspection in stylish sedan chairs, borne on the shoulders of porters. As they carry him, the bearers sing a good-humoured little song, the words of which are recorded along with the scenes. It ironically laments the burden of their work, but also highly flatters the master with their having the honour of transporting him. It contains the memorable refrain: "It is pleasanter full (the sedan chair with the deceased) than when it is empty!"[25]

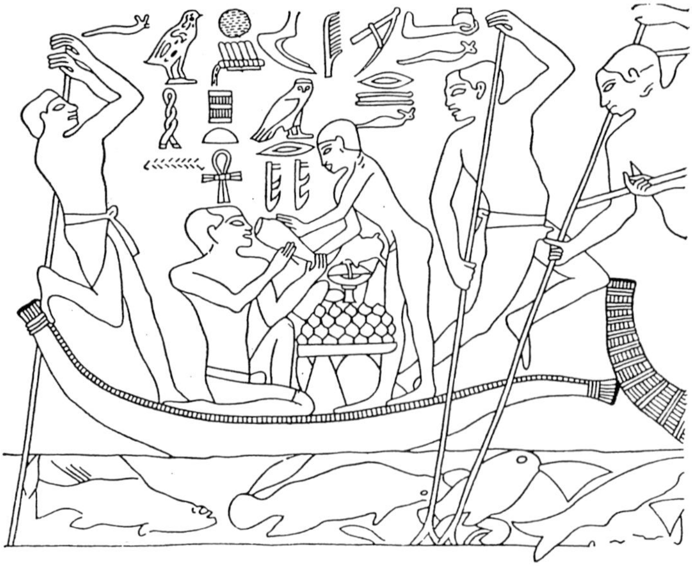

Fig. 27. Drawing of a detail of painted relief showing a unique twist on the preceding subject (see fig. 26). In a scene of a standard jousting match, a boat floats with a sole passenger on board. This is the "overseer of sculptors" Niankhptah, who left a portrait of himself in reliefs he probably carved. From the tomb-chapel of Ptahhotpe II (D 64) at Saqqara. Dynasty V.

We now turn our attention to one of the more intriguing instances of levity to be observed on an ancient Egyptian funerary monument. It exemplifies both a touching memorial for a departed friend and humour from the lives of ordinary people. It comes from a Dynasty XII limestone stela belonging to the very fat harpist Neferhotpe, which was placed in his employer's cenotaph at Abydos (fig. 28).[26] The deceased is represented in an unconventional pose, sitting on his feet and reaching out with both hands, in gluttonous anticipation, ready to devour the great meal piled high on a low table set before him. His obesity goes beyond the paunch that was always used in Egyptian art as an indicator of a comparatively prosperous life. This stela was commissioned by a humble, but caring friend of Neferhotpe's, the carrier of bricks, Nebsumenu, who was evidently well aware of the musician's love of eating and wished that he would continue this pleasure in the afterlife. Lest we should miss the obvious intent here, the standard offering formula inscribed on it ends with a rather unusual request, just above the ravenous owner and his tempting repast, asking that the gods: "Please give him what he likes best."[27] It seems reasonably certain that Neferhotpe's mate, along with another, the draughtsman Sonebau, who presumably carved the stela, and left his own signature at the bottom of it, were not without a keen sense of fun.

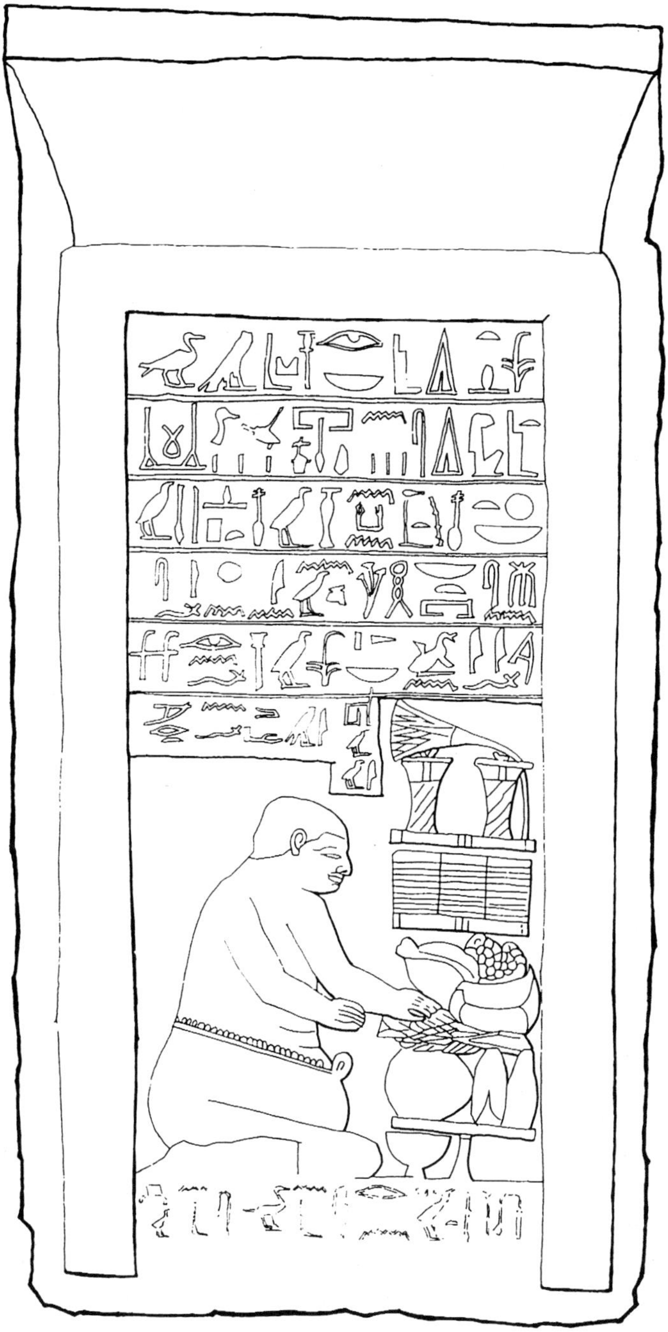

Fig. 28. Drawing of the limestone funerary stela of the grossly obese harpist Neferhotpe. The deceased is unconventionally posed, reaching out hungrily with both hands ready to devour the meal piled on an offering table. From Abydos. Dynasty XII.

The wall-reliefs in the Dynasty XII rock tombs of the nomarchs (provincial governors) at Meir, located in Middle Egypt south of Tell el Amarna, include a fine range of light-hearted elements. Again, these are primarily encountered in the scenes devoted to portraying aspects of daily life. Readily noticeable, even to the inexperienced viewer, is the ridiculously caricatured image of a ragged desert tribesman, who is depicted in several tomb-chapels at the site. He is shown presenting cattle as offerings to the deceased.[28] On one occasion, this foreigner's skeletal appearance is comically accentuated to the point of being as stick-like and crooked as the supporting staff he holds (fig. 29). In another instance of this satiric motif, his scrawny likeness stands in contrast, not only to the well-fed cattle, but to the fleshy, well-dressed Egyptian official holding a baton pictured close by (fig. 30). The humour seems clear: the herdsman has grown thin and weak while his charges have become fat and strong. He was evidently regarded as odd or funny. His features were purposefully exaggerated as an expression of derision.[29] In Egyptian iconography, however, images of glaringly grotesque humans are comparatively rare and mostly are confined to the sketches on limestone figured ostraca and on the satirical-erotic papyrus dating from the Ramesside Period (see Chapter 4). Still, the cruelly caricatured ethnic features of prisoners and enemies, on tomb and temple walls, also in the decorative arts, clearly expresses the ancient Egyptian's negative reaction towards these foreigners and a desire to ridicule them. Particularly in the New Kingdom, representations of them can sometimes verge on the grotesque and were viewed, we may well conclude, with a certain measure of amusement, arising from a position of cultural superiority.[30] In their unflattering depictions and descriptions of foreigners (see Chapter 1), the ancient Egyptians reveal themselves to be not terribly unlike peoples of other times and places down through the ages.

A favourite comic episode of those who have some acquaintance with the rock-cut chapels at Meir is one created by artisans working in the tomb of the nomarch Ukhhotpe II. The vignette pictures a cook squatting on the ground, roasting a spitted goose over a brazier of burning charcoal, his hand raised to protect his face from the intense heat (fig. 31). The accompanying text records his exaggerated bewilderment over the fowl's lengthy cooking time. He abruptly blurts out: "I have been roasting since the beginning of time! I have never seen such a goose as this one!"[31] Just to the right is a seldom-seen detail, showing men busy at work roasting an entire steer on a revolving spit, a time-consuming operation to be sure. Nevertheless, they do so without uttering even the slightest complaint, adding to the irony of the goose-cooker's remarks.

In the tomb-chapel of Senbi at the same site, an entertaining vignette

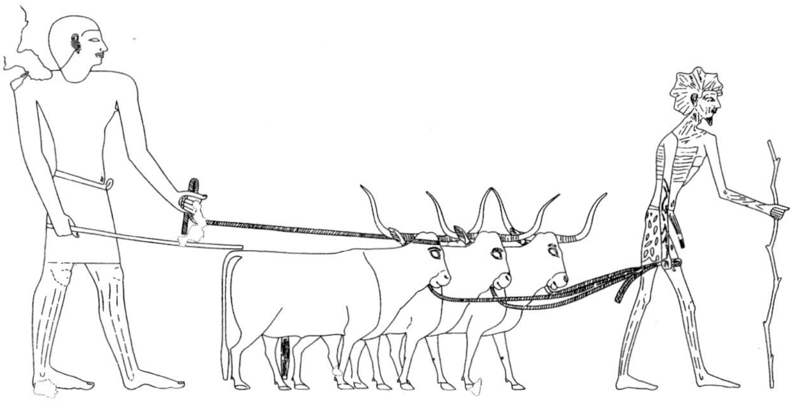

Fig. 29. Drawing of a relief portraying the rather gruesome-looking image of a ragged desert tribesman, leading three robust cattle. From the tomb-chapel of Ukhhotpe I (B. 2) at Meir. Dynasty XII.

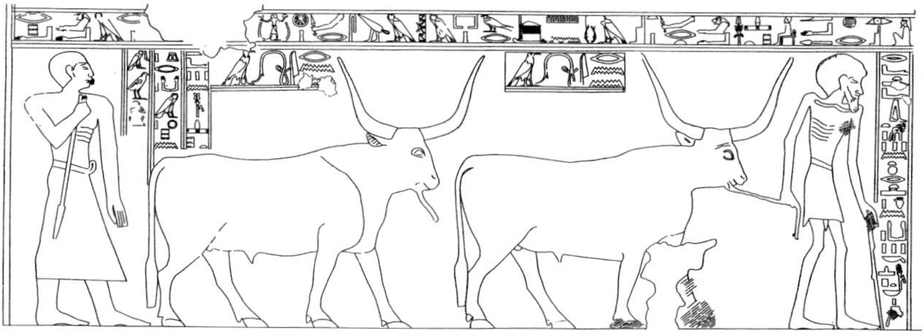

Fig. 30. Another representation of the scrawny herdsman in the tomb-chapel of Ukhhotpe I (B. 2) at Meir (see fig. 29). The foreigner's likeness contrasts with the well-fed bulls and corpulent Egyptian official. Dynasty XII.

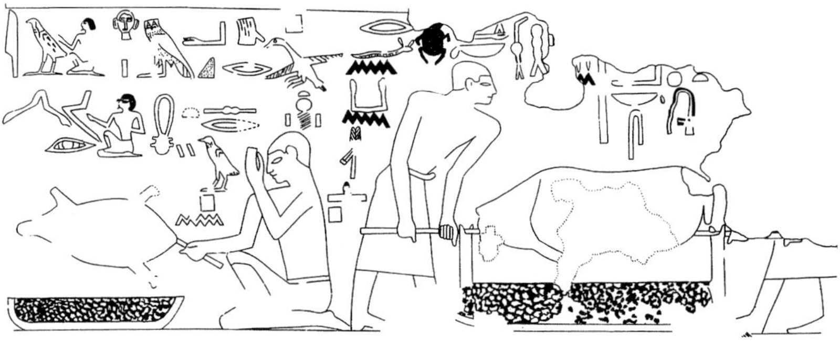

Fig. 31. Drawing of a painted relief depicting a cook roasting a goose on a spit over a brazier. The accompanying text records his bewilderment over the fowl's lengthy cooking time. From the tomb-chapel of Ukhhotpe II (B. 4) at Meir. Dynasty XII.

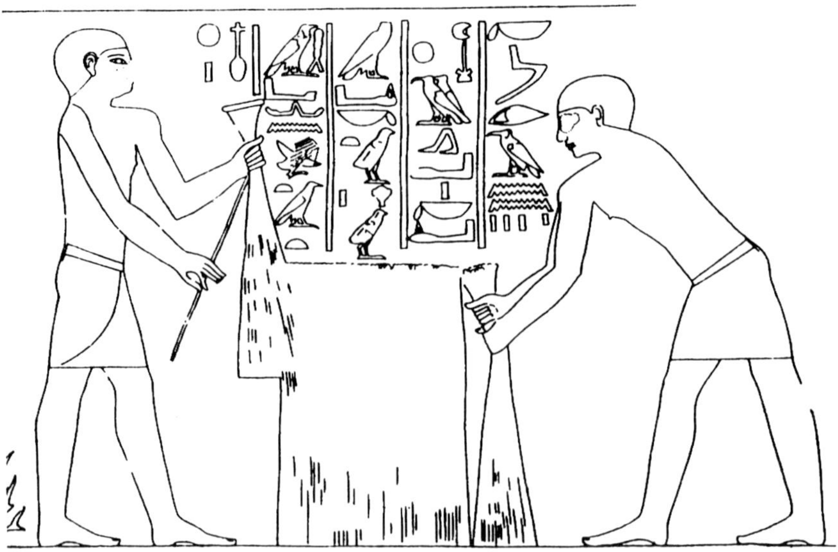

Fig. 32. Drawing of a detail of painted relief from the tomb-chapel of Senbi (B. 1) at Meir, showing field hands bickering as they harvest flax. Dynasty XII.

portrays a theme already well established under the Old Kingdom, namely the petty quarrelling amongst men doing back-breaking labour in the agricultural fields. One can easily imagine their descendants today, toiling away and having similar joshing exchanges. Here, the scene of the action is a pair of workmen busy with the harvesting of flax (fig. 32). The source of the conflict is age-old, a minor run-in with a know-it-all co-worker. The fellow on the left remarks to his comrade: "Look, you're just pulling, without picking. And the day is good for work!" The other curtly retorts: "Look to your own arm and then give a glance at us!"[32] In the same sepulchre, we see a wrestling match performed here for the everlasting thrill of the deceased owner. The sportsmen are posed in a series of holds on each other. A trace of humour is revealed in the captions that repeat their cynical quips and taunts. In one of these (fig. 33), the wrestler on the left heatedly asserts to his opponent: "Please be patient! And you'll see yourself on your face!" The other is equally sure of himself, boldly exclaiming: "I'll bring you that! Look, I make you fall on your face!"[33]

The Dynasty XII Theban tomb of the lady Senet, previously attributed to that of her son, the vizier Inyotefiqer, is remarkable on a number of grounds, but what concerns us here is its interesting wall-painting depicting various baking and brewing activities. The episodes are illuminated with the everyday speech of the characters. In one of these, two women are conversing while preparing flour (fig. 34). The one on the left,

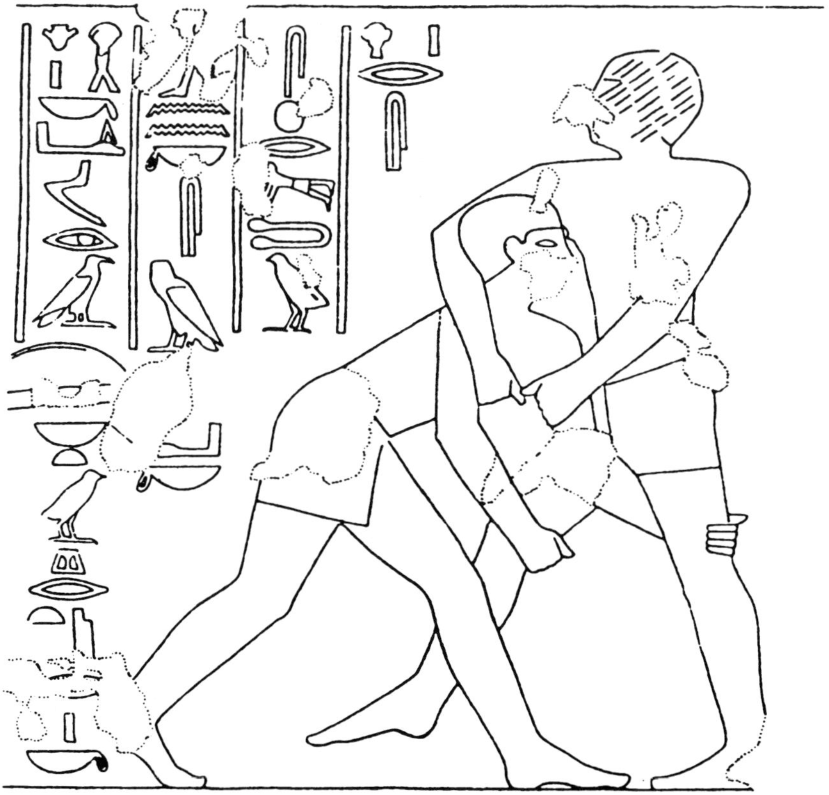

Fig. 33. Drawing of a detail of painted relief from the tomb-chapel of Senbi (B. 1) at Meir, depicting part of a wrestling match. Dynasty XII.

who is using the quern, is piously mindful of her duty to the deceased tomb-owner and recites a prayer: "O all gods of this land, make my strong master healthy!" The other, who is sieving flour, replies to her co-worker rather sardonically: "…Look, this is for my own food!"[34] In another vignette, a man is stooped over, busily combining the half-baked dough with some dates (fig. 35). As he does so, he mutters to himself, complaining about the poor quality of the dates to be used in the beer: "These dates from the store are old. If only I'd seen them when they were first issued! Then I could've done some good!"[35] In the adjoining scene, to the left, water is added to this mixture to form a mash, which having stood for the proper time, is then strained. The remaining fermented lees (*sermet*) were used for food, either eaten moist or dried in cakes. A boy with a bowl interrupts the brewer begging: "Please give me some fermented lees, look, I'm hungry!" The lad is then roundly dressed down and cursed by this annoyed and ill-humoured gentleman: "May you, and she who bore you,

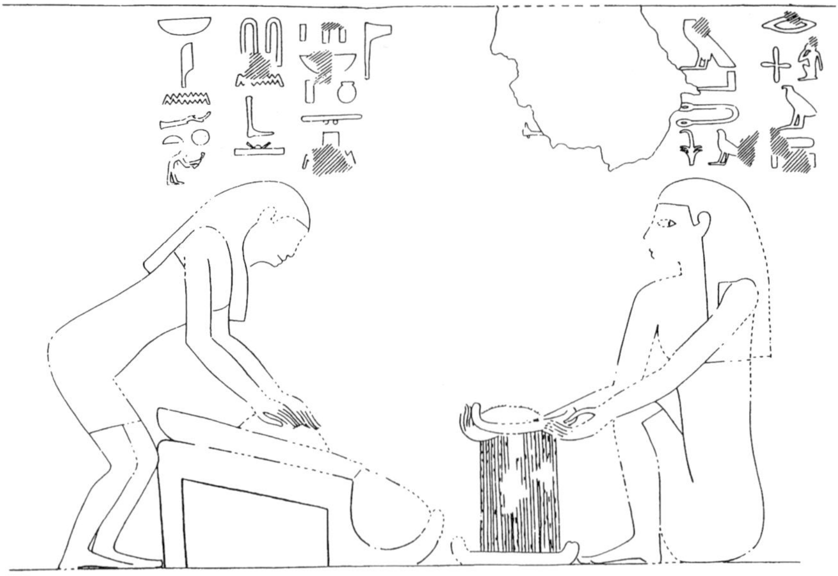

Fig. 34. Drawing of a detail from a wall-painting in the tomb-chapel of the lady Senet (TT 60) at Thebes. It depicts a pair of women chattering as they work. Dynasty XII.

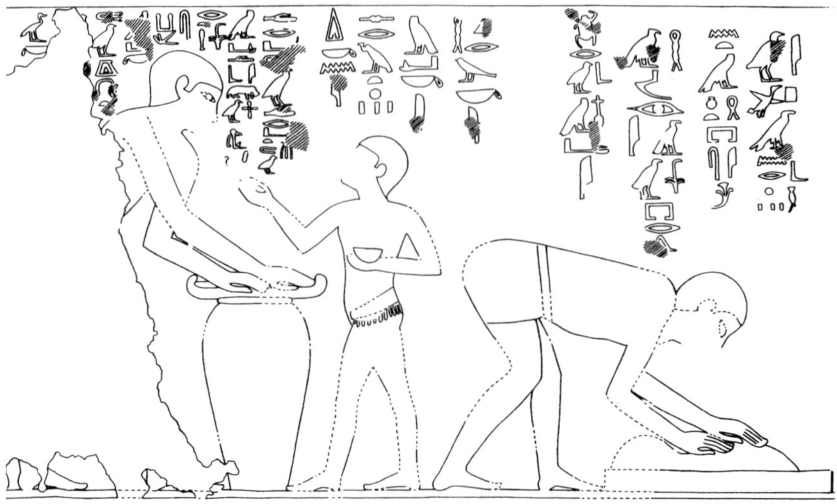

Fig. 35. This drawing comes from a wall-painting from the tomb-chapel of the lady Senet (TT 60) at Thebes. It is part of a scene showing baking and brewing activities undertaken for the eternal well-being of the deceased. It features a particularly ill-humoured individual. Dynasty XII.

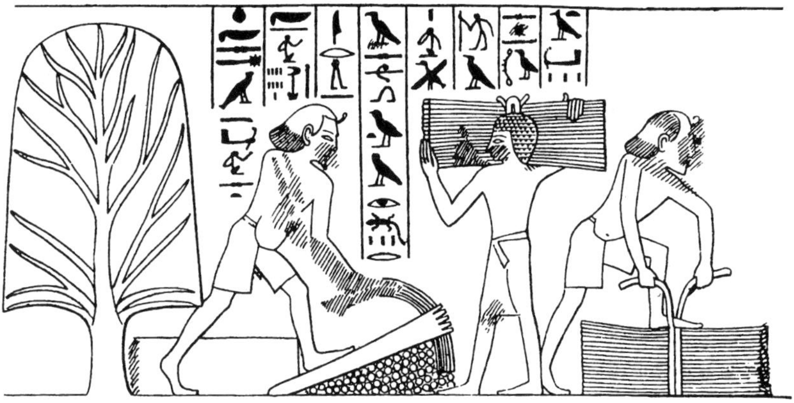

Fig. 36. Drawing of a vignette of painted relief from the tomb-chapel of Paheri (EK 3) at El Kab. To the left, an old workman is busily rippling flax as a younger labourer is bringing him another bundle, which a third field hand has tied up. The men are engaged in cheerful banter. Dynasty XVIII.

be driven off by a hippopotamus – you eat more than a royal slave at the plough! Look, you're stopping me from work!"[36] The child is, we may happily observe, in no immediate danger of starvation. By the looks of his slightly rounded belly, he's been receiving such handouts at the brewery on a regular basis for quite some time!

This witty brand of tomb-chapel humour, springing from the bickering and bantering of peasants labouring in the fields and elsewhere, may have reached its height in the painted reliefs of the Dynasty XVIII provincial rock-cut tomb of Paheri. To judge from such light-hearted vignettes on the walls his sepulchre, this highly distinguished tomb-owner seems to have hoped to partake in a fair amount of laughter in his posthumous existence.

The brightly coloured and animated agricultural scenes executed in the tomb-chapel of the mayor Paheri at El Kab, situated fifty miles south of Luxor, display in them a wealth of interest. This includes a number of situational comedies, which develop as the deceased tomb-owner looks on. In one of the more amusing pictures an elderly peasant, sporting a long wispy hairstyle and beard, enthusiastically ripples freshly harvested flax (fig. 36). As he works, he boastfully calls out to a younger co-worker delivering on his shoulder another bundle to be processed: "Even if you bring me 11,009 (bundles of flax), I will be able to comb them all!" The youth, in turn, insultingly comes back with: "Hurry up and don't talk so much, you old bald-headed field hand!"[37] On the same wall is an episode capturing two labourers with a large pannier of cut grain slung on a pole carried on their shoulders (fig. 37). They are briskly walking towards the left, taking their load to the threshing-floor. Just to the right stands the

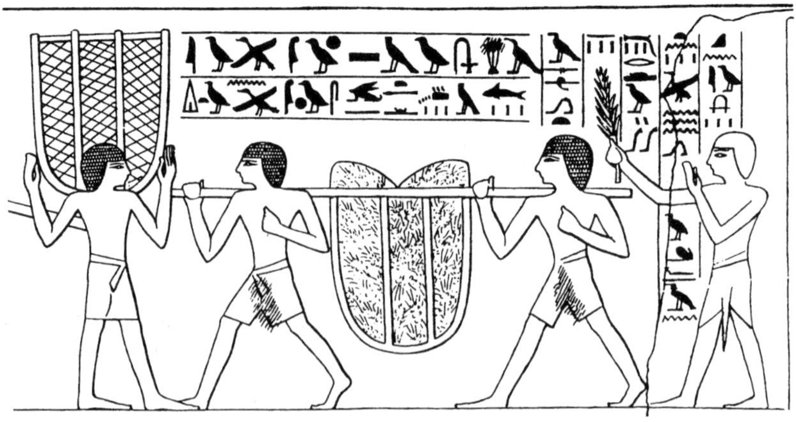

Fig. 37. Drawing of a vignette of painted relief from the tomb-chapel of Paheri (EK 3) at El Kab. The detail shows two workers with a large pannier of cut grain slung on a pole carried on their shoulders. On the right, the overseer shouts at the pair to hurry along, and one of them answers him in a joking manner. Dynasty XVIII.

overseer, brandishing a switch, who waggishly hollers at the harried pair to: "Hurry it up! The water is coming and will soon reach the baskets of grain!" The humour here lies in his hyperbole, because it is only about the end of March (harvest time), and it will be another two months or so before the first sign of the Nile's annual flooding. One of the carriers has quickly grasped the overseer's joke and responds to him cleverly: "The sun is hot! O, may the sun be given the worth of the grain in fish!"[38] By this, the fellow appears to imply that the flood can't come any too soon for him, because it would be a lot more pleasant to be catching fish in the cool water, rather than toiling in the hot fields. Finally, we come to a scene

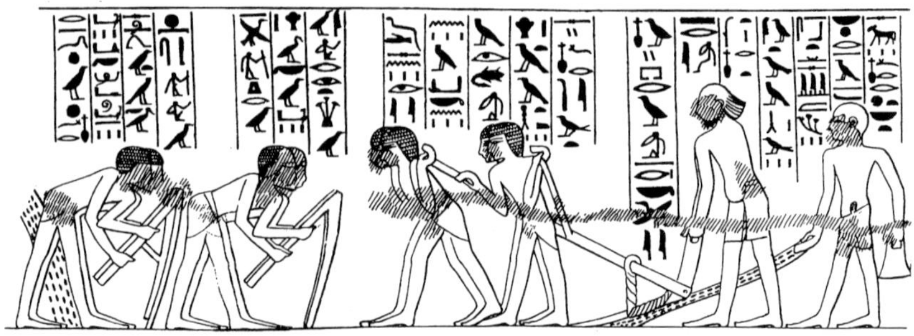

Fig. 38. Drawing of a vignette of painted relief from the tomb-chapel of Paheri (EK 3) at El Kab. Here, again, is agricultural activity on the country estates of the tomb-owner; ploughing by hand and digging with hoes is pictured. One of them, a realist, remarks that he would like to get home in a timely fashion. Dynasty XVIII.

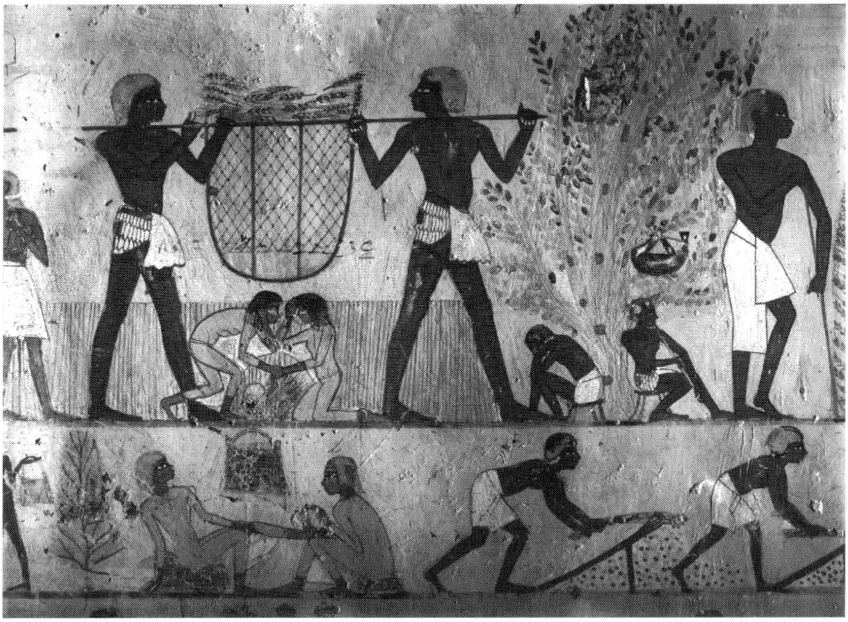

Fig. 39. A glimpse of Egyptian country life, with a number of light-hearted touches, as viewed in a detail of wall-painting from the Theban tomb-chapel of Menna (TT 69). It is the time of the harvest and two girl gleaners have got into a hair-pulling fight. Dynasty XVIII.

representing a group of peasants engaged in ploughing by hand and digging with wooden hoes (fig. 38). These extremely difficult jobs are undertaken with much eagerness, as the men's speeches in the brief captions make clear. One of the hoers boastfully exclaims to his comrades that: "I will do even more work than the master wants!" However, the man next to him does not share this unbridled devotion and pragmatically tells him: "My friend, hurry up with the work so we can get back home in good time."[39]

Such minor troubles in the fields will already be familiar to many readers from the often reproduced episode of two young gleaners having a set-to in the famed Dynasty XVIII tomb-chapel of Menna at Thebes (fig. 39). The gathering of gleanings during harvest time seems to have been rather competitive, at times leading to squabbles, probably over territorial infringements. In a wall-painting in Menna's tomb, it has escalated into a scuffle. Beneath a large wickerwork basket filled with freshly cut grain, two girls are pictured pulling on each other's hair; the ears of wheat they have already collected are spilled in a pile between them. Off to the right, a labourer can be seen dozing under a tree, sitting next to a fellow relaxing and playing the flute. In the lower register, in happy contrast to the previous pair, another gleaner, a slightly older girl has come to the aid of a

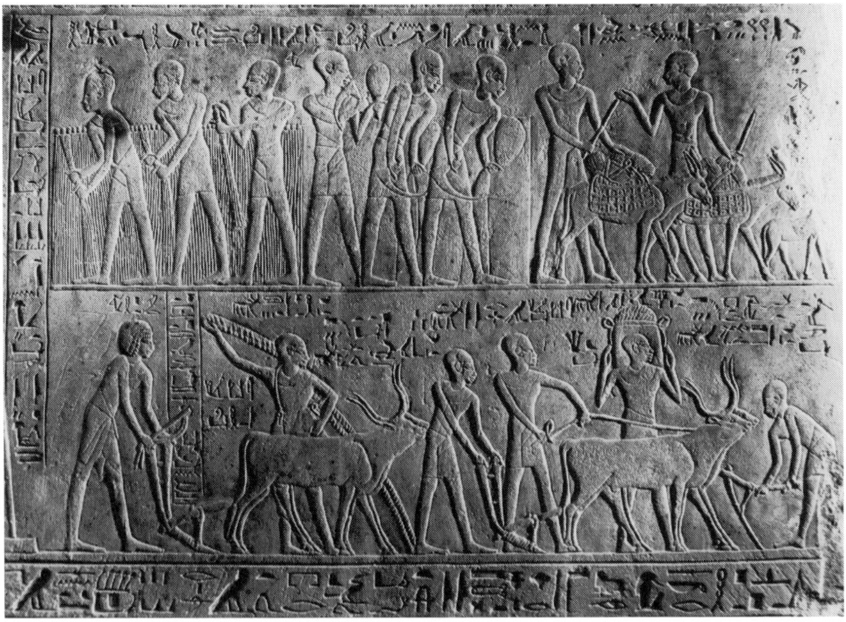

Fig. 40. Detail of carved limestone wall-relief containing several agricultural episodes, with brief descriptive inscriptions. From the tomb-chapel of Merymery at Saqqara. Dynasty XVIII.

companion and is extracting a thorn from her foot. These are only but a few of the amusing and vivid glimpses of country life that enliven the agricultural and related scenes of this fine tomb-chapel.[40] Some of these intimate details were closely copied, including both vignettes featuring the pairs of girls, and admiringly included in the tomb decoration of the most high-ranking Theban notable of Dynasty XXVI, the mayor Mentuemhat (TT 34), who lived seven-and-a-half centuries after Menna's time.[41] Although his reliefs have only survived in fragments, they still retain much of the charm of the earlier examples that inspired them.

A further humorous incident encountered in a bucolic composition worthy of our attention unfurls in a wall-relief from the late Dynasty XVIII tomb-chapel of Merymery at Saqqara. It illustrates a group of hard-working field hands going about their chores for the eternal benefit of the tomb-owner: ploughing, sowing, and reaping (fig. 40). In the upper register, at the right, a pair of donkey drivers is having a bit of a row. The jocularity derives from the blunt dialogue between them. One turns to his comrade and declares: "I'm going to get myself four jars of beer quickly!" Thereupon, the other driver vigorously blames him for already being negligent of his job: "While I was driving off 202 donkeys, you remained sitting on your backside!"[42]

The mention of going off to get some beer allows us to neatly segue into another subject area of ancient Egyptian humour, one that is routinely linked with the promotion of laughter and good cheer the world over, namely comic situations revolving around the generous or over-consumption of alcoholic beverages. The ancient Egyptian wisdom (instructional) texts urge moderation in the drinking beer and wine, and strongly discourage public drunkenness. In one of these, in the Dynasty XVIII *The Teaching of Ani*, the sage despairingly describes a drunkard:

> "Don't indulge in drinking beer, lest you utter evil speech and don't know what you're saying. If you fall and hurt your body, none holds out a hand to you; your companions in the drinking stand up saying: 'Out with the drunk!' If one comes to seek you and talk with you, one finds you lying on the ground, as if you were a little child."[43]

If Dynasty XVIII tomb-chapel scenes are an accurate reflection of reality on this matter, however, intemperance at festive banquets was not at all uncommon and may well have even been considered as a compliment to the hospitality of the host. Drunken guests of both sexes are often pictured at these rollicking affairs being horribly sick, in the act of vomiting, much to the general hilarity of the other partygoers (fig. 41).[44] At the end, some of the participants had to be assisted to their homes. In the rock tomb of Paheri at El Kab, we see a banqueting composition with a bout of exuberant drinking in full progress, attended by various relatives and close friends of the deceased and his wife, Henuterneheh. A notable detail pictures five female guests sitting on mats, looked after by male servants who are plying them with wine and yet more wine (fig. 42). They appear on the surface to be rather sedate, but this belies their revelry as expressed in the captions around them. The second woman on the left, likely already half inebriated, announces to the server before her: "Bring me 18 cups of wine. I want to get drunk. My inside (throat?) is as dry as straw!" However, he has just poured a cup of wine for another woman sitting close by and says her to: "Drink to drunkenness. Celebrate the good day! Hear what your neighbour is saying and don't tire of your pleasure!" The other servant is waiting on a more abstemious guest, who has her hand raised to refuse his offer of drink. He tells her: "Stop resisting and drink. I'm not going to leave you alone (until you do)!" Upon hearing this, her companion sitting on the right, who is sniffing the pleasant fragrance of a lotus blossom and also well on the way to being drunk, cries out: "Drink, and don't be vexed. At least try some, and then let me finish the rest of the jar. The lord Paheri (gave it to us) for drinking!"[45] The humour here comes, needless to say, from the eagerness of the banqueters to become deliriously drunk, especially the hard-drinking lady who

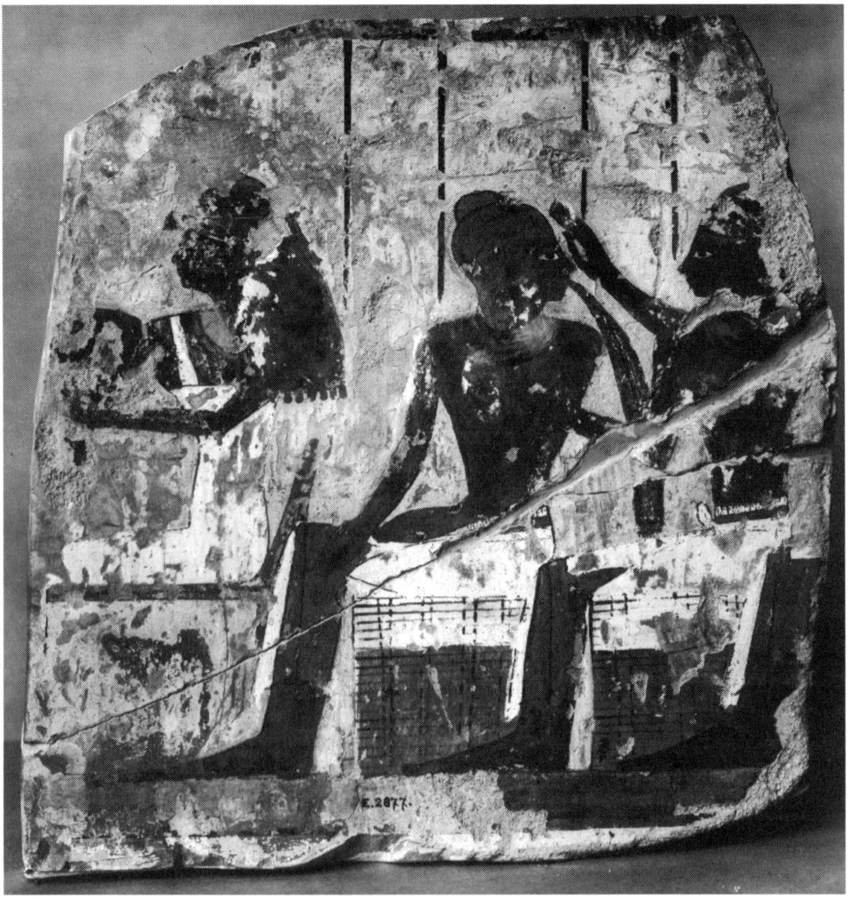

Fig. 41. Fragment of wall-painting depicting an overindulgent drinker at a banquet, the poor fellow now paying the price by being disgustingly sick. He is receiving some comfort from a fellow partygoer. Dynasty XVIII.

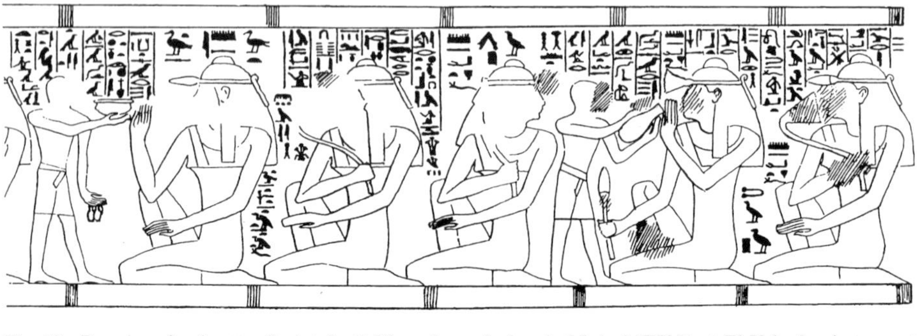

Fig. 42. Drawing of a vignette of painted relief from the tomb-chapel of Paheri (EK 3) at El Kab, showing a group of women at a lavish banquet, attended to by male servants. One of these hard-drinking guests announces that she wants to get drunk. Dynasty XVIII.

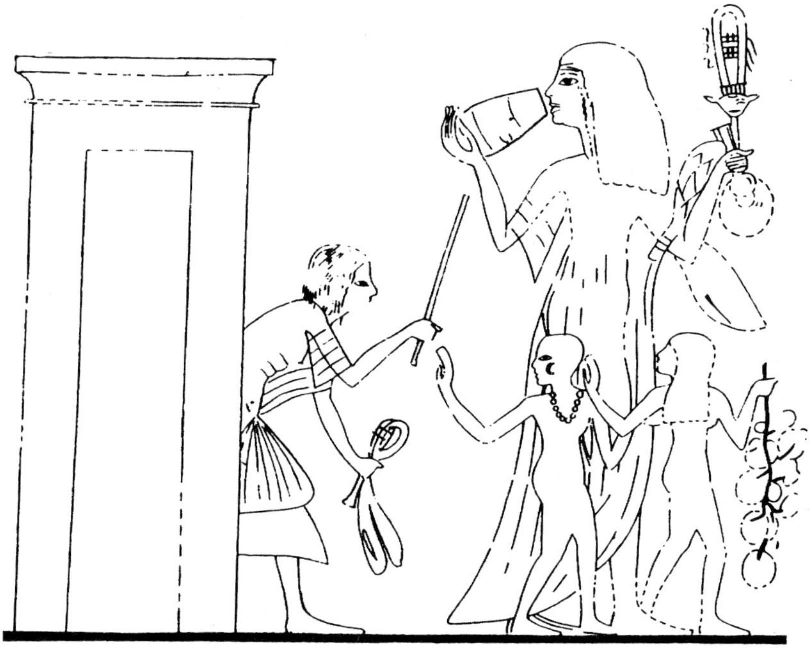

Fig. 43. Drawing of a charming vignette from a wall-painting in the tomb-chapel of Neferhotpe (TT 49) at Thebes. It pictures an angry doorkeeper chasing away revellers attending a garden party with a short stick. Dynasty XVIII.

exaggeratedly calls for 18 cups of wine, and then quips that her inside is parched. It is also found in the celebrants' attempts, joined by the hosts' pushy servants, urging the other women to drink long and deeply.

In the Dynasty XVIII tomb-chapel of Neferhotpe at Thebes, a wall-painting captures a delightful scene of merry-making. Attending this garden party are a young girl and boy, accompanied by their nurse or governess, who is busily shown gulping down beer from a jar and rattling a sistrum (fig. 43). This small group of revellers has evidently awoken a grumpy doorkeeper from his sound sleep and he is amusingly pictured chasing them away by brandishing a short stick. The figure of a sleepy doorkeeper is known from other occurrences and one might easily think of this being an expression of something approaching a running joke. This theme reappears, for example, on a block of relief from a late New Kingdom tomb-chapel at Saqqara. There the doorkeeper is represented *en face* and snoozing while standing on one leg, leaning against the doorpost of his charge during the funerary ceremonies of his master, which is attended by some high-ranking dignitaries (fig. 44). What in heavens name will it take to wake this bored fellow up?

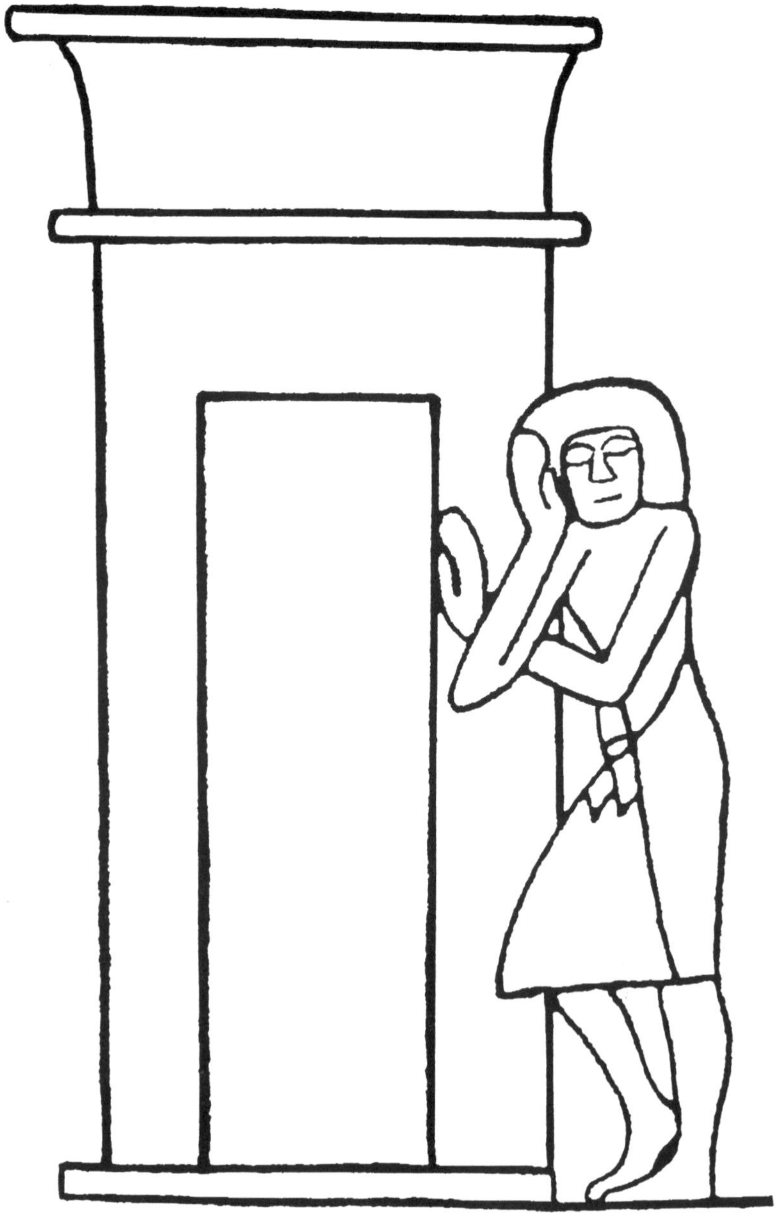

Fig. 44. Drawing of a droll detail on a block of relief. It depicts a doorkeeper dozing while on the job. From a late New Kingdom tomb-chapel at Saqqara.

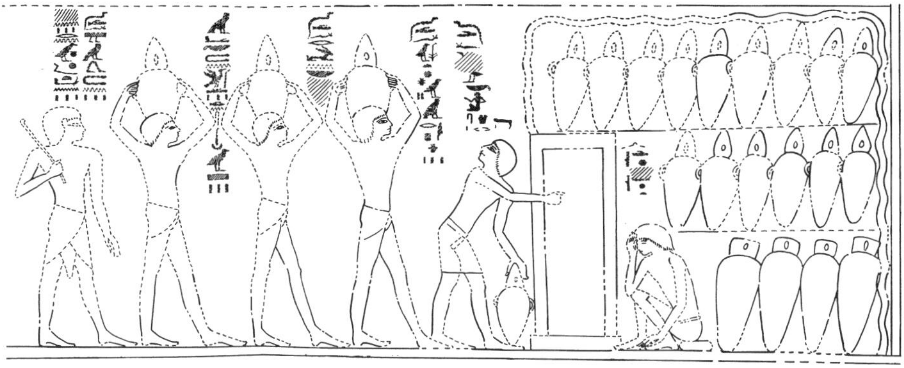

Fig. 45. Drawing of a delightful vignette from a wall-painting in the tomb-chapel of Intef (TT 155) at Thebes. A foreman is supervising four porters carrying wine amphorae for storage in the tomb-owner's cellar, but the doorkeeper is asleep on the job! The episode is enlivened by the inclusion of texts containing the remarks of the men. Dynasty XVIII.

Far and away the funniest instance of this motif of the dozing doorman is found in a wall-painting in the Dynasty XVIII tomb-chapel of Intef at Thebes. The vignette reads almost like a modern comic-strip, which shows humour both in the drawing and in the accompanying texts, and everybody has something to say (fig. 45). An overseer with a short stick is supervising an orderly procession of four porters carrying freshly pressed wine in large stoppered amphorae for storage in the tomb-owner's cellar, shown on the right; but the progress of the group has been held up by an amusing incident. The overseer, who hasn't noticed what is happening at the head of the file, calls to his men: "Move on! We will scorch ourselves (out here in the sun)!" The fourth porter, directly in front of the overseer, bearing a heavy wine-jar on his shoulder, mutters that: "The load is burdensome!" The third porter responds to him with an affirmative: "Really!" The first porter, who has set down his jar, is knocking at the door of the cellar, but without any response. He turns and says to the second porter behind him: "The doorkeeper has probably fallen asleep!" His comrade likewise finds the silence very curious and says of the cellar's doorkeeper: "He's just drunk on the wine!" But from inside the wine-cellar there finally comes a faint voice, the doorkeeper now rubbing his eyes, having clearly fallen asleep on the job, claiming: "I haven't been sleeping at all!"[46] Whether his dozing off was, in fact, related to drinking wine remains unknown, although he had ample opportunity to indulge in some among all those rows of full wine-jars. In antiquity, as today, this jolly episode cannot fail to produce a smile. Its bright joking immediately transcends the millennia.[47]

The British Egyptologist, Norman de Garis Davies, a brilliant interpreter of Egyptian painting and relief, saw a wealth of humorous

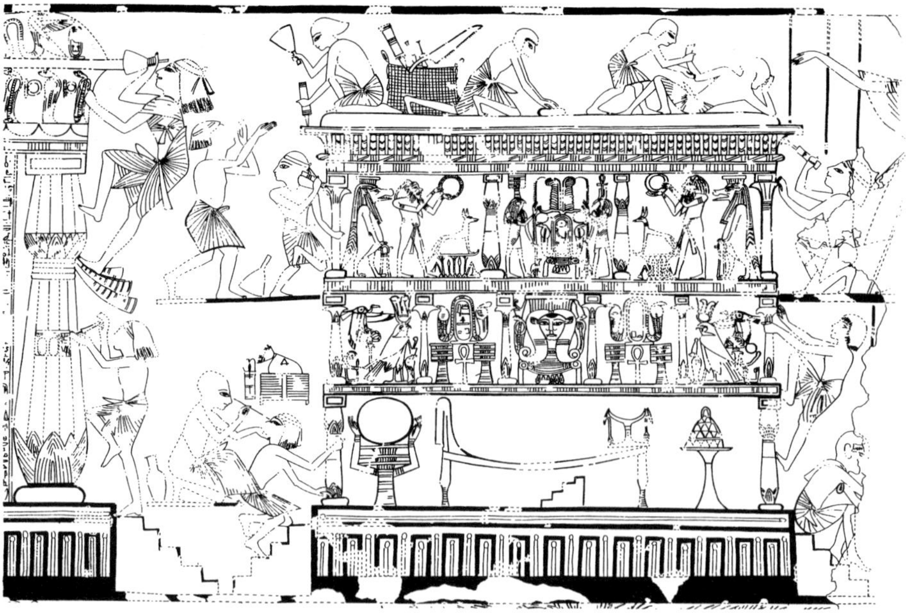

Fig. 46. Drawing of a remarkable scene illustrating craftsmen at work, from a wall-painting in the tomb-chapel of Ipuy (TT 217) at Deir el Medina. The antics include a man on the top of the shrine who has dozed of; a friend is trying to arouse him. Another fellow has dropped his mallet on the toes of an unlucky co-worker. Dynasty XIX.

touches in tomb-chapel decoration from early times. But for him, there was none where laughs were so deliberately plotted as in the Dynasty XIX tomb-chapel of Ipuy at Deir el Medina, a sculptor during the reign of Ramesses II.[48] The scene Davies probably had foremost in his mind is an especially rollicking and delightful one (fig. 46). The action centres on a group of craftsmen clambering about, finishing the work on an elaborate shrine or catafalque for use in the popular cult of the defied King Amenhotpe I. The painter has introduced several conspicuous comic incidents into his composition.[49] On top of the shrine a craftsman is smoothing off its surface with a piece of sandstone, while just to the right another has seized the opportunity to lie down for a snooze. On the right, however, is the tomb-owner (much damaged), who has noticed the slacker and is shouting at him to wake up or else; a comrade is trying to arouse him. Another man on the top has just dropped a big wooden mallet on the toes of a hapless co-worker; the poor fellow is now hopping around on one foot as the overseer standing next to him bellows at the guilty individual above to be more careful. We can only imagine their ribald language, since there are no captions attached to the figures. Just below them, another craftsman is taking some time off have his eyes made up by a kohl-painter instead of doing his job, while on the construction project

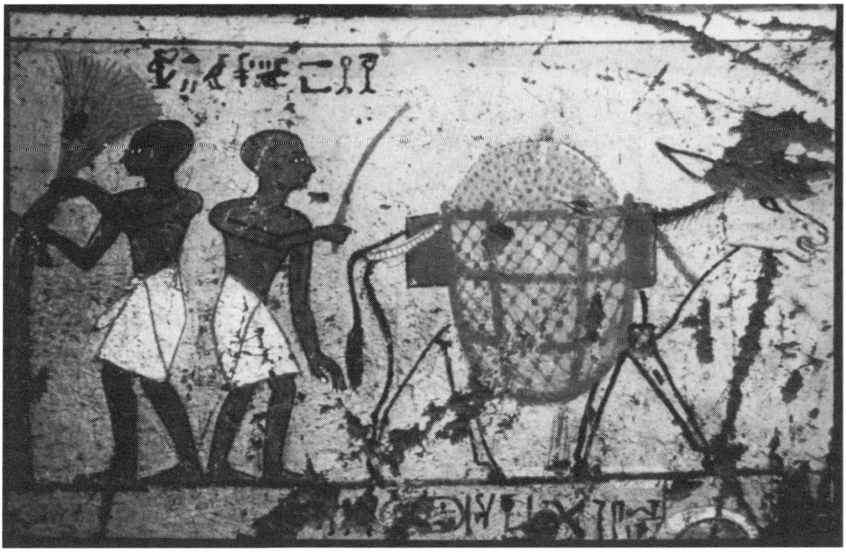

Fig. 47. This small episode of country life comes from a wall-painting in the tomb-chapel of Panehsy (TT 16) at Thebes. It pictures a reluctant donkey carrying a huge load of newly cut grain in wickerwork panniers on its back. The beast is being whacked into action by the driver wielding a stick, loudly brays in protest, and has an terribly displeased look in its eye. Dynasty XIX.

at the left, a carpenter is clinging perilously and is close to taking a tumble onto a co-worker standing beneath him. There are other details in Ipuy's tomb-chapel that are also ripe with a gentle humour.[50] In one, even the deceased himself is not wholly spared from this, being illustrated in a composition with a charming little kitten perched on his lap, ready for some mischief, while the mother-cat is curiously shown full face under the chair of his wife.

Although rarer and certainly less striking than in earlier times, artisans of the New Kingdom continued to see amusing moments in the behaviours of birds and beasts and included some of their antics in private sepulchral art (figs. 14, 16 and 47-49). The Egyptian farmer was always bedevilled by stubborn or defiant domestic animals that have determined minds of their own. Not surprisingly, these are often over-worked and belaboured donkeys (fig. 24). Wall-paintings in the Dynasty XIX tomb-chapel of Panehsy at Thebes contain several vignettes in this time-honoured tradition (figs. 47 and 48). The most inventive, which has a caption, records an incident of discontent in the fields. A team of oxen hitched to a scratch-plough is working when one of them suddenly decides to have a rest, lies down and refuses to budge an inch, despite the repeated blows or threats of a field hand with a stick (fig. 48). Finally, the frustrated ploughman, Prehotpe by name, shouts vituperation at the obstinate

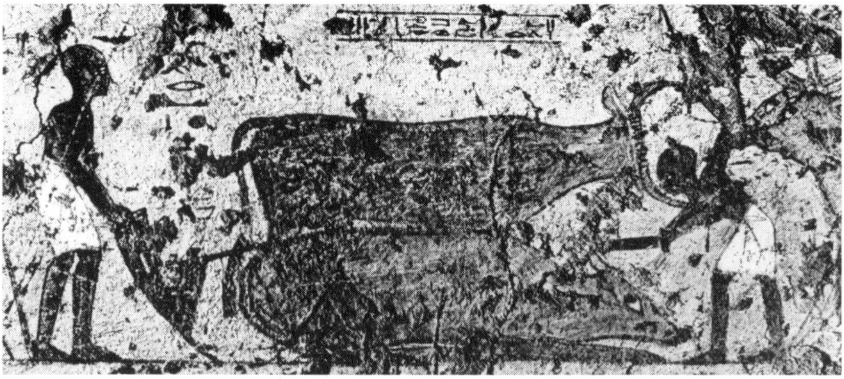

Fig. 48. Vignette of a wall-painting capturing an amusing incident of trouble in the fields. From the tomb-chapel of Panehsy (TT 16) at Thebes. Dynasty XIX.

creature: "Get up, get moving, stop playing dead, you (brute)!"[51] At this, the beleaguered beast drolly glances back at him as if to say: "In my own time!"

The extremely rich iconography of Theban tomb paintings and reliefs provide a wide assortment of entertaining images of peasants and craftsmen, which are often portrayed with the standard features of those belonging to the lower rungs of Egyptian society (figs. 50-52).[52] Take, for example, the figure of an old carpenter in a workshop from the Dynasty XVIII tomb-chapel of Nebamen and Ipuky, who is shown laboriously sawing an ebony board tied to a wooden post. He is treated in the spirit of caricature, being characterised by an aged and toil-worn look: balding head with thin, straggling long hair, stubble on his chin, paunch with a distended navel, and gaping mouth, suggesting that he is out of breath (fig. 53). Details such as this clownish lout go a long way to enliven and create light-hearted moods in the less prominent secular scenes of a number of private tomb-chapels at Thebes.

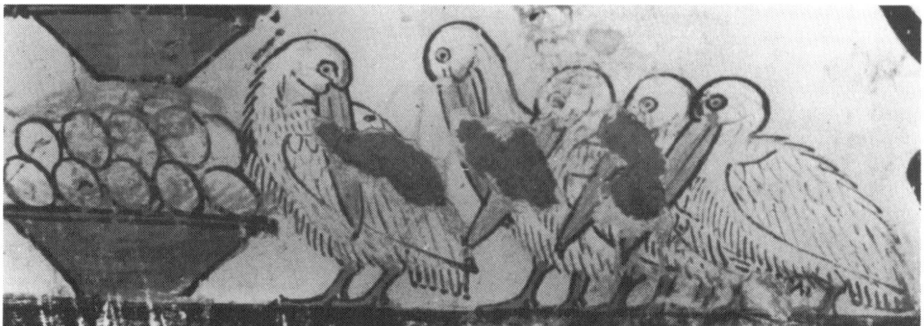

Fig. 49. This appealing vignette of wall-painting is from the tomb-chapel of Horemhab (TT 78) at Thebes. A flock of pelicans has been playfully observed engaging in some social interaction. Dynasty XVIII.

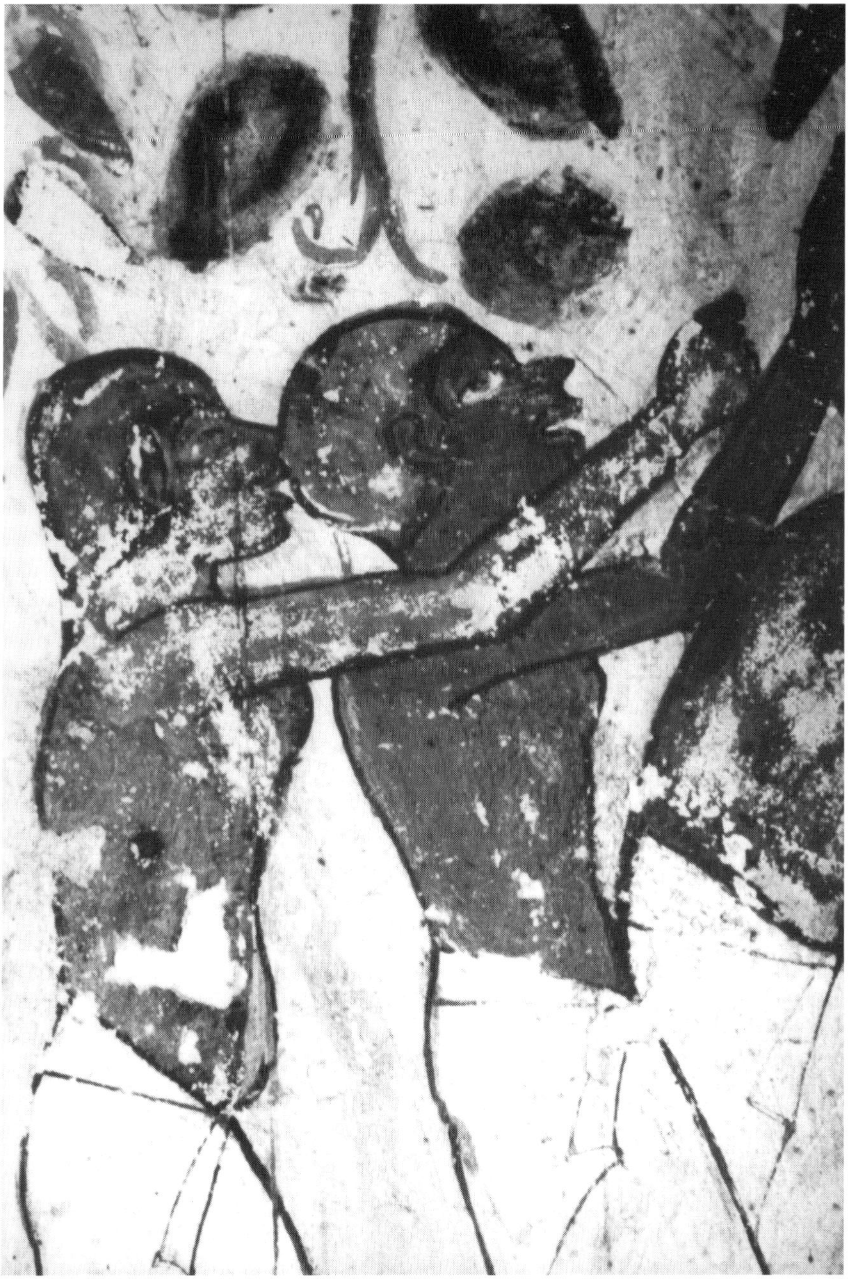

Fig. 50. Detail of wall-painting from a wine-pressing scene in the tomb-chapel of Userhet (TT 56) at Thebes, portraying the happy faces of two workmen, singing as they tread out the grapes in the crushing vat – or have they been enjoying some wine? Dynasty XVIII.

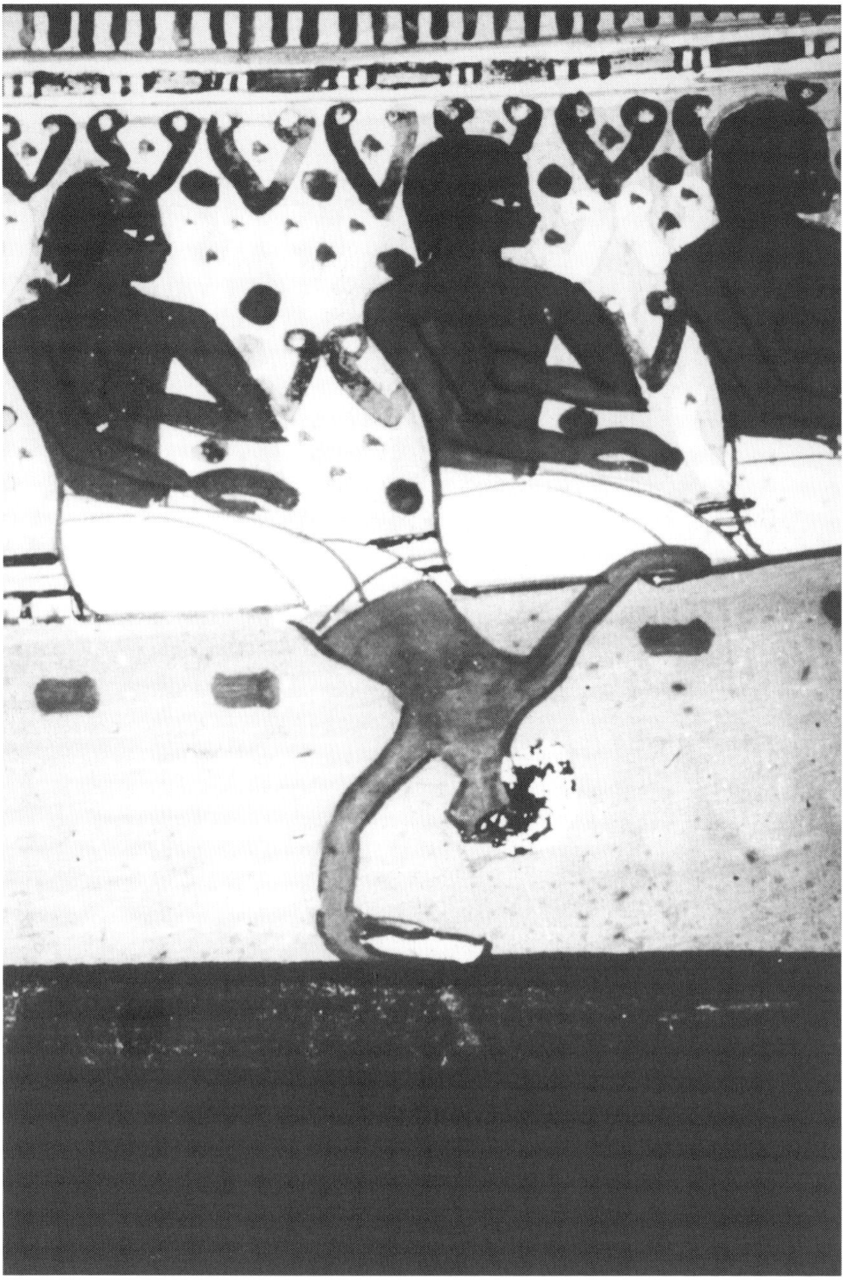

Fig. 51. This amusing detail of a thirsty sailor leaning down over the side of a ship to draw a cup of water from the Nile comes from a wall-painting depicting the tomb-owner's funerary voyage to Abydos. From the tomb-chapel of Menna (TT 69) at Thebes. Dynasty XVIII.

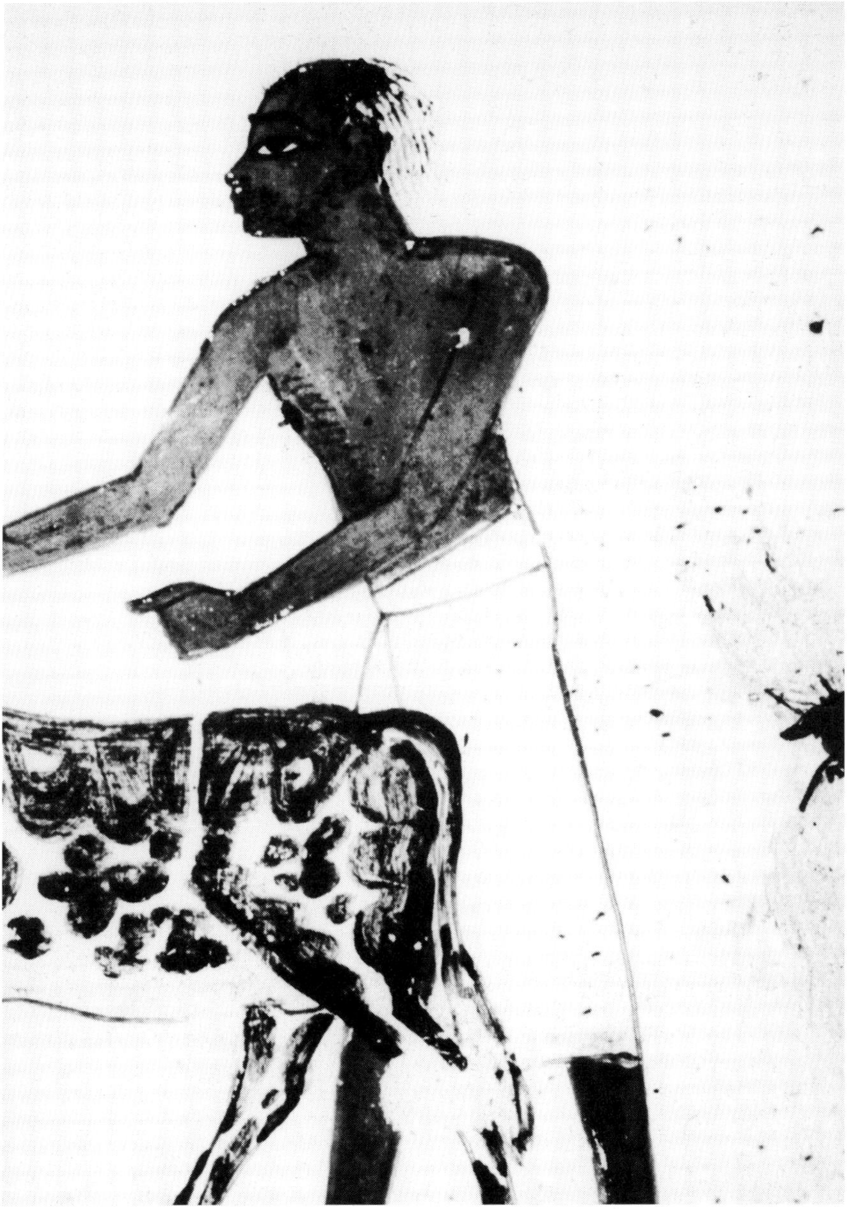

Fig. 52. This detail of wall-painting illustrates a cowherd bringing a sacrificial calf. His balding head and wispy hair, stubby beard and hairy chest, associate him with the lower orders of society. From the tomb-chapel of Menna (TT 69) at Thebes. Dynasty XVIII.

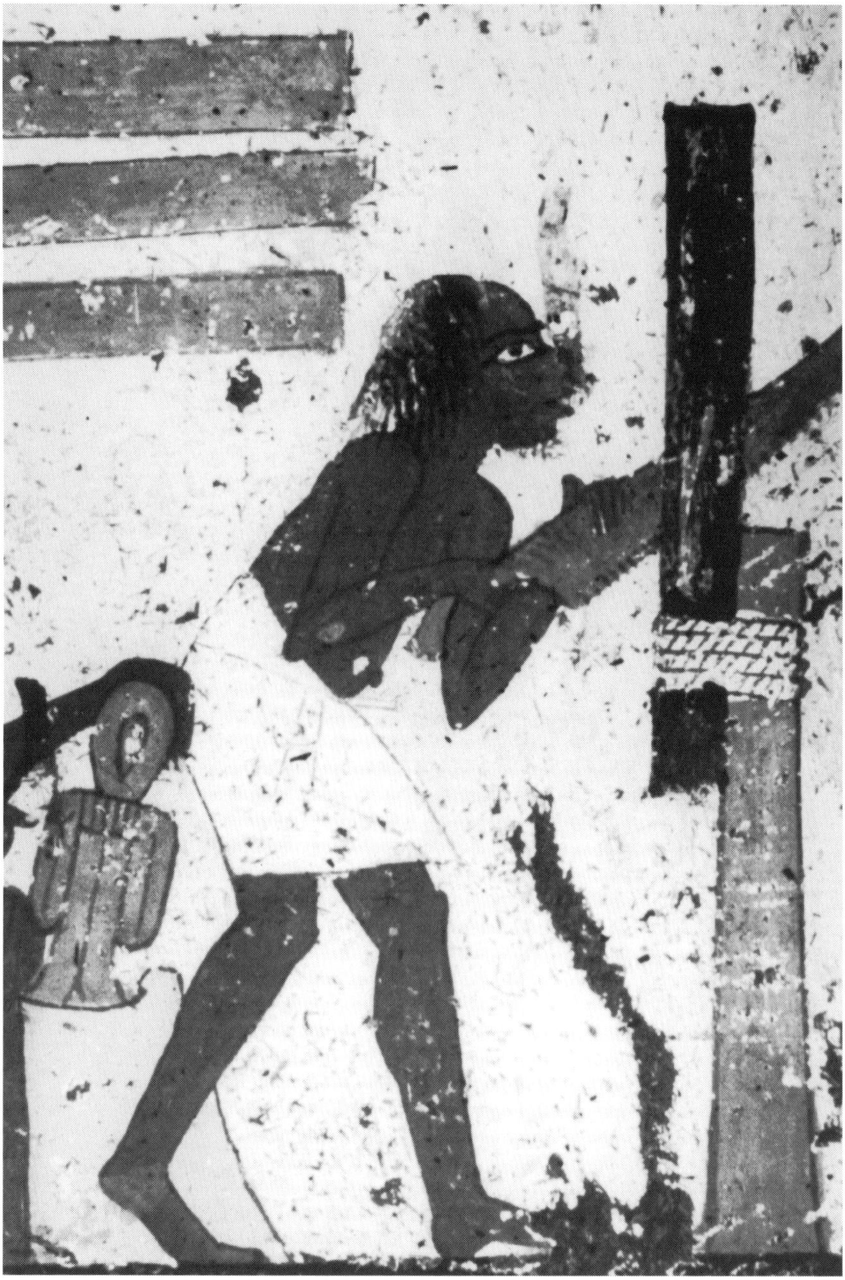

Fig. 53. Detail of a wall-painting showing an amusing old carpenter labouring in a workshop. From the tomb-chapel of Nebamen and Ipuky (TT 181) at Thebes. Dynasty XVIII.

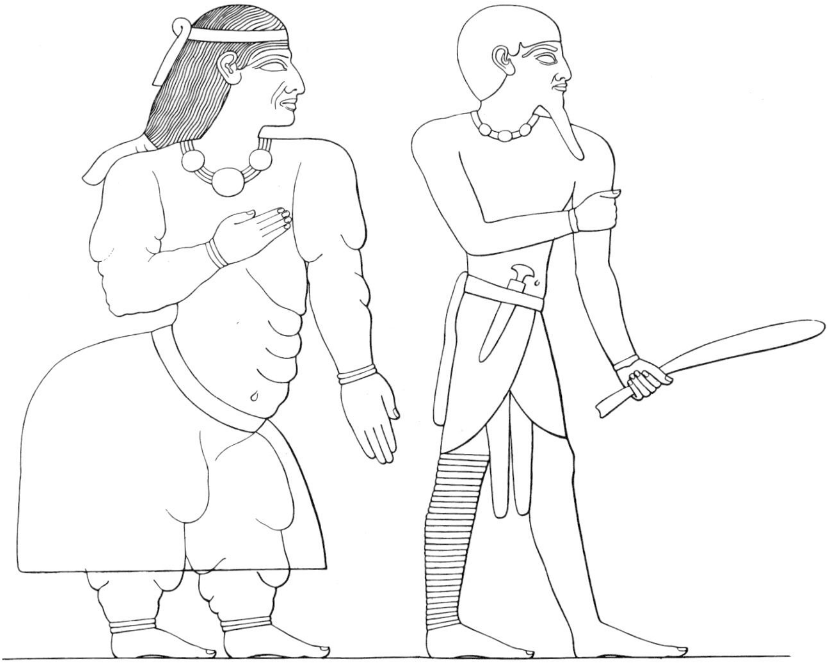

Fig. 54. Drawing of the ruler of the African land of Punt Parehu, with his monstrously fat wife Ati, as portrayed on a fragment of painted relief from the mortuary temple of Queen Hatshepsut at Deir el Bahri. Ati's portrait was later copied by a draughtsman of the Ramesside Period (see fig. 129). Dynasty XVIII.

While the decorative programme of Egyptian temples seldom permitted the inclusion of humour, elements of comic relief can occasionally be glimpsed in monumental art. These generally relate to the depiction of foreigners. The most widely known occurrence is found on a wall in the southern half of the middle colonnade of Queen Hatshepsut's Dynasty XVIII mortuary temple at Deir el Bahri. In a splendid series of scenes celebrating the events of her sea-borne expedition to the far-off African land of Punt, we encounter Parehu, the Puntite chief, accompanied by his extraordinary-looking wife, Ati (fig. 54). The couple have been realistically observed in regards to their ethnic features and dress; note for example, that Parehu's right leg seems encased from ankle to knee with metal or ivory rings. In stark contrast to the slender figure of the Puntite sovereign, the Queen of Punt is mountainously obese and deformed.[53] Rather than suffering from a disease, as has frequently been suggested, her fatness is likely to have been a symbol of her royal station in Puntite culture, and even her daughter is rather enormous. The humour here has been much heightened by fact that the queen, who definitely was in no condition to do much walking, is followed by a little saddled donkey, that has a brief

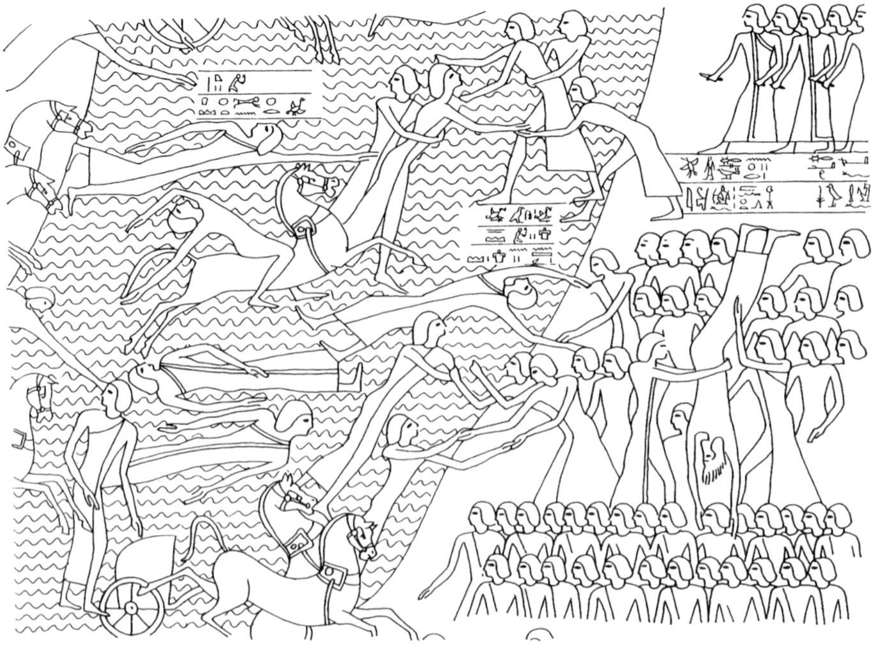

Fig. 55. Drawing of a scene carved on the mortuary temple of Ramesses II (or Ramesseum) at Thebes, picturing the mighty Hittite prince of Aleppo being humiliatingly emptied out of water he swallowed while fleeing across the Orontes River. Dynasty XIX.

caption written just above it, identifying the creature as the queen's trusty mount.[54] What a backbreaking task for that poor beast! One can readily imagine the joking and roars of scurrilous laughter this outlandish portrait must have aroused among some of the sharp-witted visitors to the temple in antiquity. It obviously also struck a passing draughtsman of the Ramesside Period some two centuries later, who may have found her likeness hideously amusing. He paused long enough to execute a lively impression of it on a small limestone ostracon (fig. 129).

One of the more hilarious instances of visual derision of an Egyptian foe is represented on a wall of the Dynasty XIX mortuary temple of Ramesses II (or Ramesseum) at Thebes. It illustrates an episode from the famous story of the king's battle against the Hittites at the city of Qadesh in Syria (fig. 55).[55] We see the routed enemy, in utter disarray, forced to plunge into the Orontes River to escape, the Egyptian chariotry in close pursuit. On the opposite bank, helping hands are outstretched to rescue floundering comrades. A touch of malicious humour is afforded at the right as "the wretched prince of Aleppo" is absurdly being held up-side-down by his soldiers to empty him out of all the water that he had swallowed while swimming across the river. This humiliating portrayal could hardly have

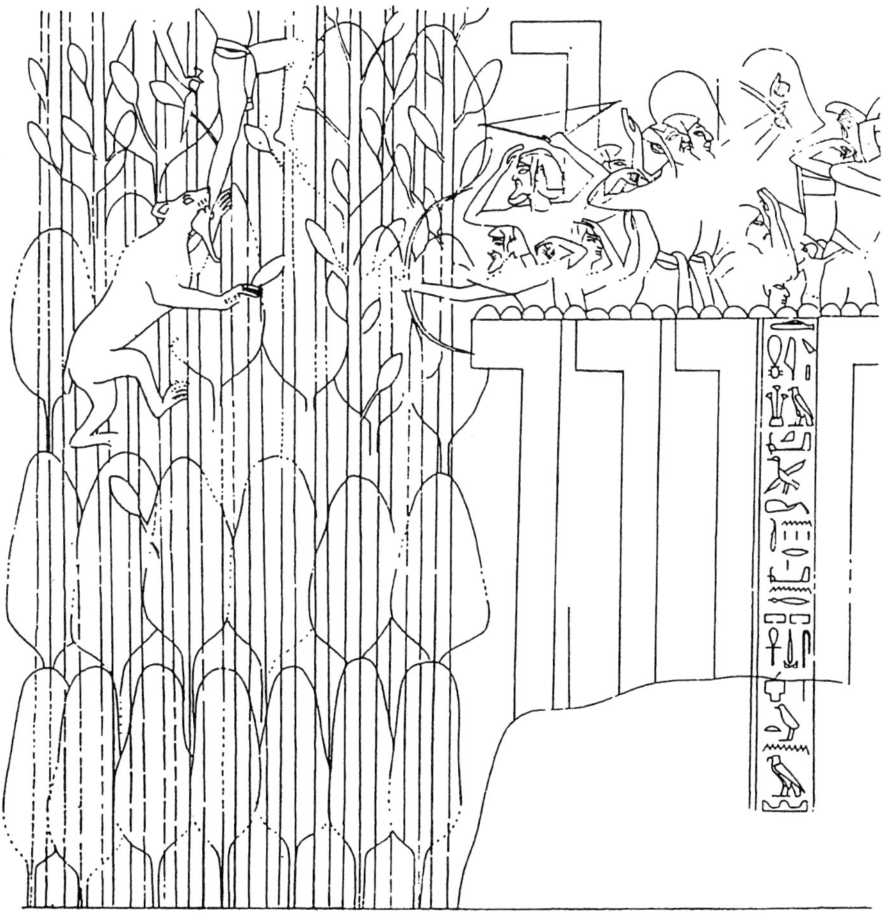

Fig. 56. Drawing of an episode carved on a wall of Luxor Temple. It depicts Ramesses II attacking a Syrian fortress at Satuna. A fugitive is climbing a tree in a cedar forest to escape a bear that has already seized his leg. Dynasty XIX.

been unintentional and would not have been missed on its audience. Not only could foreign enemies be pictured with their facial features grossly exaggerated, but also in highly undignified postures and situations, as shown here. In a similar vein, depictions of Egypt's traditional foes are routinely displayed during the New Kingdom tightly fettered, and sometimes prostrate, adorning the king's footrest, sandals, the dais on which his throne stood, and the like. In this way they would be magically subjected to the shame and agony of his daily trampling on them.[56]

In another public example of mockery, also from Dynasty XIX, carved on Luxor temple, an Asiatic fortress at Satuna is being stormed by the Egyptian army under Ramesses II. A Syrian fugitive can be seen attempting to climb a tree in a wood to escape a hungry wild bear which already has seized one of his legs (fig. 56).[57] This vignette of relief recalls precisely the reference made in a contemporary epistolary schoolboy exercise, *The Satirical Letter* in Papyrus Anastasi I, to the prince of Asher being found in a balsam tree by a bear, where the incident is used as a literary device to express ridicule. It is a welcomed touch of drollery to the intense atmosphere this standard battle scene. These all too few and brief moments of lightness help to relieve some of the formality permeating the official themes traditional to Egyptian temple decoration.

3 Humorous Drawings on Papyri and Ostraca

Visual pharaonic humour is best attested, and found its widest and most creative expression, during Dynasties XIX and XX, which is often referred to as the Ramesside Period (when the most common royal name was Ramesses). Three fragmentary illustrated papyri, now housed in museum collections in London, Cairo, and Turin, each contain on them a carefully composed series of comic drawings.[1] These reveal an energetic humour that is still capable of raising a smile on faces after more than thirty centuries, even if the full impact or point of the jokes may now be lost on the modern viewer. They are an early precursor of the familiar cartoons and comic-strips in today's newspapers and magazines (fig. 147). Unlike these, the juxtaposed vignettes represented on ancient Egyptian papyrus scrolls have minimal, or lack any, narrative sequence to them and, by and large, appear to exist entirely independently of each another. Nor is the speech of the characters indicated on the papyri; ideas were merely conveyed pictorially. The exceptions to this are the brief hieratic captions giving part of the sexually explicit dialogue between the human protagonists in the obscene portion of the celebrated satirical-erotic papyrus in Turin. From what has now been preserved on these fragmentary papyri, it should be noted that it is not known whether there might have been texts which served to introduce or follow the drawings.[2] At any rate, the rollicking good fun and laughs on them are immediately recognizable and are able to successfully transcend the absence of written language. The group of "satirical papyri", as they have today come to be known, in all likelihood share the same provenance.

It was a secluded village housing the workmen and the highly-skilled artisans, along with their families, who were responsible for the excavation and decoration of the splendid New Kingdom royal tombs in the nearby (less than a mile away) Valley of the Kings and Valley of the Queens, on the western bank of the Nile at Thebes. This small walled community of privileged state employees was nestled in a narrow desert valley near the southern end of the Theban necropolis, at a place today known as Deir el Medina.[3] The ancient name of the site was *Set-Maat*, "the Place of Truth". We are extremely fortunate in having a tremendous wealth of information on the personalities and workaday lives of this village's inhabitants, largely afforded by papyri and inscribed ostraca. They enjoyed a standard of living and level of literacy that were substantially above the vast majority of the Egyptian population. It has been estimated that during Dynasty XX at least forty percent of the residents of Deir el Medina could read and write.[4] There seems little doubt that all three of the illustrated satirical papyri were produced by draughtsmen belonging to this distinguished group of artisans. The precise date when they were composed, though, remains a bit uncertain. There is general consistence of opinion among scholars, however, that they were created sometime during the Ramesside Period, the time when this isolated settlement was at its greatest strength and work on the royal tombs was in full flourish. This very prosperous village was finally abandoned during the closing years of Dynasty XX, after nearly five centuries of habitation, when the royal burials ceased and local conditions grew unstable due to marauding bands of Libyans in the area.

When not engaged in tomb-building for their royal patrons, the gifted draughtsmen of Deir el Medina spent a portion of their off-work hours working on private drawings for practice and pleasure. These included casual sketches that were outside the traditional repertoire of iconographic subject matter associated with funerary and religious themes. These drawings often display enormous vitality and a freedom of imagination that is rarely met with in their official commissions. The ancient Egyptians were a cheerful and fun-loving people who dearly appreciated a good laugh. A wider secular sphere of artistic expression to amuse and parody is suggested by the appearance of informal drawings on satirical papyri and figured ostraca (disposable limestone flakes and potsherds).[5] The existence of the painted sketches on the costly medium of papyrus scrolls definitely indicates that they were intended to be kept, and were probably shared with colleagues, close friends, and family in the village, and not simply tossed away after a few chuckles. Together they give an idea of a genre of lighthearted work that may have been more widespread, but which otherwise has not survived in the archaeological record.

This sizable collection of drawings on papyri and figured ostraca features immensely appealing images of wild and domestic animals exuberantly acting out human roles. The theme of a world turned upside-down with laughable incongruities was especially popular in this brand of humour. Here predators, often cats, herd or wait on their natural prey, birds and mice, or are otherwise subservient to them in some fashion, rather than devouring them. The most routinely depicted of these anthropomorphising motifs revolves around the eternal enmity between cats and mice, documented in numerous cultures the world over, and even

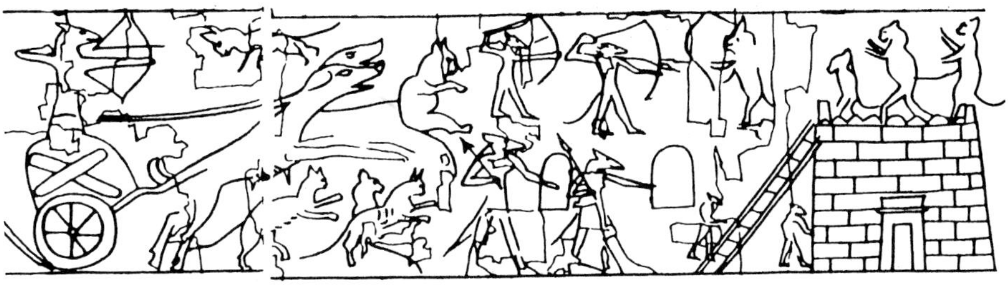

Fig. 57. Drawing of an exciting battle-scene from the satirical-erotic papyrus in the Turin Museum (see fig. 66). A fortress defended by cats is under siege from an army of attacking mice. A heroic mouse-warrior, in the spirit of a pharaoh such as Ramesses II, fires arrows from a speeding war-chariot drawn by a pair of galloping female dogs. Ramesside Period.

well-known down to the present-day from animated films and cartoons such as Tom and Jerry.[6] Egyptian audiences must have derived enormous enjoyment from these as well. Perhaps it is not too surprising then that, just as their familiar modern counterparts, the clever mice always seem to manage to outwit their feline adversaries and win the day. One particularly celebrated vignette on the Turin papyrus represents a pharaoh-like warrior mouse driving a dog-drawn chariot, and valiantly charging a cat-fortress, which is about to fall (fig. 57). A number of these same scenes reappear in varied forms on different comic works. Many, it would seem, were improvisations on widely-known or stock motifs.

While the bulk of the satirical subjects encountered on Ramesside Period papyri and figured ostraca are rarely known in other media, some of the motifs do have antecedents in other forms. As we have previously seen, Egyptian artisans always had a predilection to treat animal life, especially household animals, in an affectionate and merry manner, even including some of their clownish antics and pranks in tomb-chapel scenes (see Chapter 2). Already during the Middle Kingdom, limestone figurines of monkeys playing musical instruments appear. These are followed in Dynasty XVIII by additional stone statuettes of monkeys imitating musicians, along with a range of additional humorous types, which were discovered at Tell el Amarna.[7] The highlights of these include such tomfoolery as a boat being rowed by a crew of monkeys, and a painted limestone children's toy representing two monkeys riding in a chariot drawn by another monkey, as if it were a horse, with a fourth monkey in front serving as the groom (fig. 58). This latter cheery object was thought by its excavators to have been fashioned as a parody of the heretic King Akhenaten and the royal family driving through his capital city, which they evidently did on a regular basis.[8] Another popular series of figurines uncovered at the site depicts one or more hungry monkeys attempting to

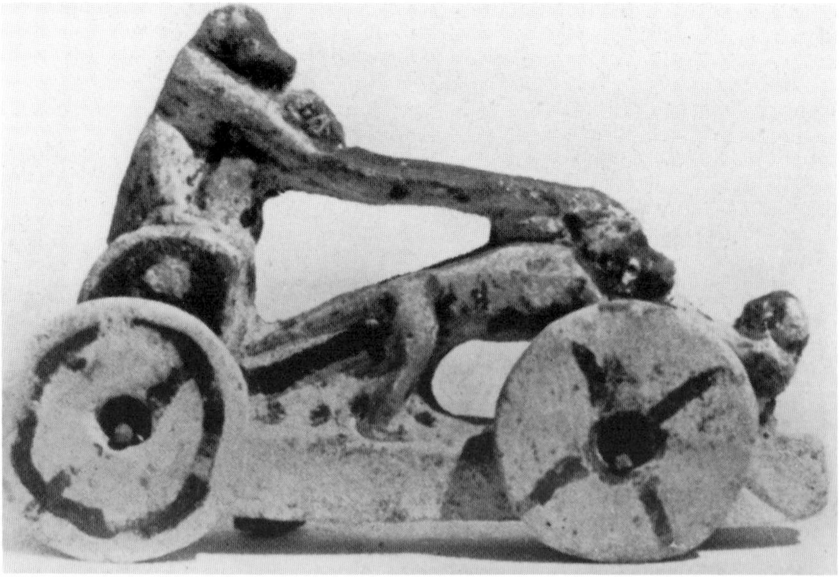

Fig. 58. A painted limestone children's toy of two monkeys riding in a chariot drawn by another monkey, with a fourth monkey in front acting as a groom. The excavators of Tell el Amarna, Akhenaten's short-lived capital, thought that this object was intended to directly parody a representation commonly found in the rock-cut tombs of the élite at the site, illustrating the king driving his chariot through the residence city. Dynasty XVIII.

pilfer sacks of appetizing *dôm*-nuts (the apple-sized fruit of the *dôm*-palm), a theme that reappears in force later on figured ostraca. Other types show them as acrobats, mutually grooming, and tending their young. Similar statuettes of monkeys have reportedly been found at Kom Medinet Ghurab and Deir el Medina as well.[9] The function of this kind of minor work was probably little more than to delight and amuse their owners. In any event, this three-dimensional material serves as a splendid introduction to the greatly-expanded and even more imaginative variety of entertaining animal motifs seen on papyri and ostraca during the Ramesside Period.

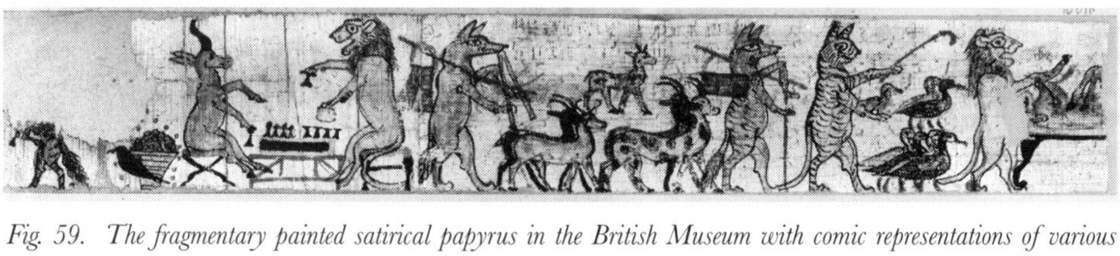

Fig. 59. The fragmentary painted satirical papyrus in the British Museum with comic representations of various animals behaving like common people, but where the roles of the real world are reversed. On this large sheet an antelope is shown playing a board game with a lion, foxes herd goats, and a cat tends a flock of poultry. Probably from Deir el Medina. Ramesside Period.

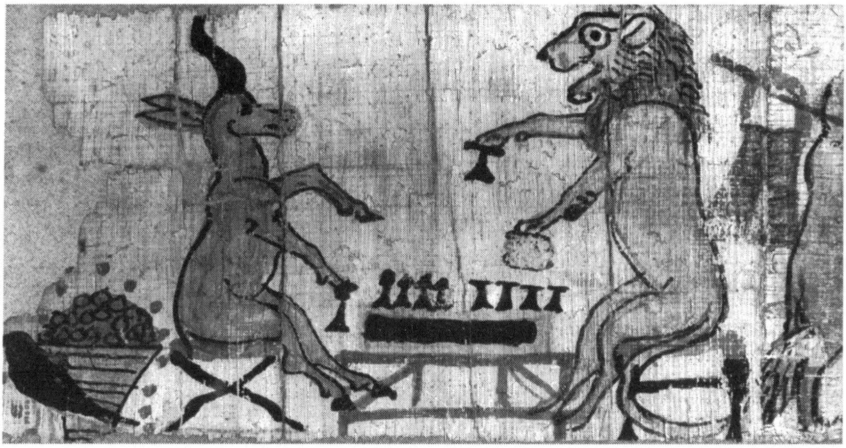

Fig. 60. Delightful vignette of a lion and an antelope playing the board game senet *from the satirical papyrus in the British Museum. Ramesside Period.*

Some of the finest examples of these comic animal representations are found on the fragmentary painted satirical papyrus now in the British Museum, London (figs. 59-61).[10] The document illustrates a range of birds and beasts engaged in everyday human activities, but with an additional wrinkle, the roles of the real world are reversed and pandemonium reigns. The largest fragment of the papyrus is (9 x 54.5 cm), in general well-preserved (fig. 59). It displays, from the left, a large crow standing under a tree, next to a full basket of brightly-coloured fruit. This damaged vignette may have been similar to one on the Turin papyrus (fig. 68). Next we encounter a timid antelope and the king of beasts sitting across from each other on low stools, peacefully immersed in playing *senet*, a board game reminiscent of our draughts (fig. 60). The match thus pits the hunter against the hunted, and from the gleeful expression on the face of the wide-eyed lion, he appears to be in a winning position. This is followed by a pair of foxes, normally the legendary enemy of farmyard animals, acting as good shepherds for a flock of goats, each

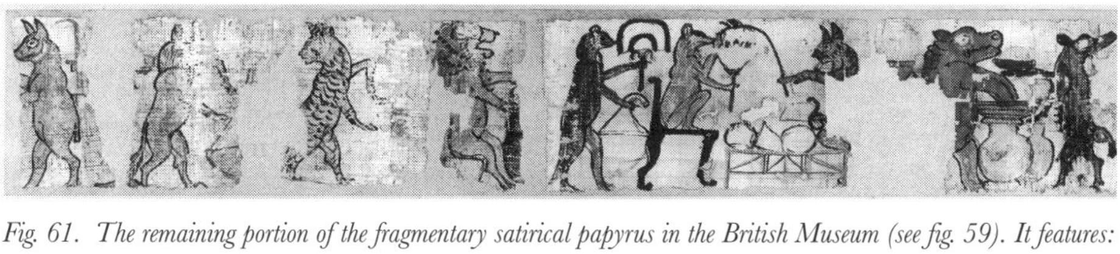

Fig. 61. The remaining portion of the fragmentary satirical papyrus in the British Museum (see fig. 59). It features: a canine(?) and a cat carrying a basket slung on a pole, a seated lion, a well-heeled mouse attended to by her servants, and a brawny hippopotamus beer-brewer. Ramesside Period.

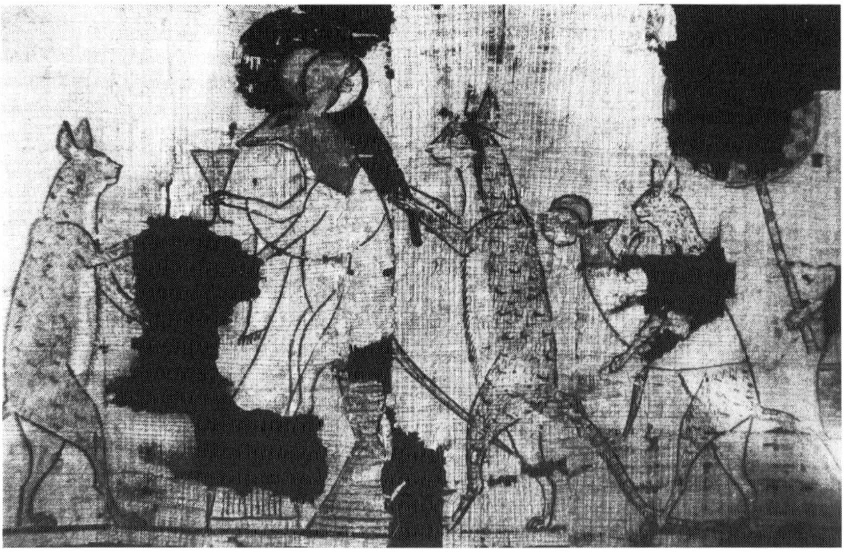

Fig. 62. A vignette from the fragmentary painted satirical papyrus in the Cairo Museum. It displays a procession cats attending to a seated and fashionably-dressed lady mouse at her toilette. Purchased at Tuna el Gebel, but probably from Deir el Medina. Ramesside Period.

with a bag of provisions slung over its shoulder on a long stick. One of these erstwhile predators is playing a tune on a double oboe. Further along, a tabby cat is wielding a long crook, driving a flock of plump ducks or geese. As a crowning touch of irony, the diligent creature is gently carrying a fledgling, apparently too young to keep up with the others, balanced on its arm. At the right, there is an astonishing, though now unfortunately incomplete vignette. It depicts a lion reared on its hind legs, with a jovial look on its face, having sexual intercourse with a hoofed-creature of some species (is it a donkey?) which is lying on its back in a bed.[11] Conversely, could this be the same antelope we already saw the lion defeat at *senet* earlier on the fragment, as has been proposed?[12] Possibly, but the colourings of the two beasts do appear to be somewhat different, so doubts about its precise identity will persist.

The remaining vignettes of this papyrus are much less well-preserved and, therefore, the interpretation of several of them cannot be given with a great deal of confidence (fig. 61). Nor is it known whether the fragments are correctly mounted in their original order, and the length of the lacunae between them is uncertain.[13] From the left, work in the fields is depicted. A beast, now missing, was holding a sickle or crook. Next, several creatures are depicted performing diverse activities. These include a canine(?) and a tabby cat carrying a long pole on their shoulders, over which a large basket of grain(?) is slung. Then comes a seated lion, who is either sieving flour or making beer. He has three rows of black dots around his mane, which could be interpreted as a beaded necklace or the like. This is followed by a well-known motif on satirical papyri and figured ostraca. A pair of servants, one a mouse the other a cat, is tending to an eminent lady(?) mouse. She is sitting on a high-backed chair, knees in a tucked position, and holding a large flower in her hand. There is a table loaded with food offerings before her. The mouse and cat are fanning their mistress with cool air. Finally, at the far right, a brawny hippopotamus is portrayed, along with a female assistant of some species, brewing a batch of beer.

The painted satirical papyrus in the Egyptian Museum, Cairo, consists of a single tattered sheet and a loose fragment (13 x 55.5 cm), displaying two unrelated vignettes (figs. 62-65).[14] On the left side, a procession of four house-cats is attending to a *grande dame* mouse at her toilette. She is sitting on a tall wickerwork birthing-stool, resting her legs on a footrest, and is fashionably dressed in an ankle-length sheer robe. One of the felines has served her a goblet and she is about to raise it to her lips. Another acts as a hairdresser and is arranging the locks of her massive wig. Note that this creature sports a chic long black curl of her own, held in place with a long hairpin. A third tabby cat charmingly parodies a nursemaid, and is tenderly carrying her baby mouse, which has Mickey Mouse-like round ears, swaddled in a sling (fig. 63). The fourth, following close behind, bears a large sunshade, and a jar of liquid. In the vignette on the right side, which is incomplete, the animal characters proceed in the opposite direction (fig. 64). Using a shoulder-yoke, a fox serves as a water-carrier, as his companion of the same species pours the water from one of these large jars into a trough for a recumbent ox in a pen. At the far right, on a small loose fragment, a third fox, wearing what looks like a shawl, can just be glimpsed, walking on top of the enclosure.

The famous painted satirical-erotic papyrus in the Museo Egizio, Turin, which is officially known as Papyrus 55001, while now sadly fragmentary with many lacunae (25 x 259 cm), is both the best known and most spectacular of all the extant comic works (figs. 57 and 66-68).[15] This extraordinary document has two highly distinct sections, which are separated from one another by a vertical line. In the smaller portion (85 cm), on the right side of the papyrus, a topsy-turvy animal world unfolds in two registers. It exhibits fifteen delightful episodes of hilarious bird and beast activity, in the familiar vein of animals imitating human activities. The larger part of this papyrus (174 cm), however, which is on the left side, is devoted to twelve vignettes of caricatured sexual encounters between men with enormous, erect phalli and one or more scantily clad young women (figs. 136 and 141-146). This is the only surviving major work

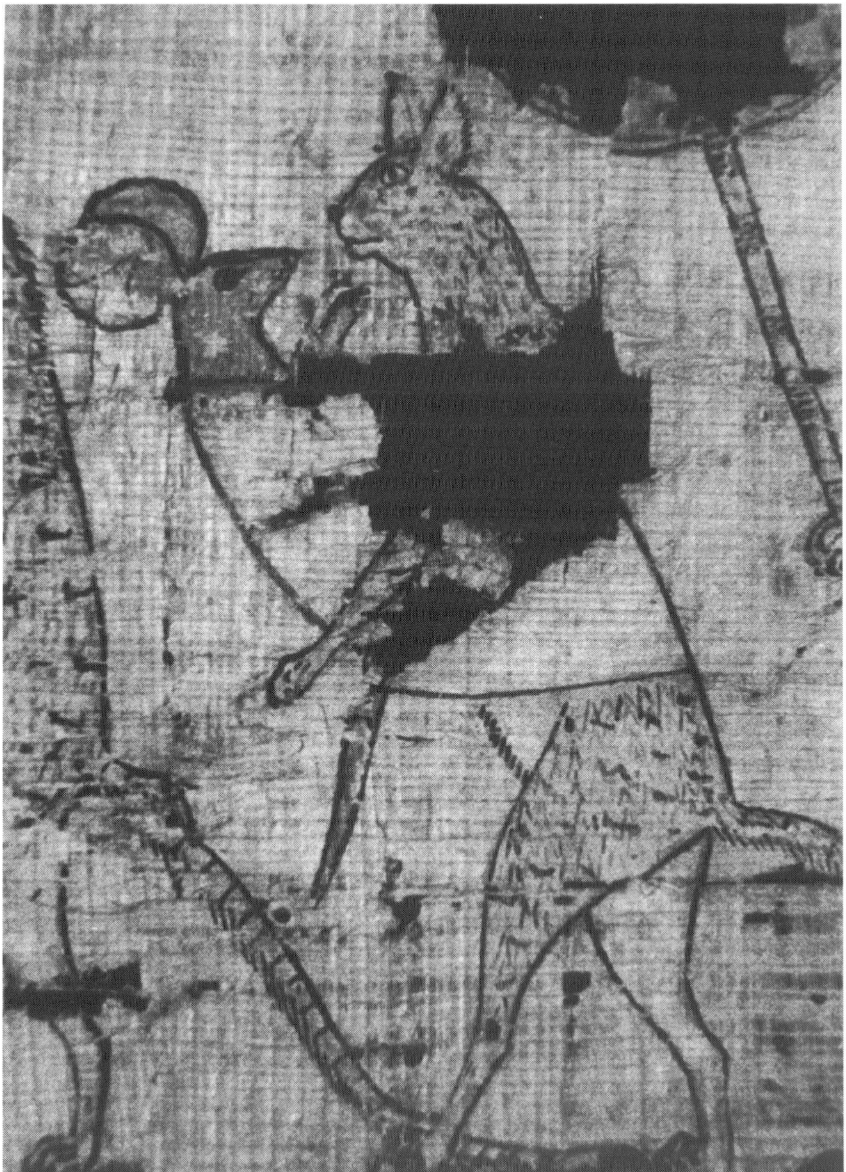

Fig. 63. This charming detail is from the satirical papyrus in the Cairo Museum. It playfully illustrates a cat as a nursemaid, providing mouse child-care, tenderly carrying the baby swaddled in a sling. Ramesside Period.

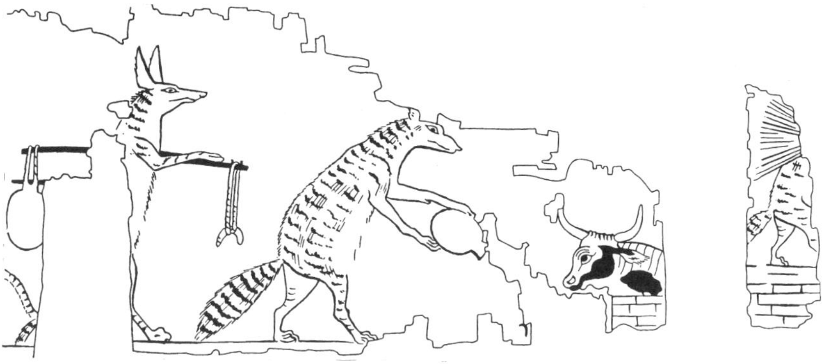

Fig. 64. Drawing of the poorly preserved second vignette on the satirical papyrus in the Cairo Museum (see fig. 62). Ignoring natural roles of predator and prey, a pair of dutiful foxes is delivering water to an ox lying in a pen. Ramesside Period.

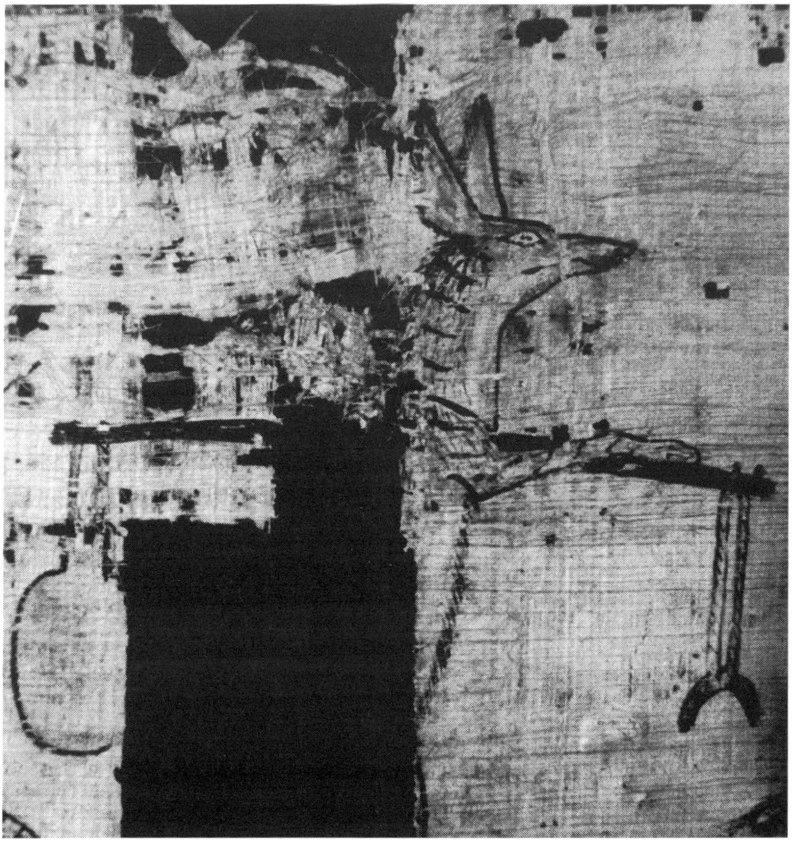

Fig. 65. Detail of the fox bearing a yoke on the satirical papyrus in the Cairo Museum. Ramesside Period.

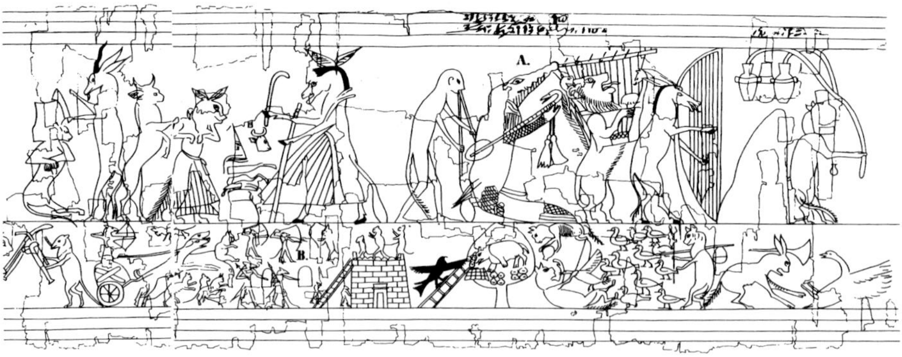

Fig. 66. Partially restored drawing of the fragmentary painted satirical-erotic papyrus in the Turin Museum. It displays vignettes of bird and beast characters burlesquing various human pursuits. In the upper register, a donkey-judge is holding court, followed by an all-animal musical quartet. In the lower register, warrior mice are laying a full-scale assault on a cat-fortress. Further along, a crow climbs a ladder to reach a tree where a hippopotamus is roosting, and house cats are tending a rather rebellious flock of poultry. Probably from Deir el Medina. Ramesside Period.

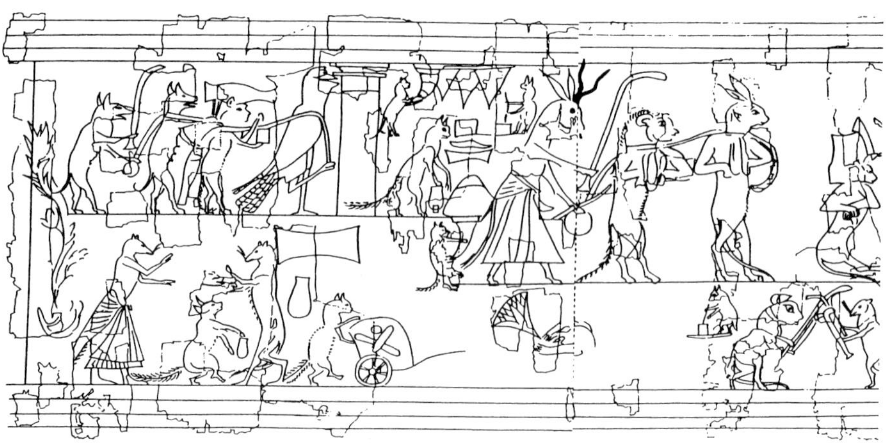

Fig. 67. Partially restored drawing of the poorly preserved adjoining section of the satirical-erotic papyrus in the Turin Museum (see fig. 66). It shows, in the upper register, a procession of bound animal-prisoners which are being escorted by guard-animals wielding long sticks. The lower register features a cat(?) and a mouse fighting a duel using curved sticks. Ramesside Period.

celebrating carnal exploits from pharaonic Egypt. The juxtaposition of the two different sections strongly indicates that the contents of the whole scroll were intended to be thought of as being satirical (see Chapter 4). There is also no reason for thinking that the viewing audience of this papyrus was not a mature one. This helps dispel the notion advanced by some writers that the fairy-tale-like animal images depicted on the satirical papyri and figured ostraca were primarily meant to be enjoyed by Egyptian youngsters.

The first part of the satirical-erotic papyrus with comic animal scenes includes (fig. 66), in the upper register, from the left, a lowly donkey, dressed in the fine garment of a well-to-do man. The beast is holding a long staff and crook, as he serves as a high and mighty magistrate, pronouncing judgment on the bound creatures brought before him. Directly in front of his honor there is a tall pile of choice offerings. At the far left, a billy-goat appears to be meting out the stern punishment of the donkey's verdict. This is followed by a memorable vignette of a spirited four-member musical ensemble, consisting of a monkey on a double oboe, a crocodile on a lute, a donkey on a boat-shaped harp, and showcasing the king of beasts, who is raucously singing the lead vocal and accompanying himself on a lyre. On the right, there is a much damaged detail, picturing a cat blending wines, using a siphoning tube, possibly for a now lost banqueting vignette. In the lower register, from the left, a formidable fortress defended by cats is undergoing a full-scale siege from a host of determined mice, some armed with bows and arrows, others carrying shields and spears (fig. 57). A heroic pharaoh-like mouse, an obvious a tongue-in-cheek allusion to a great warrior-pharaoh such as Ramesses II, fires arrows from a racing chariot drawn by a pair of female dogs, that rear like horses, trampling the retreating enemy beneath their paws. The infantry is about to storm the high walls with a scaling-ladder; the cats standing on top of the fortress have their arms raised and appear ready to capitulate. All looks lost for the feline foes! It almost defies keeping a straight face. Further along, there is another remarkable and often reproduced drawing (fig. 68). It is a superlative piece of comedy. It drolly pictures a clever black crow, laboriously climbing up the rungs of a ladder to reach a sycamore fig tree. An ungainly hippopotamus is already perched high in its branches, gathering fruit in a basket.[16] At the right, tabby cats are tending a flock of poultry, but the natural antagonism between the two species has resulted in an altercation. An enraged duck is attacking one of its feline herders, which has fallen to the ground on its back. Another cat appears to be dousing the pair with a jug of water to cool the combatants off. Finally, at the far right, a cat, wearing a lotus blossom on top of its head, is embroiled in another wrangle with a duck or goose.

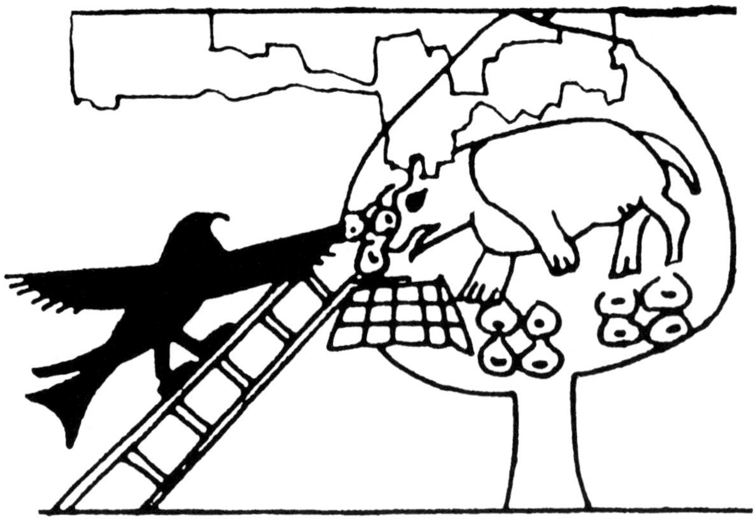

Fig. 68. Drawing of a well-known vignette from the satirical-erotic papyrus in the Turin Museum (see fig. 66). It depicts a clever crow climbing a ladder to reach a sycamore fig tree. A huge hippopotamus is laughably already in its branches gathering fruit in a basket. Ramesside Period.

The adjoining part of the satirical-erotic papyrus devoted to humorous animal episodes is not as well-preserved, the result being that the scenes are imperfectly understood (fig. 67). The upper register is composed of vignettes portraying the bringing of various animals and a large bird (a falcon?) as bound captives. Some of the creatures are secured by manacles and ropes about the neck. This recalls the long files prisoners from foreign wars, helpless in fetters, being led away and paraded before the gods or victorious pharaoh in temple wall decoration during the New Kingdom. They are being escorted forward by watchful guard-animals, who brandish long sticks, and are assisted by several small housecats. The group of captives on the left is heading towards a large (temple?) doorway. In the lower register, at the left, a cat seems to be pleading or submitting before an important mouse. This has been interpreted by some scholars as being the cat-general from fortress seen earlier, making a gesture of obeisance and surrendering to the victorious mice (fig. 57).[17] However, since this area of the papyrus has only survived in highly fragmentary state, the exact reading of it is uncertain from what has now been preserved. This is followed by a much broken detail of cat walking behind a chariot – or is he fabricating it? To the right of this, a cat(?) and a mouse are engaged in a heated one-on-one combat using curved sticks.

A zany world of animal burlesques, with creatures often parodying their human counterparts, also provided the source of inspiration for numerous drawings on ostraca (the singular is ostracon) during the Ramesside Period.[18] In ancient Egypt, potsherds and smooth pieces of limestone were extensively used as a cheap alternative to high-priced papyrus for writing and drawing surfaces. On average, ostraca are about the size of a man's hand, but a few examples of more than a metre in length are known. The Theban necropolis, in particular, has yielded a vast quantity of them. The small, cream-coloured hard limestone chips obtained during the course of constructing a rock-cut tomb, or just picked up from the base of the mountain, provided an inexhaustible supply of ready-made flakes. The residents of Deir el Medina were very fond of using ostraca as notepads ("scrap paper") for sketches, memorandums, letters, copies of literary works, and *ex votos*, among other functions. Excavations undertaken by the Institut Français d'Archéologie Orientale du Caire (IFAO) at the village, in an area of it that was used as a dump, have turned up many thousands of them. Well over fourteen-hundred ostraca decorated with scenes from Deir el Medina have been published so far, along with many others with this site being the probable find-spot. The types of drawings executed on figured ostraca, so-called because of the illustrations on them, do vary. They can range anywhere from simple childish doodlings to advanced student trial pieces with corrections, or deftly crafted master studies in anticipation of the image being transferred to a full-scale context, such as on a tomb-chapel wall or stela. It is often difficult, however, to precisely classify the type of sketch one finds on these small fragments of limestone.[19] Other figured ostraca are of a much different sort.

In this category, there are spontaneous sketches which appear to have been explicitly created by draughtsmen for a quick dose of comic relief during idle moments away from their formal work. The French Egyptologist Jeanne Vandier d'Abbadie, who was responsible for publishing most of the corpus of figured ostraca discovered at the village of Deir el Medina, has observed that the amusement of the draughtsmen was the chief reason for the majority of the drawings.[20] Some of the jokes were pleasantries which cropped up during the course of the job. It might well be imagined that they were then passed around within the artists' small circle of close friends or others to excite laughter and relieve boredom. They give us a glimpse into the humorous imagination of the men who decorated royal tombs. Though unlike the painted sketches on the satirical papyri, these rapidly created works were likely to have been discarded soon after being executed. It is also very possible that a portion of these figured ostraca may have been intended as preliminary drawings for illustrations on papyrus scrolls. It is has also been argued that some of the comic motifs could even be small-scale patterns for the transfer of

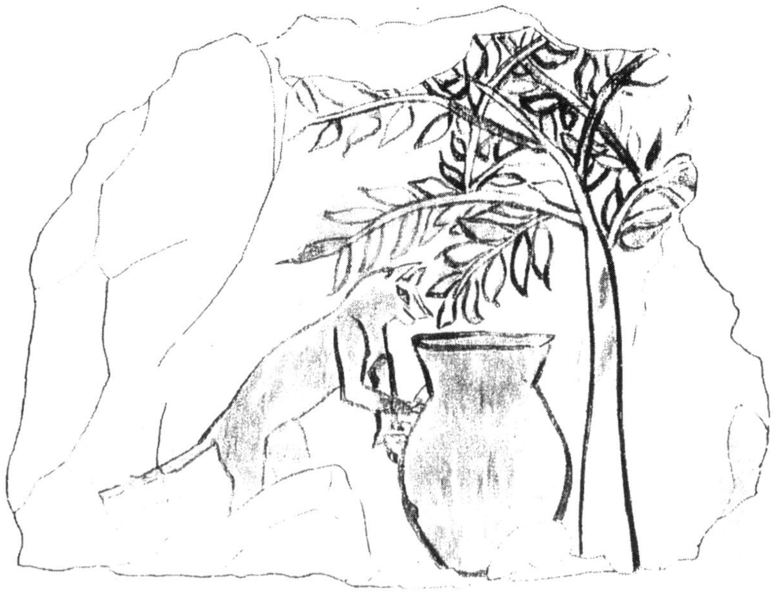

Fig. 69. Drawing of a figured limestone ostracon showing what appears to be a cat acting like a thirsty human, peering down into a water amphora in the shade of a large (persea?) tree. From Deir el Medina. Ramesside Period.

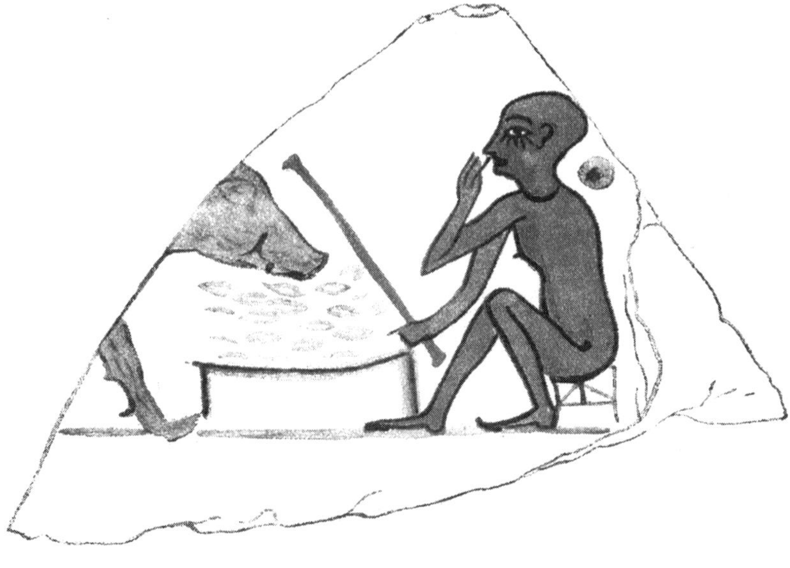

Fig. 70. Drawing of a figured limestone ostracon portraying a weeping, nude young boy, sitting on a low stool and holding a long stick, who is reduced to eating from the trough of a filthy village pig. Probably from Deir el Medina. Ramesside Period.

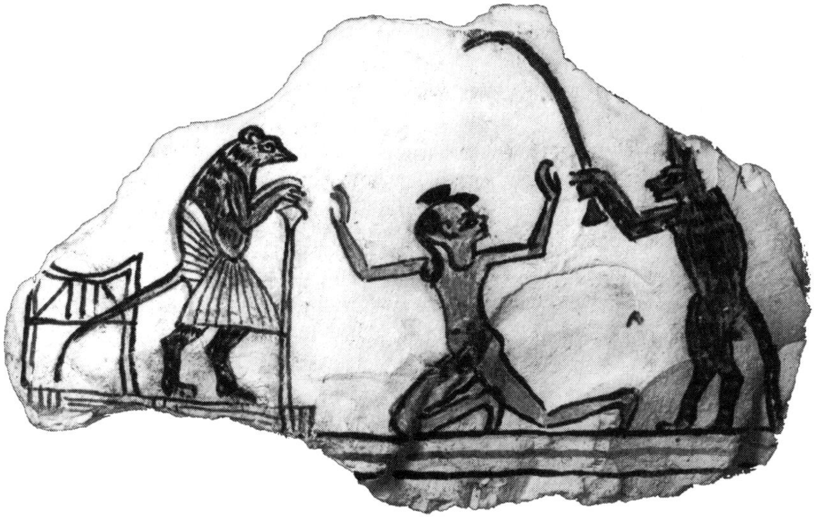

Fig. 71. Figured limestone ostracon with an amusing drawing in red and black ink depicting a lord-like mouse-magistrate, and a cat acting as his servant (or policeman). The creature is about to deliver a thrashing to the pleading culprit, a kneeling nude boy, who sports the side-lock of youth hairstyle. Probably from Deir el Medina. Ramesside Period.

these images to large-scale wall-paintings decorating secular buildings, houses and shops, now entirely lost.[21] Taken together, figured ostraca are clearly among the most insightful of the minor works of art from ancient Egypt.

There is a huge assortment of humorous subject matter represented on figured ostraca. While some motifs are attested from only a single flake (figs. 69 and 70), others are known with variations on a dozen examples. From this entertaining corpus, we call attention to a courtroom presided over by a distinguished mouse-judge, who hears the charges brought against wrongdoers and then oversees their punishments. Two distinct versions of the drama are known. On two flakes it is a young boy who receives a sound thrashing from a cat, while on a third, their roles are switched, and the cat is beaten (figs. 71-73). The reverse side of the most carefully executed of these bears an inscription in hieratic and, unusually, would seem to be the caption for the picture on the obverse (fig. 71). It reads: "The cat and the mouse arrest the small boy."[22] A baboon or dog nobleman quietly relaxes on a folding stool in the shade of a reed pavilion, enjoying his jar of beer, sipping it by means of a long tube (fig. 74). Another whimsical drawing on a limestone chip captures the rather tense negotiations among two age-old enemies, hunting hounds and hyenas (fig.

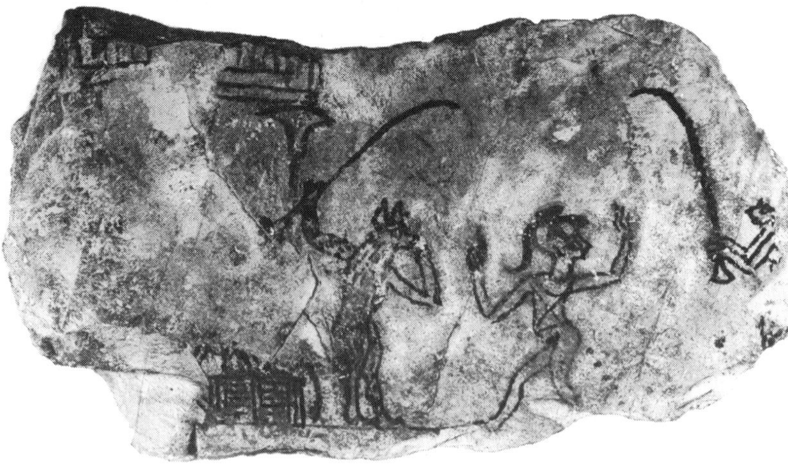

Fig. 72. This figured limestone ostracon bears a damaged drawing of a young offender entangled in a predicament which closely resembles the situation on the preceding flake (see fig. 71). Here the wrongdoer, who spontaneously defecates out of fear, is about to be beaten by a pair of cats flourishing long sticks. A mouse-judge once sat in the pavilion on the left, but only traces of this character are now extant. Probably from Deir el Medina. Ramesside Period.

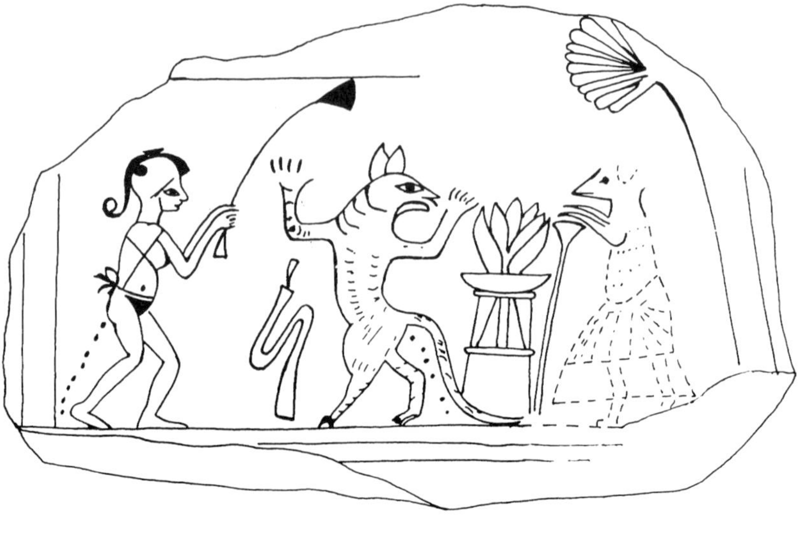

Fig. 73. Drawing of a figured limestone ostracon with a variant scene of the theme represented on the last two ostraca (see figs. 71 and 72). On this flake, the resourceful youth, although he is defecating, has managed to turn the tables on the cat, and is now meting out punishment to the offender. The panic stricken cat, also dropping feces, appeals to the mouse-magistrate for mercy. Probably from Deir el Medina. Ramesside Period.

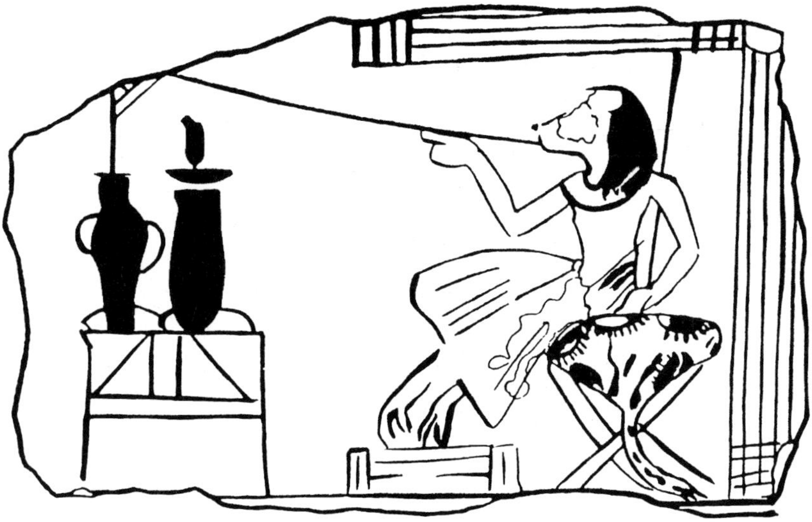

Fig. 74. Drawing of a figured limestone ostracon portraying a baboon or dog in the shade of a reed pavilion sitting on a folding stool, feet on a footrest, sipping a beverage from a jar on a stand by means of a long drinking tube. From Deir el Medina. Ramesside Period.

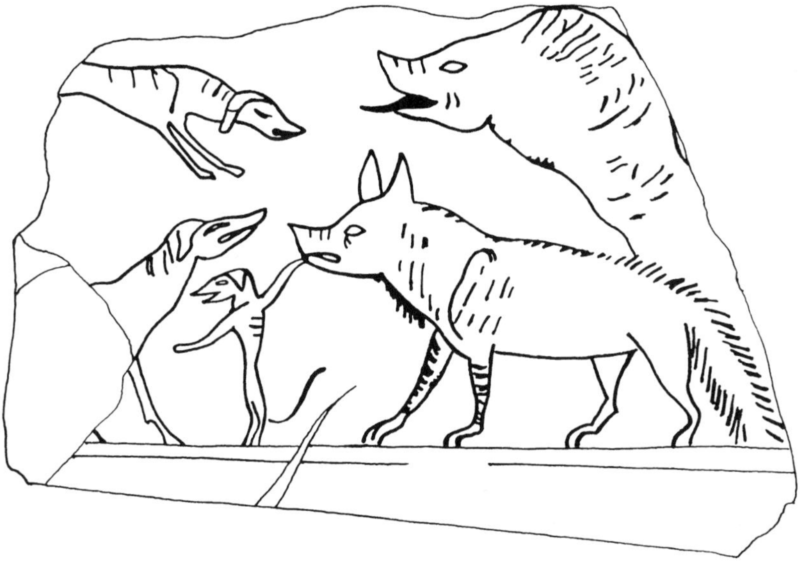

Fig. 75. Drawing of a figured limestone ostracon with a droll depiction of the delicate negotiations involving two traditional enemies, hunting hounds and hyenas. A small, perky puppy appears to be arbitrating the quarrel between the respective parties, still glaring and snarling at each other. From Deir el Medina. Ramesside Period.

75). A perky little puppy serves as the skillful arbitrator between the quarrelling parties, still glaring and distrustfully snarling at each other. While a totally different class of ostraca is decorated with comic scenes explicitly of an erotic nature (figs. 139-140).

Among the most richly documented motifs are those featuring tabby cats, occasionally joined by other creatures, in which they attend to mice dressed in fine human costume and poses. The theme has already been encountered several times on the satirical papyri. Here, humble servant cats are portrayed waiting on mice, cooling them with fans, doing their *coiffure*, plying them with food and drink, playing music for them, and offering them bouquets, among other menial duties (figs. 76-80). The felines are sometimes described in the Egyptological literature as having been captured and forced into servitude by the conquering mice, but this assumption, in my judgment, surely overreaches what is actually known. The scenarios underlying these episodes can only be hypothetically reconstructed, much must remain speculative, and cross-cultural comparisons are of limited assistance. What does seem fairly certain, though, is that for the ancient Egyptians the comic abilities of natural foes, particularly between cats and mice, made them a popular butt for humour.

Another favourite incongruous situation, also well-attested on the papyri, renders predatory species shepherding their natural prey, opening the way for absurdities such as foxes or jackals donned in human attire tending a flock of poultry (figs. 81-83, but, conversely, fig. 84). Animals carrying out recognizable human occupations was yet another extremely popular subject matter, like when a talented mouse is delightfully shown as a juggler and a chariot driver (figs. 58, 85, 86 and 87), or when creatures work as butchers (fig. 88). A monkey charmingly assumes the burdensome task of a water-carrier for a garden plot, complete with a small companion sitting on his shoulders supervising the job, while other beasts are engaged in brewing beer (figs. 89 and 90). Musical and dancing animals, either performing solo or in mixed troupes, are abundantly attested in vignettes on figured ostraca. Foxes merrily dance, with arms swinging, to a lively tune played by goat-musicians, one on a double oboe, the other beating out the rhythm on a drum (figs. 91-100). There are several series of limestone flakes with drawings centering around the curious shenanigans of baboons, their young human handlers, and the gathering of the ripe fruits from small *dôm*-palms. There is also a colourful competition between these tame monkeys and hungry crows over the tasty *dôm*-nuts (figs. 102-107).[23] In the present state of our knowledge, however, the precise meaning of these groups remains elusive. It is plausible that they reproduce incidents from popular stories (see below).

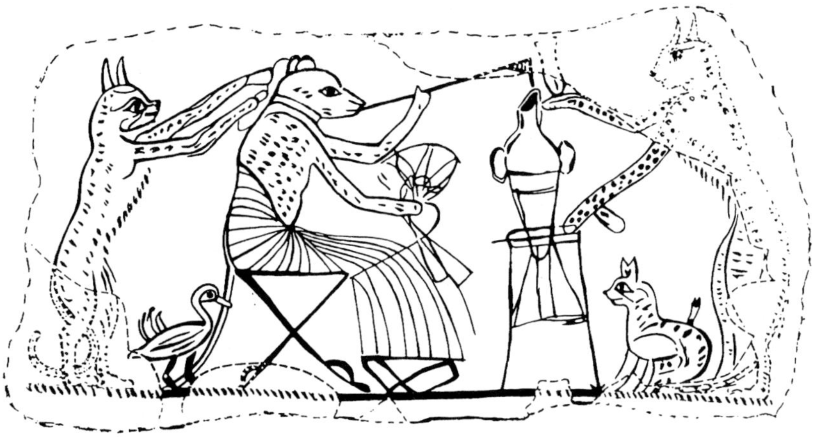

Fig. 76. Partly reconstructed drawing of a vignette on a now destroyed figured limestone ostracon. A mouse is dressed as an elegant noblewoman, wearing a fine pleated linen garment and holding a flower. Her faithful handmaids, two tabby cats, are in attendance, one of whom arranges her mistress's coiffure and the other helps her to take refreshment from a jar on a stand by means of an drinking siphon. Her pets, a duck and a cat, also sit close by. Probably from Deir el Medina. Ramesside Period.

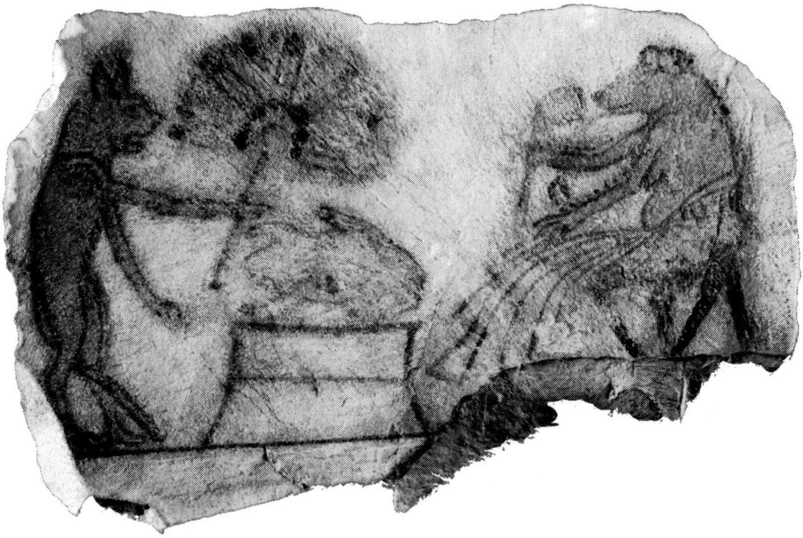

Fig. 77. Figured limestone ostracon with a red and black ink sketch of a cat and a mouse. On the flake a thin servant cat, who seems to be speaking or singing, fans a corpulent noblewoman mouse sitting on a folding stool. Between them there is a table with a roasted duck or goose. Amusingly clad in finery, Madame mouse is shown holding a flower to her nose to smell its fragrance. Probably from Deir el Medina. Ramesside Period.

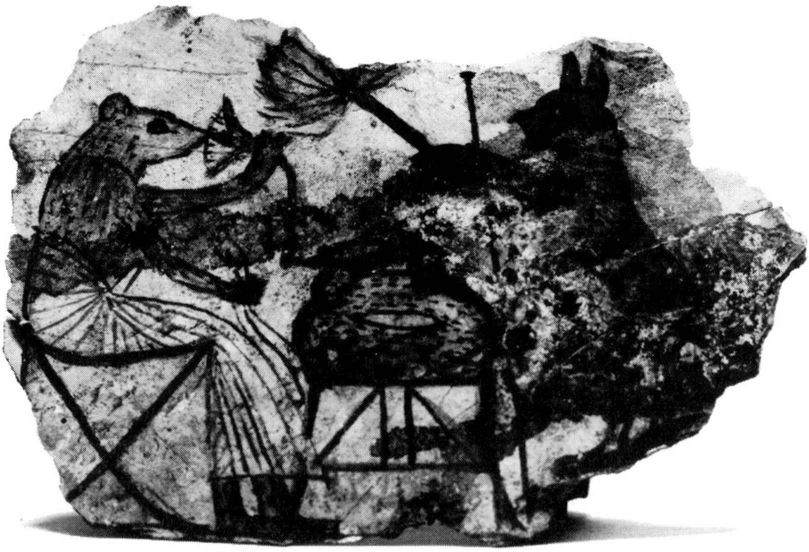

Fig. 78. The drawing of a cat and mouse on this figured limestone ostracon directly parallels the domestic situation on the preceding flake (see fig. 77). A meek servant tabby with a fan is gently cooling a seated lady mouse. Probably from Deir el Medina. Ramesside Period.

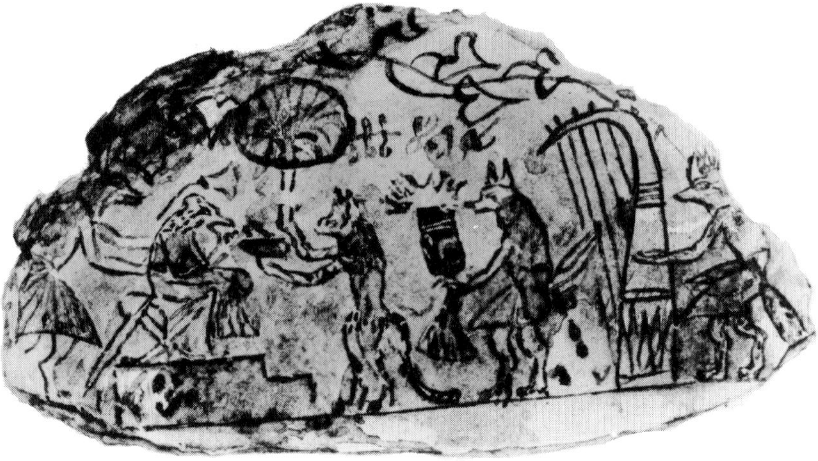

Fig. 79. Figured limestone ostracon with a drawing which relates to the theme pictured on the two previous flakes (see figs. 77 and 78). From a stepped dais, a seated lady mouse, who wears a lotus blossom on her head, impatiently receives her harried servants. The first, a cat, is holding a large sunshade and presents her with something; next a fox brings her other items. Another fox is positioned close behind the mistress mouse. At the right, a fox plays a tune on a boat-shaped harp. Probably from Deir el Medina. Ramesside Period.

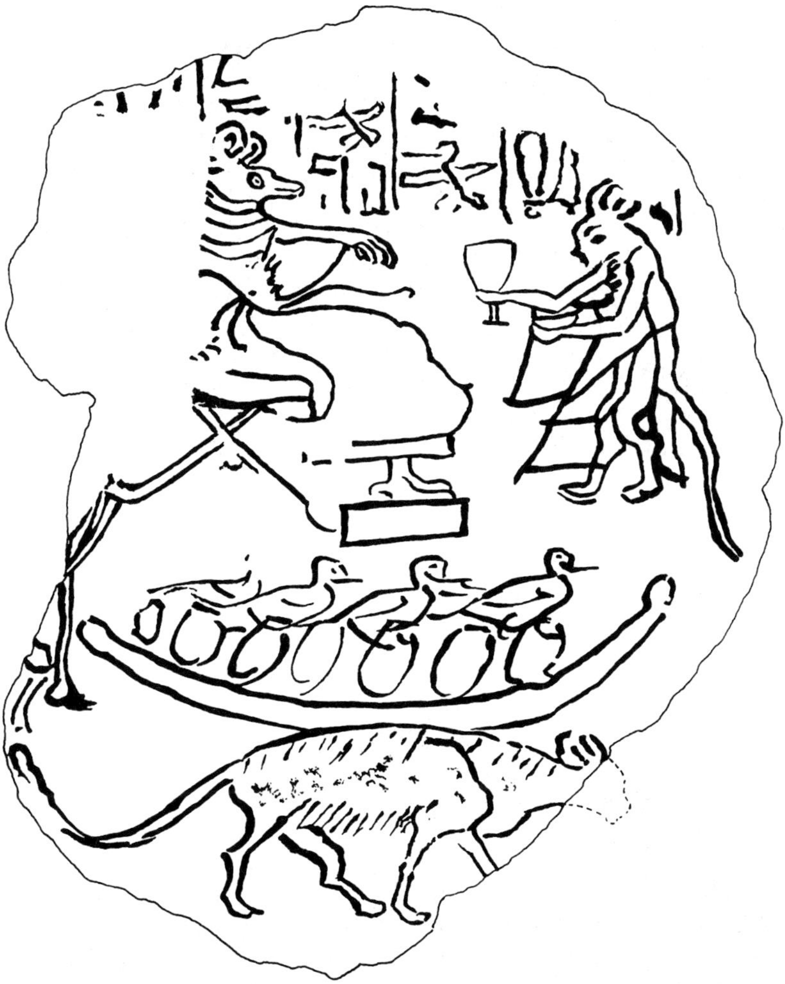

Fig. 80. Drawing of a figured limestone ostracon with two playful, but unrelated sketches. The upper scene captures a mouse nobleman sitting on a folding stool and resting his feet on a footrest, as his humble cat servant offers him a goblet and dish. The fragmentary inscription over them refers to "the cat". Below this pair, a feline of some sort is transporting on its back a large nest filled with newly hatched ducklings. This recalls the wild cats shown robbing birds' nests in swampland scenes on tomb-chapel walls. Probably from Deir el Medina. Ramesside Period.

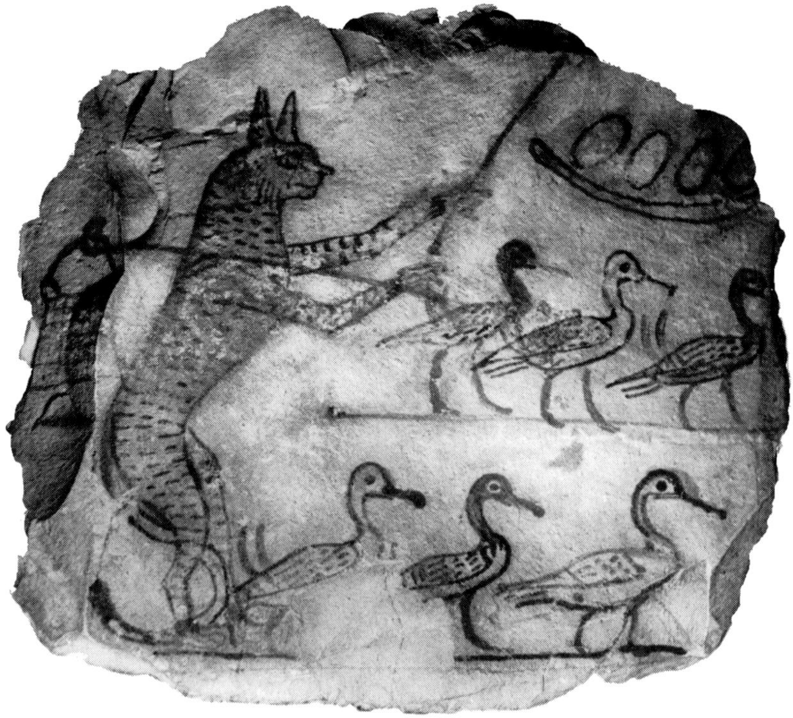

Fig. 81. Figured limestone ostracon with a black and red ink drawing, showing a cheery episode of an Egyptian tabby wielding a long staff herding a flock of six ducks or geese, arranged in two registers. Above the birds, there is a nest which is filled with a clutch of eggs. The cat is equipped with a small bag of provisions suspended from the end of a long crook that is carried over its shoulder, precisely as shepherds appear in tomb-chapel decoration. From Deir el Medina. Ramesside Period.

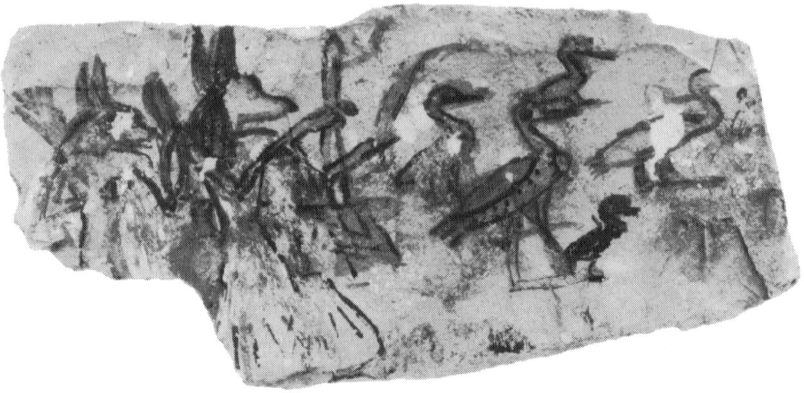

Fig. 82. Figured limestone ostracon with an ink drawing of a pair of foxes or jackals, bewigged and dressed in fine human clothing, comically shepherding a flock of domestic poultry. Probably from Deir el Medina. Ramesside Period.

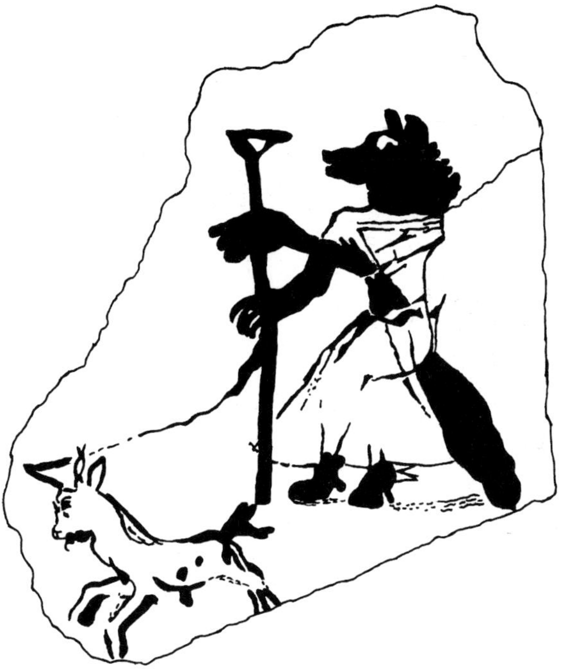

Fig. 83. Drawing of a figured limestone ostracon portraying a cunning fox or a hyena standing with a tall staff and clothed in human attire. This predator is holding a young goat on a leash, a member of his flock, not his next meal! Probably from Deir el Medina. Ramesside Period.

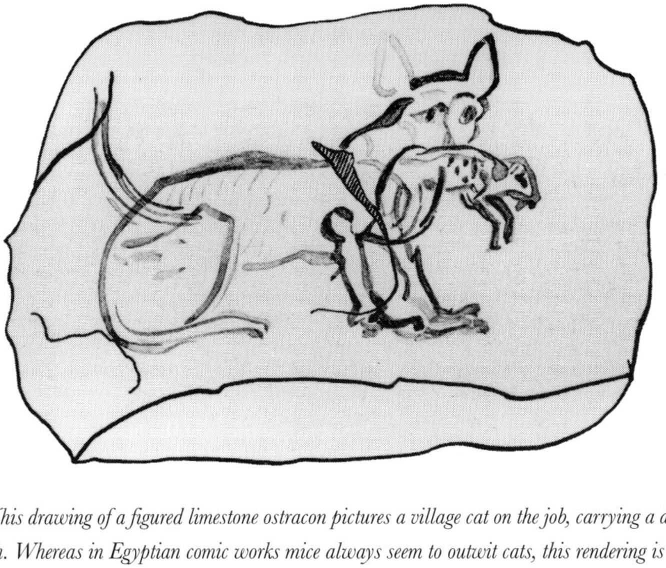

Fig. 84. This drawing of a figured limestone ostracon pictures a village cat on the job, carrying a dead mouse in its mouth. Whereas in Egyptian comic works mice always seem to outwit cats, this rendering is very much grounded in the brutal realities of the real world. From Deir el Medina. Ramesside Period.

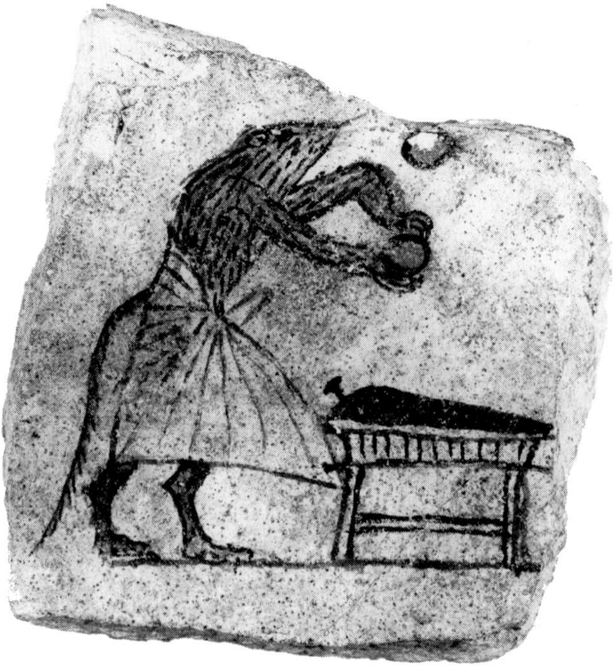

Fig. 85. This appealing image of a mouse wearing the long, pleated, flaring kilt of a well-to-do man, is drawn in black and red ink on a limestone ostracon. The little creature is depicted performing a juggling act with two balls. To the right of him there is a wooden storage chest, likely the place where the balls were kept when not in use. Probably from Deir el Medina. Ramesside Period.

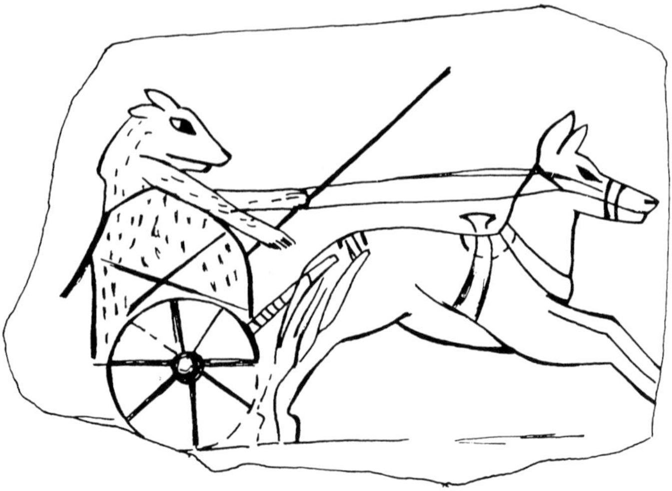

Fig. 86. Drawing of a figured limestone ostracon depicting a mouse driving a speeding chariot, drawn by a dog. From Deir el Medina. Ramesside Period.

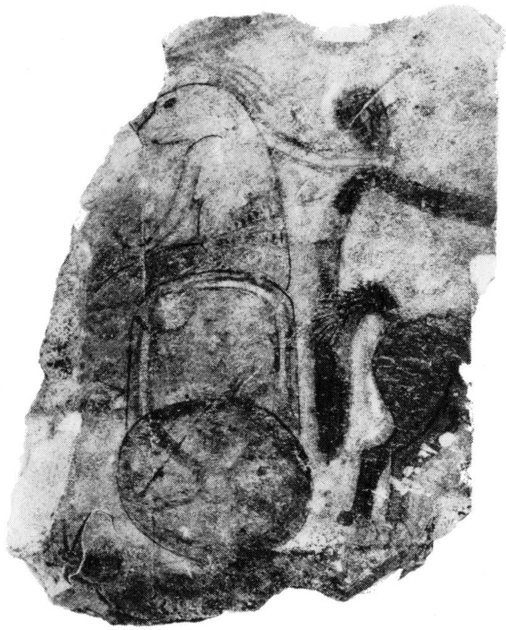

Fig. 87. Fragment of a figured limestone ostracon with a sketch of a mouse dressed as a nobleman driving a horse-drawn chariot, sitting in the wagon facing backwards, perhaps viewing bound prisoners behind him, and holding onto the reins in his outstretched arm. Probably from Deir el Medina. Ramesside Period.

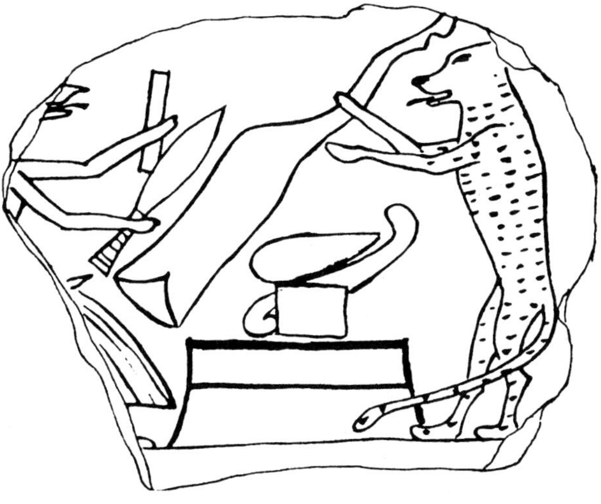

Fig. 88. Drawing of a limestone ostracon preserving part of a scene showing animals at work as butchers- or are they about to dine? On the right side of a low table piled with produce, an Egyptian cat receives a large cut of meat, the prized right foreleg of an ox, from the creature on the left, who dons a human costume, and is holding a knife and sharpener. Probably from Deir el Medina. Ramesside Period.

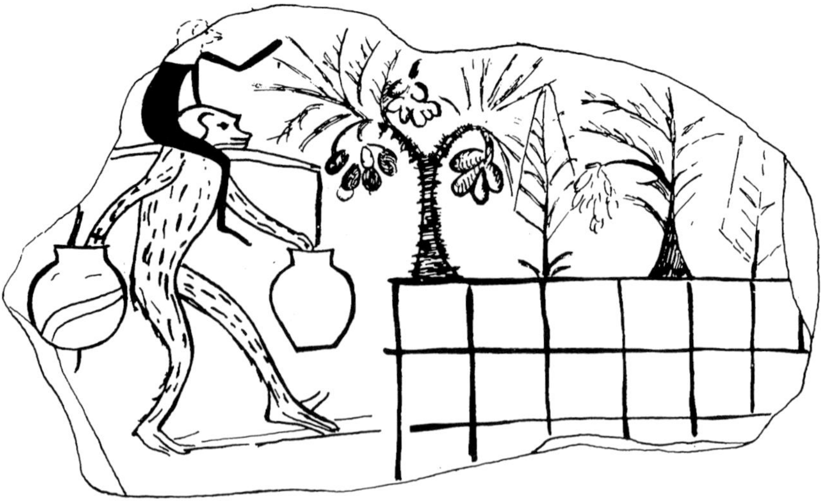

Fig. 89. This figured limestone ostracon is decorated with a very entertaining vignette of a monkey toiling as the water-carrier for a garden plot. The ambling beast bears a yoke from which two large jars are suspended. A smaller monkey is perched on the shoulders of the larger one, the perfect location for directing this hilarious operation. Probably from Deir el Medina. Ramesside Period.

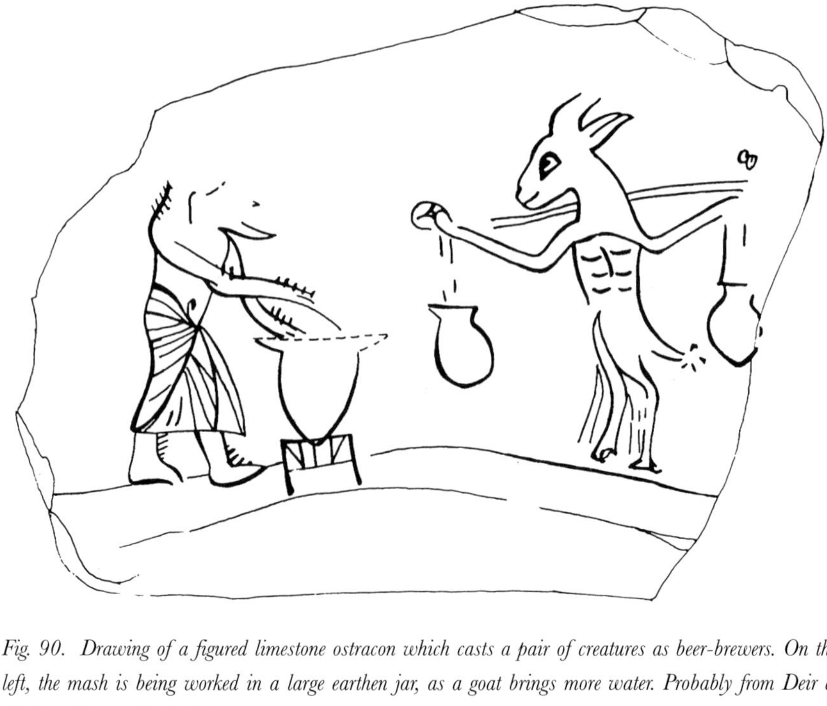

Fig. 90. Drawing of a figured limestone ostracon which casts a pair of creatures as beer-brewers. On the left, the mash is being worked in a large earthen jar, as a goat brings more water. Probably from Deir el Medina. Ramesside Period.

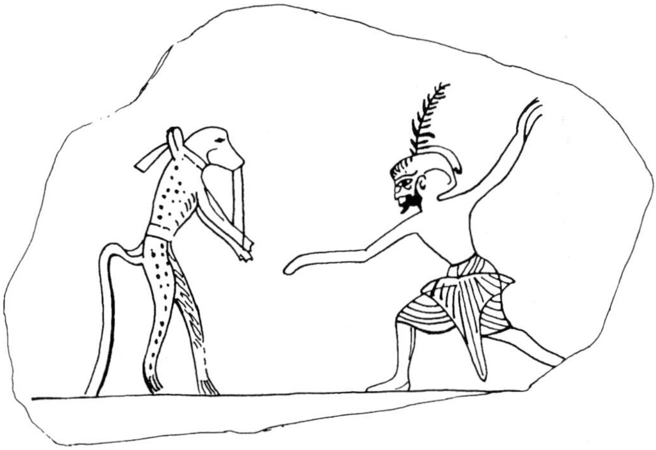

Fig. 91. Drawing of a small figured limestone ostracon with a sketch of a dark-skinned man, who is likely to be a Nubian soldier, his arms outstretched and with a protruding feather on his head, performing a dance before a monkey playing a double oboe, which is wearing a girdle and necklace. Probably from Deir el Medina. Ramesside Period.

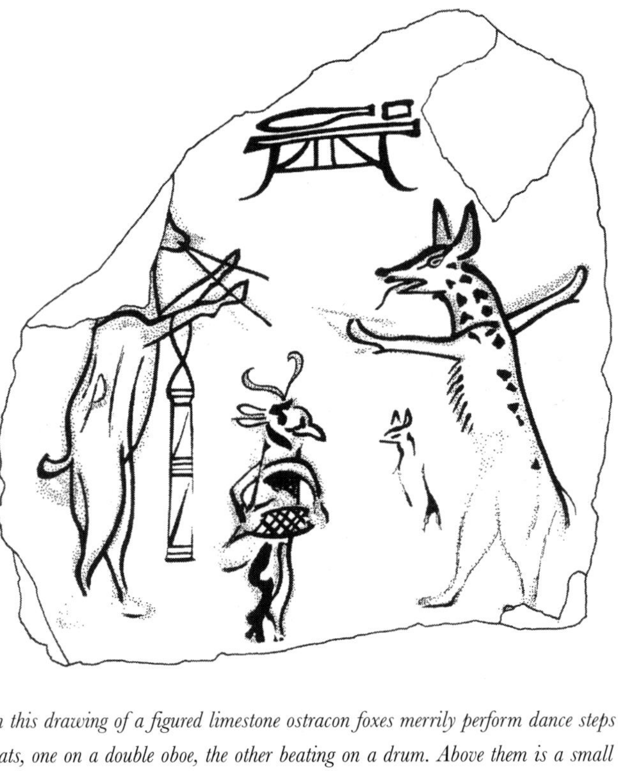

Fig. 92. On this drawing of a figured limestone ostracon foxes merrily perform dance steps to a lively tune played by goats, one on a double oboe, the other beating on a drum. Above them is a small table. Probably from Deir el Medina. Ramesside Period.

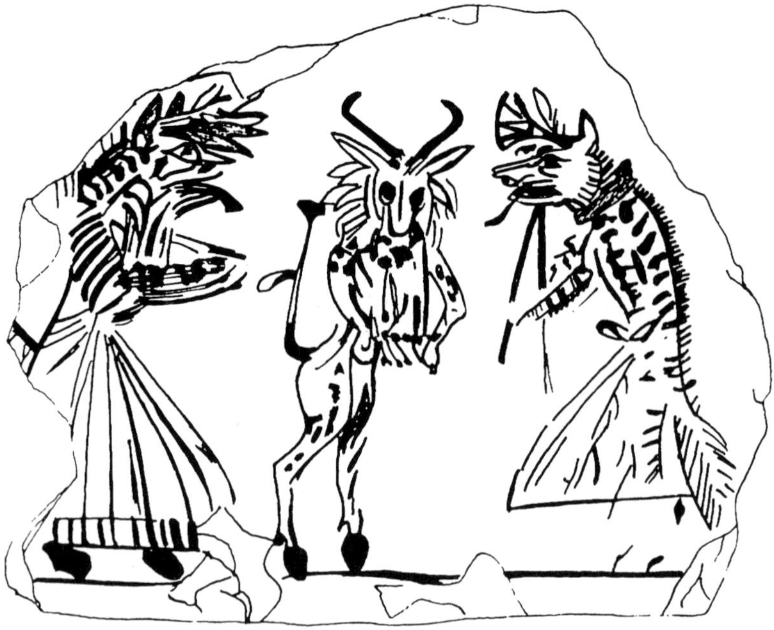

Fig. 93. Drawing of a figured limestone ostracon with a sketch of a troupe of animal musicians dressed in fine human attire. At the left, a hyena appears to be singing and keeping time by clapping his hands, as a goat plays a drum, and another hyena plays a double oboe. From Deir el Medina. Ramesside Period.

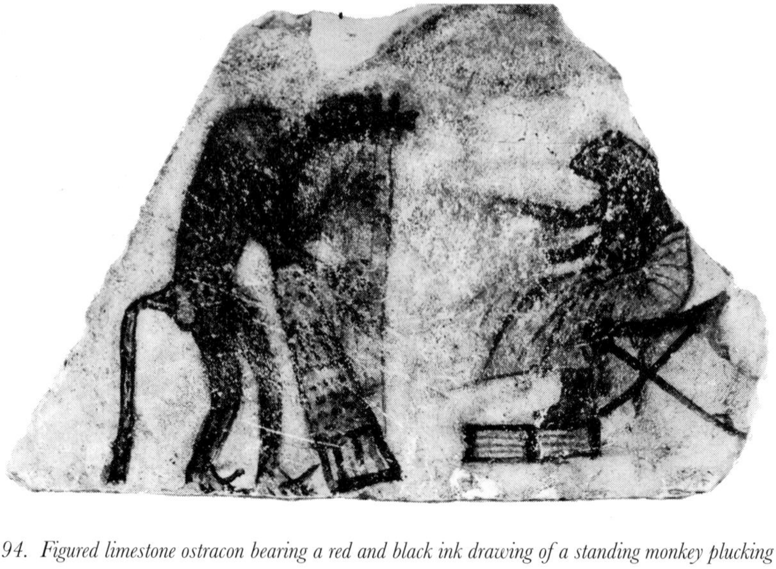

Fig. 94. Figured limestone ostracon bearing a red and black ink drawing of a standing monkey plucking the strings of a large boat-shaped harp before a mouse dressed as a nobleman, who is sitting on a folding stool and making use of a footrest. Probably from Deir el Medina. Ramesside Period.

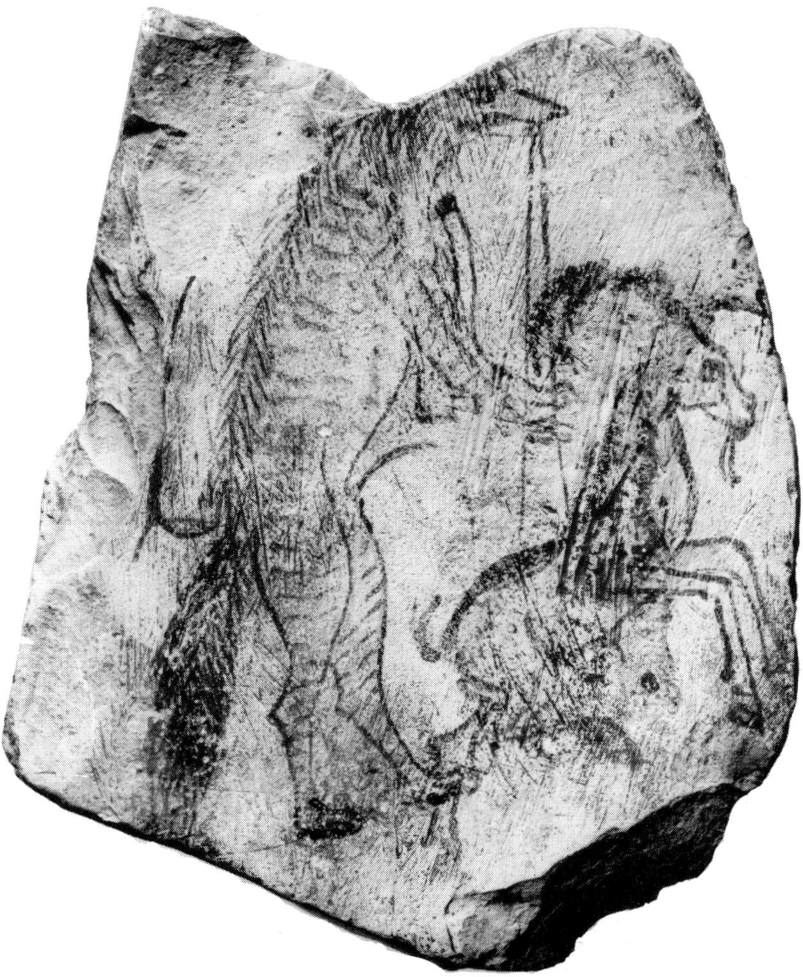

Fig. 95. Figured limestone ostracon with sketches of a hyena playing a double oboe and a dancing or frolicking goat. From Deir el Medina. Ramesside Period.

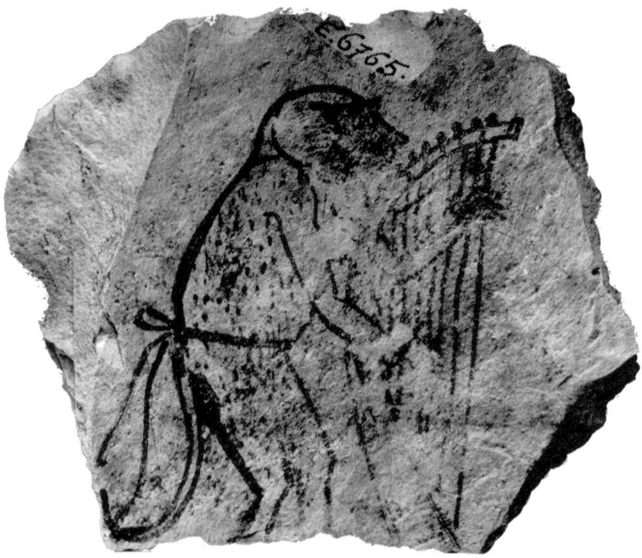

Fig. 96. Figured limestone ostracon with a black and red ink drawing of a monkey harpist, which wears a girdle tied round its waist, indicating that this is a tame household animal. Probably from Deir el Medina. Ramesside Period.

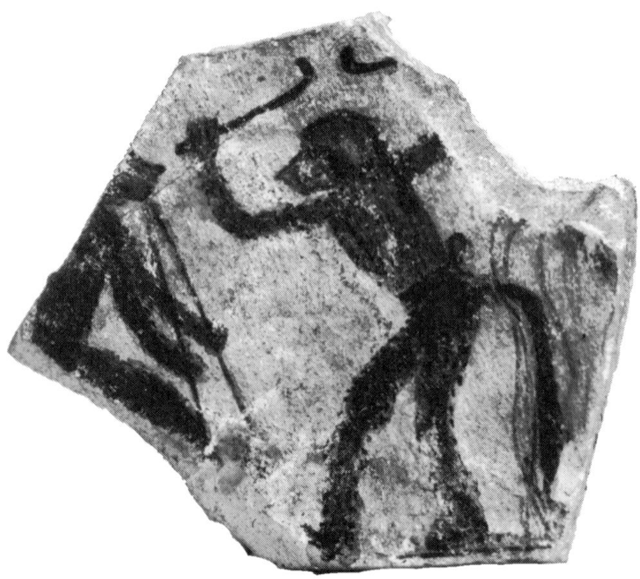

Fig. 97. Small fragmentary figured limestone ostracon with an ink drawing of a pair of simians, one an oboist, the other performing a dance. The latter is holding a pair of short crooks above his head, just the type of stick used by humans to control monkeys, but here used as clappers. Probably from Deir el Medina. Ramesside Period.

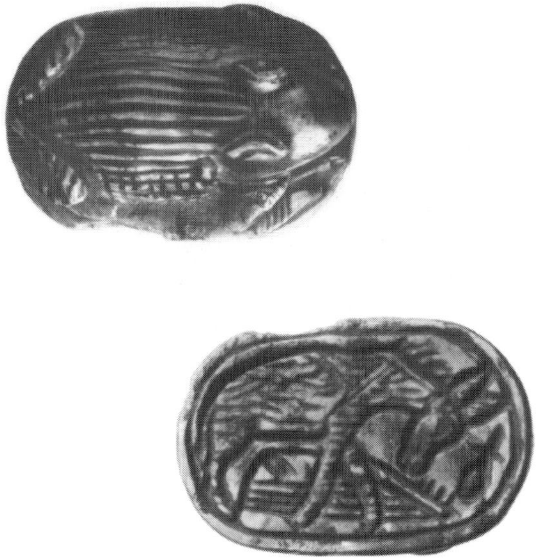

Fig. 98. A glazed steatite frog-backed scaraboid. It is decorated on the underside with a portrayal of a donkey strumming a harp, and a nefer*-sign, meaning "good". New Kingdom or later.*

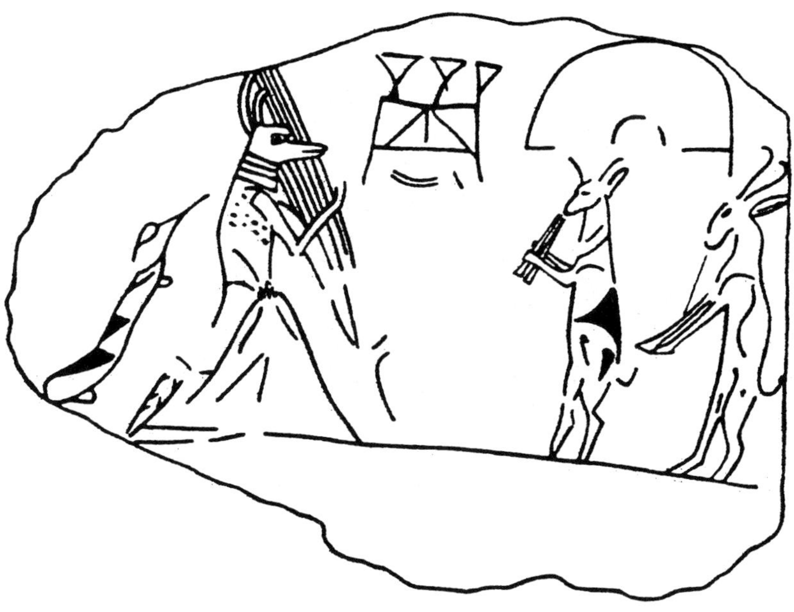

Fig. 99. Drawing of a figured limestone ostracon showing a musical concert performed by an animal ensemble. From Deir el Medina. Ramesside Period

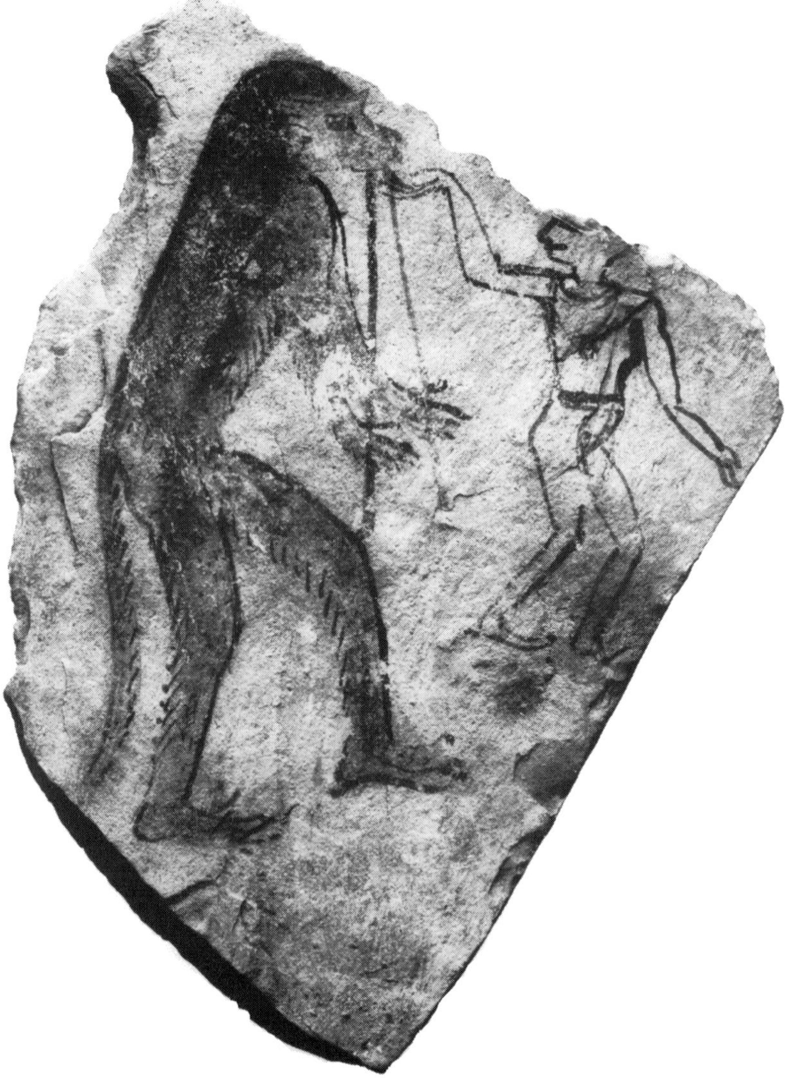

Fig. 100. On this figured limestone ostracon a monkey has been carefully depicted playing a double oboe. And if this motif were not already droll enough, there is the later rapidly drawn addition of a girl tickling(?) the musician's chin. From Deir el Medina. Ramesside Period.

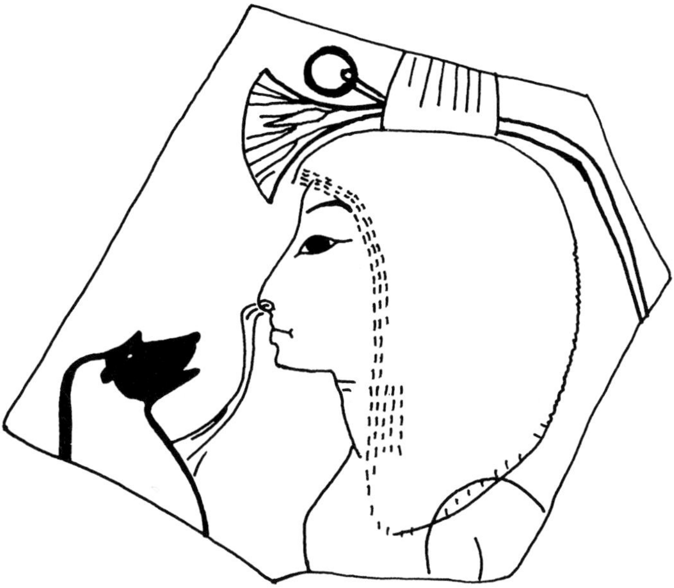

Fig. 101. A potsherd displaying a second sketch added to a figured ostracon for humorous effect (see fig. 100). The primary drawing is composed of the head and shoulder of a young woman facing left. At some later point, another hand has rendered a monkey scratching(?) her prominent nose. Found in the mortuary temple of Ramesses II (or Ramesseum) at Thebes. Ramesside Period.

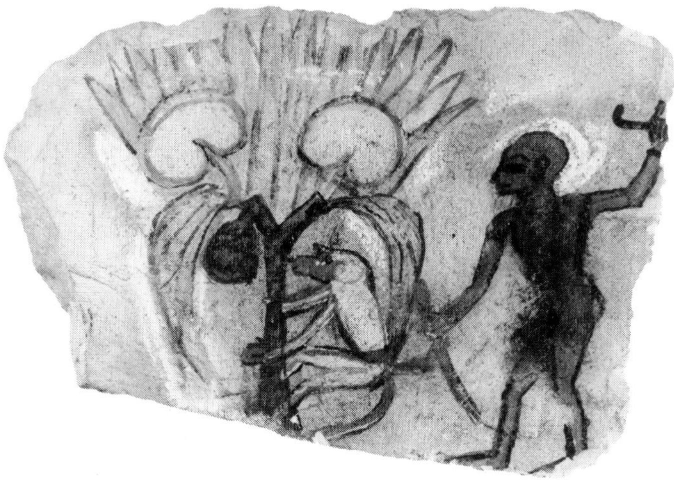

Fig. 102. Painted limestone ostracon bearing a scene of a leashed monkey, wearing a halter around its waist, climbing up the trunk of a dôm*-palm to reach the fruits. Its handler, a young boy, shown disproportionately large, is standing to the right of the tree, wielding a short crook and holding the other end of the leash. From Deir el Medina. Ramesside Period.*

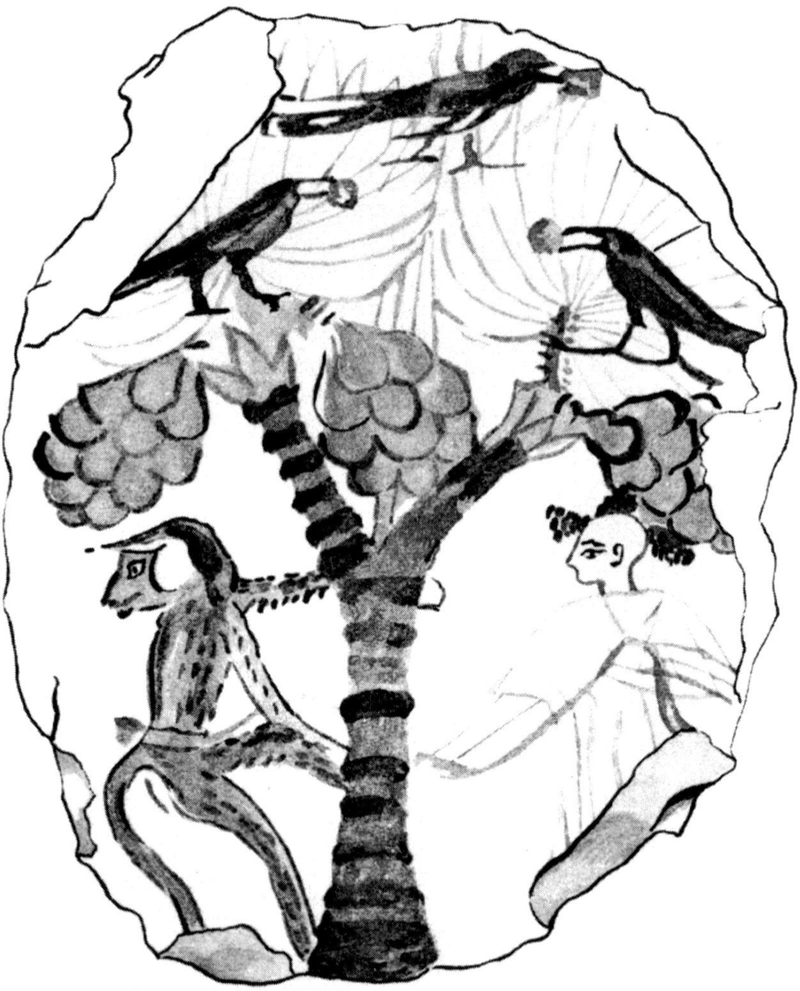

Fig. 103. On this drawing of a figured limestone ostracon a leashed monkey is represented climbing up the truck of a small dôm*-palm, and in its branches three crows are nibbling on ripe fruit. The animal's handler, a young boy wearing a long linen garment, is standing to the right of the tree, holding on to the leash (see fig. 102). The monkey and birds seem to be engaged in a droll race for the fruits. From Deir el Medina. Ramesside Period.*

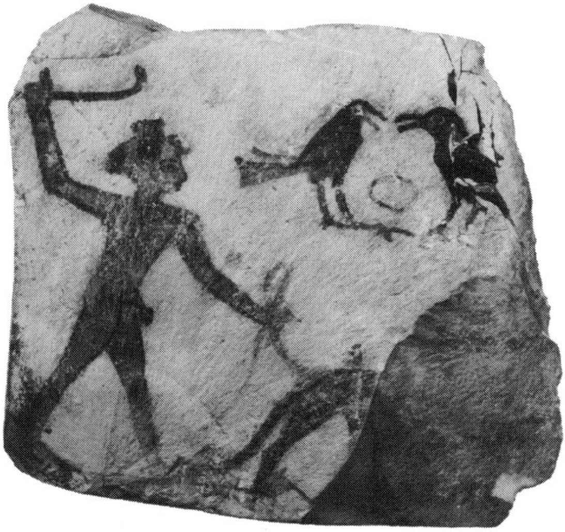

Fig. 104. Figured limestone ostracon with a drawing of a nude young boy in the act of driving a monkey (damaged) and brandishing in his right hand a short crook, used to prod the animal along, while in his left he holds onto a leash, the other end of which is tied around the monkey's waist. Above them there is an amusing sketch of two large chattering crows, whose lively discussion probably centres on the action below. Probably from Deir el Medina. Ramesside Period.

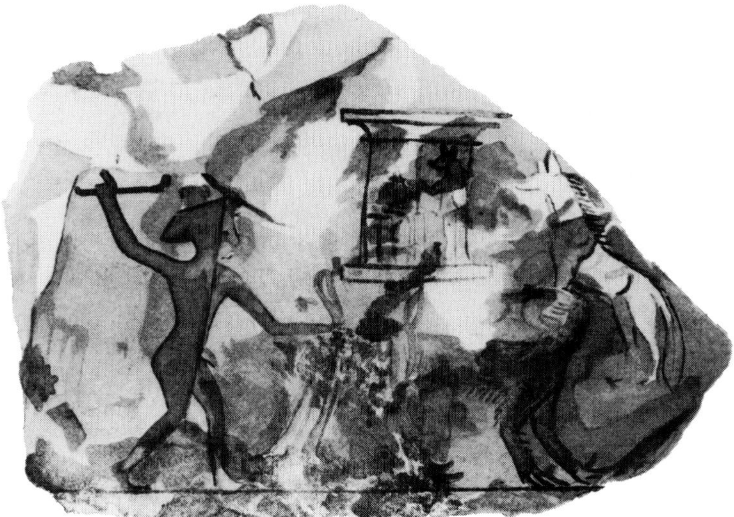

Fig. 105. Drawing of a figured limestone ostracon on which two apparently unrelated motifs have been executed. The larger one depicts the same subject as the preceding flake (see fig. 104), a young boy driving a protesting monkey forward. An earlier sketch seems to show a hyena on the staircase(?) leading to a shrine, where a mouse(?) deity sits on a throne. From Deir el Medina. Ramesside Period.

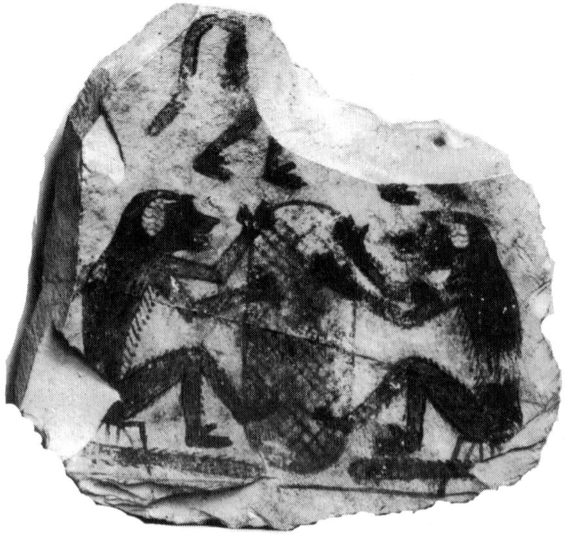

Fig. 106. A figured limestone ostracon with an animated drawing in red and black ink of two highly excited monkeys, each sitting in human fashion on a low stool, and attempting to rifle a large net bag filled with dôm*-nuts, one of their favorite foods. Above, a third monkey (damaged) is represented leaping over the group. Probably from Deir el Medina. Ramesside Period.*

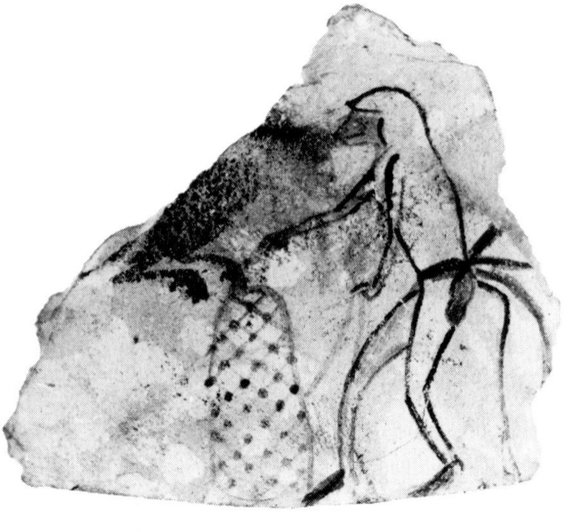

Fig. 107. On this figured limestone ostracon a monkey, wearing a halter around its waist, and a black crow are pictured on either side of a large net bag filled with ripe dôm*-nuts, a favorite food of both. The clever monkey appears to be undoing the netting to get the fruit inside. The flake is another instance of these two highly intelligent species cast together (see figs. 103-104). Probably from Deir el Medina. Ramesside Period.*

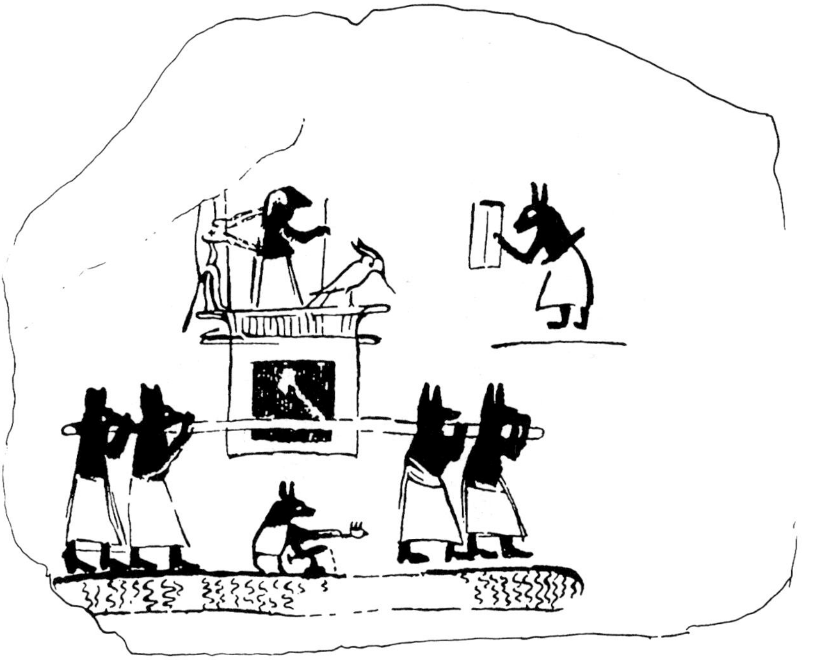

Fig. 108. Drawing of a figured limestone ostracon illustrating one of the more extraordinary scenes preserved on ostraca. It depicts a religious festival or ceremony, in which a statue of a mouse-deity, holding a staff, is being carried in a procession by jackal-priests in human clothing. Its satirical intent seems clear enough. From Deir el Medina. Ramesside Period.

Incidents of a quasi-religious nature are also evident on ostraca. Several flakes would appear to be conspicuous examples of irreverent humour. One of the more extraordinary scenes to have come down to us on a figured ostracon is a deliciously mischievous and daring satire on the sacred sphere (fig. 108). A religious festival or ceremony is depicted, in which a statue of a mouse-deity (mice were not sacred in ancient Egypt) in a portable shrine is being carried in a procession by four jackal-priests, clad in human garb. At the right, a jackal piously recites the liturgy before the god, and another one is kneeling on the ground beneath the shrine, solemnly burning incense in a censer and pouring a libation. This act of blasphemy could hardly have been unintentional. Another noteworthy flake pictures a hippopotamus and a crow perched on either end of a balance beam (fig. 109).The sketch recalls and, moreover, seems to directly parody or poke fun at the traditional weighing scene during the final judgment in the netherworld, as illustrated in a vignette accompanying Chapter 125 of the *Book of Going Forth by Day*.[24] An owl and a cat are positioned below the scale, which resembles the *ankh* "life" hieroglyph, to determine the outcome

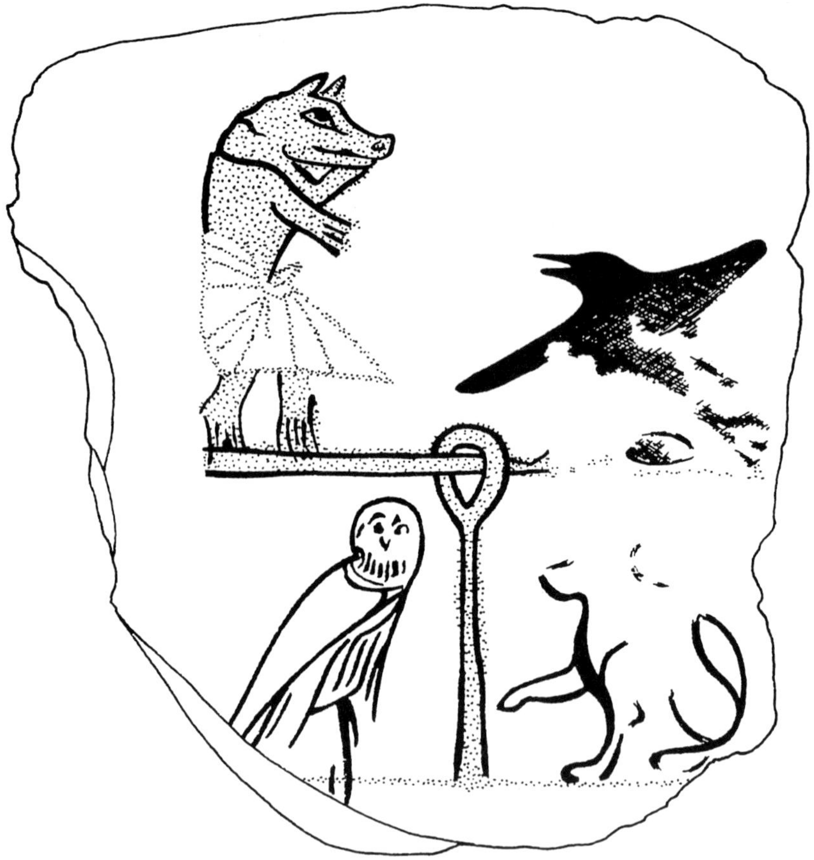

Fig. 109. Drawing of a figured limestone ostracon with a ludicrous weighing scene. It features a hippopotamus and a crow standing on either end of the balance beam. The shape of the scale vaguely resembles the hieroglyphic sign for "life" ankh. *If correct, this would have the animals being weighed on a balance representing life. Below, an owl and a cat serve as the judge and jury to determine the outcome. Probably from Deir el Medina. Ramesside Period.*

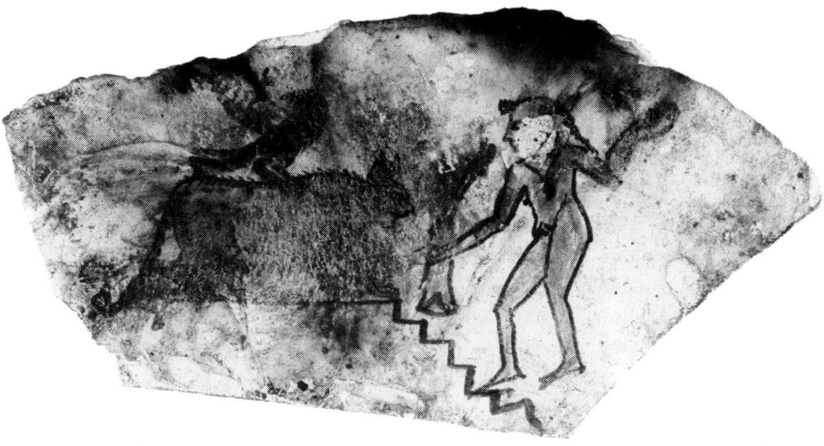

Fig. 110. Figured limestone ostracon with a unique and enigmatic drawing of a nude boy, sporting the sidelock of youth hairstyle, walking up the staircase leading to a raised platform, carrying the foreleg of an ox, a sacrificial offering for the animal deities(?) at the top, a large cat, and a black crow roosting on its back. This scene could possibly be a parody of a religious ceremony – or does it refer to a religious tale? Probably from Deir el Medina. Ramesside Period.

of this delightful farce. For the time being, the crow's luck is holding, as the balance arm is shown in perfect equilibrium. On another intriguing limestone flake (fig. 110), a naked young boy is walking up the staircase leading to a raised platform, carrying a sacrificial offering for the curious animal-deities(?) standing at the top: a none too friendly-looking feline, with a crow roosting on its back. What are we to make of this unique and enigmatic vignette? While little can be said with absolute certainty, it does seem as if there is an element of religious parody at work here but, of course, it remains open to other interpretations.[25] Elsewhere, a devout dog can be seen on a figured ostracon slowly making its way up a staircase in order to visit a temple (figs. 111 and 112), and another flake bears the sketch of a hyena on the steps leading to a shrine where a mouse(?) deity sits on a throne (fig. 105). It is very satisfactory to know that behind the pomp of official compositions on tomb-chapel and temple walls, that Egyptian artisans were capable of now and then cracking merciless jokes connected with religious beliefs.

While no one can deny the amusing side of the illustrations on satirical papyri and limestone ostraca, the precise meaning of these fairy-tale images for the ancient Egyptians is not clearly understood, owing to the absence of detailed texts accompanying them. So, is there an underlying significance to them beyond being a display of popular humour? Several explanations to account for these works have been

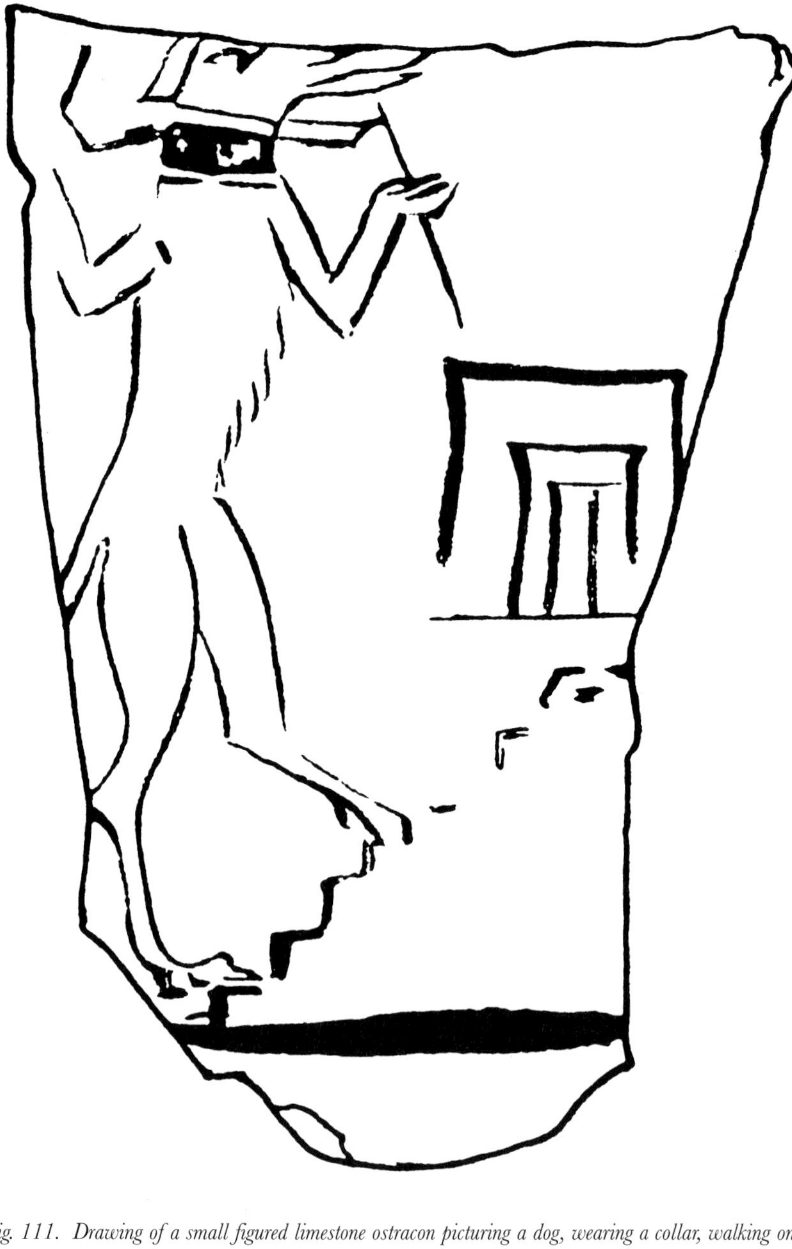

Fig. 111. Drawing of a small figured limestone ostracon picturing a dog, wearing a collar, walking on its hind legs up the staircase leading to a temple or shrine. From Deir el Medina. Ramesside Period.

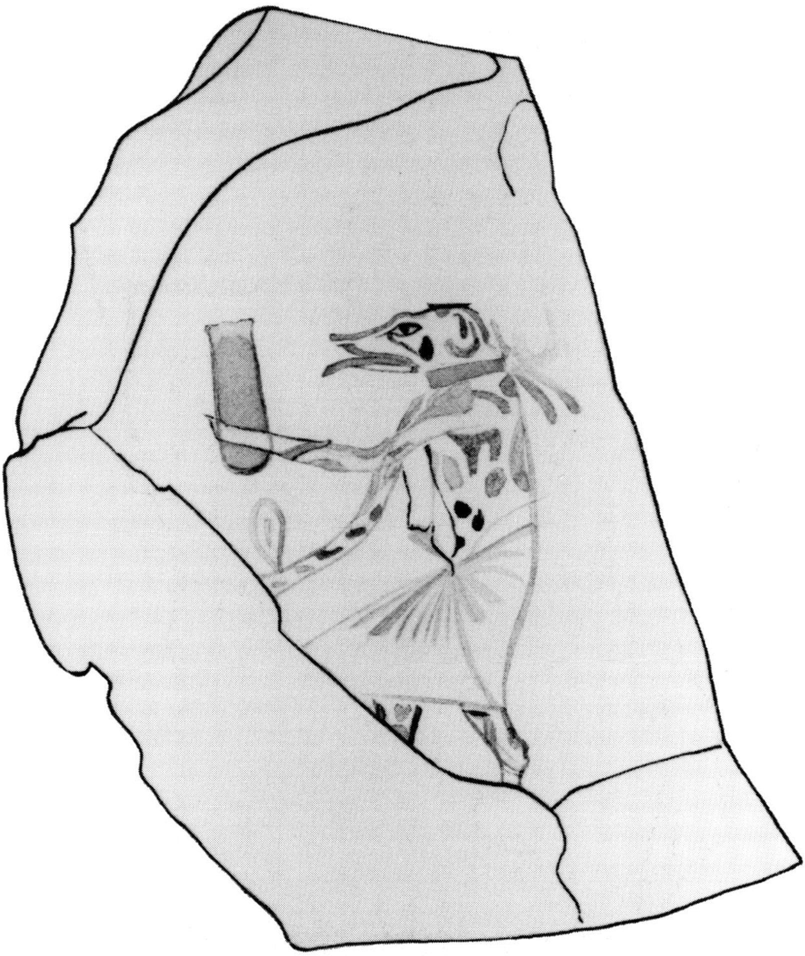

Fig. 112. This drawing of a figured limestone ostracon shows a collared dog standing on its hind legs, wearing a linen kilt, and carrying a small vase and a piece of cloth. From Deir el Medina. Ramesside Period.

offered. It has long been reasoned that a satirical element in the drawings is clearly shown by the fact that many of the animal motifs are modelled on formal activities traditionally displayed in the wall decoration of tomb-chapels: herding, banqueting, brewing, dancing, music-making, and the like. This brand of humour, with its subversion of the natural order of things, may have served as trenchant wit, parody, or a kind of social satire, ridiculing the aristocratic classes and funerary art in general. These sketches, it is posited, reflect a growing cynicism resulting from the disorder that Egyptian society experienced at the close of Dynasty XX. Parallels describing a time when total anarchy reigned in the land, with role reversals between those of humble station and members of the élite, is a theme known in official literary works such as *The Admonitions of Ipuwer*, composed in the late Middle Kingdom, but preserved in a papyrus from Dynasty XIX: "O, but beggars have become lords of wealth; someone who could not earn sandals for himself is a lord of riches." This pessimistic wisdom text would have been familiar during the Ramesside Period.[26] A different line of thought would connect the reversals illustrated on papyri and ostraca, and a few similar types of scenes carved on later temple walls, with the topsy-turvy carnival atmosphere and drunken revelry associated with the celebration of the New Year feast and religious festivals.[27] Another possibility that has been extensively investigated over the course of many years by the eminent German Egyptologist Emma Brunner-Traut is that these illustrations are brief episodes of ancient Egyptian folk-tales and fables, now lost, which centered around the antics of these highly animated animal characters.[28] The stories would presumably have included motives of parody, satire, and sheer whimsy, to be enjoyed for their comedy and possible instruction too. They must have been orally passed down from generation to generation, but were never actually written down (until much later); only the pictorial snippets from them survive. To what extent, however, any of these stories may have been truly fables, that is, conveying moral lessons, has yet to be satisfactorily proven. No fable texts are known to exist before the time of the Graeco-Roman Period. In the meanwhile, they should probably be thought of as merely animal tales. As such, they were probably not unlike the folk-tales which have been documented from numerous cultures around the world. Tales based on the lives of birds and beasts are still told in rural Egypt nowadays.[29] We can readily dismiss as folly the proposed theory attributing the madcap behaviour of cats and mice on the satirical papyri and figured ostraca as being the consequence of the ingestion of a naturally occurring form of LSD.[30]

Whatever the correct explanation may be for the majority of the drawings in the corpus, it has been reasonably shown that a very few figured ostraca must have had a certain degree of religious significance attached to them and do, in fact, depict illustrations from stories.[31] This connection is most strongly supported by a Ramesside Period painted limestone chip from Deir el Medina, bearing a motif of three characters, a lioness, a baboon, and what is probably a vulture (fig. 113). This trio of animal-actors makes their appearance together in the lengthy literary story known as *The Myth of the Eye of the Sun*, preserved on three demotic papyri dating from the Roman Period (Second Century CE), and fragments of a Greek translation of the myth. The narrative of this work recounts the search for, and the return of, the goddess Tefnut, the daughter and fiery "eye" of the sun-god Re to Egypt, who fled south into Nubia after quarreling with her father. The god Thoth, in the guise of a baboon, serves as Re's envoy and persuades the lion-goddess to return home to Egypt and, in so doing, relates to the goddess a cycle of six beast fables (two of which also occur in *Aesop's Fables*), one mentioning a vulture.[32] That these creatures are pictured together on the flake is unmistakable evidence that the story, or a close variant of it, was already current in the late New Kingdom. Moreover, it suggests that at least a portion of the later fables are based on ancient Egyptian traditions, which are derived from genuine Ramesside sources. A few other figured ostraca are also suspected of possibly alluding to animal stories (figs. 110, 114 and 115). An explicit religious meaning must surely also account for the surprising appearance of a satirical scene which decorated a wall of a Dynasty XXV temple, perhaps dating from the time of the god's wife of Amen, Shepenwepet II, at the site of Nag el Madamud (figs. 116 and 117), a little northeast of modern Luxor.[33] The sandstone blocks picture a festive banquet with animals behaving like people, which is set against the backdrop of a dense papyrus thicket. The larger relief features an elegantly dressed noblewoman mouse sitting on a high chair or throne, using a footrest, a fragrant flower in hand, and attended to by a tabby handmaiden, positioned close by. Standing before her there is a puzzling portrayal of a man, though some authorities have described the figure as depicting a monkey, who is wearing a long robe and a tall conical head-dress. Could this curious figure represent a king? He is evidently about to have something to eat or drink, to be served by a jackal. The entertainment for the feast is provided by a lute-playing crocodile, partnered with a naked young woman standing on its back, plucking the strings of her large angular harp. The exact significance of this extraordinary composition for an ancient audience is difficult to explain. That a purely satirical or humorous scene would be allowed to appear in a sacred temple is highly unlikely, to say the least. Clearly, therefore, this depiction must have held an additional layer of meaning for the ancient Egyptians beyond the obvious comic appeal. Its accurate meaning aside, it is refreshing to see this

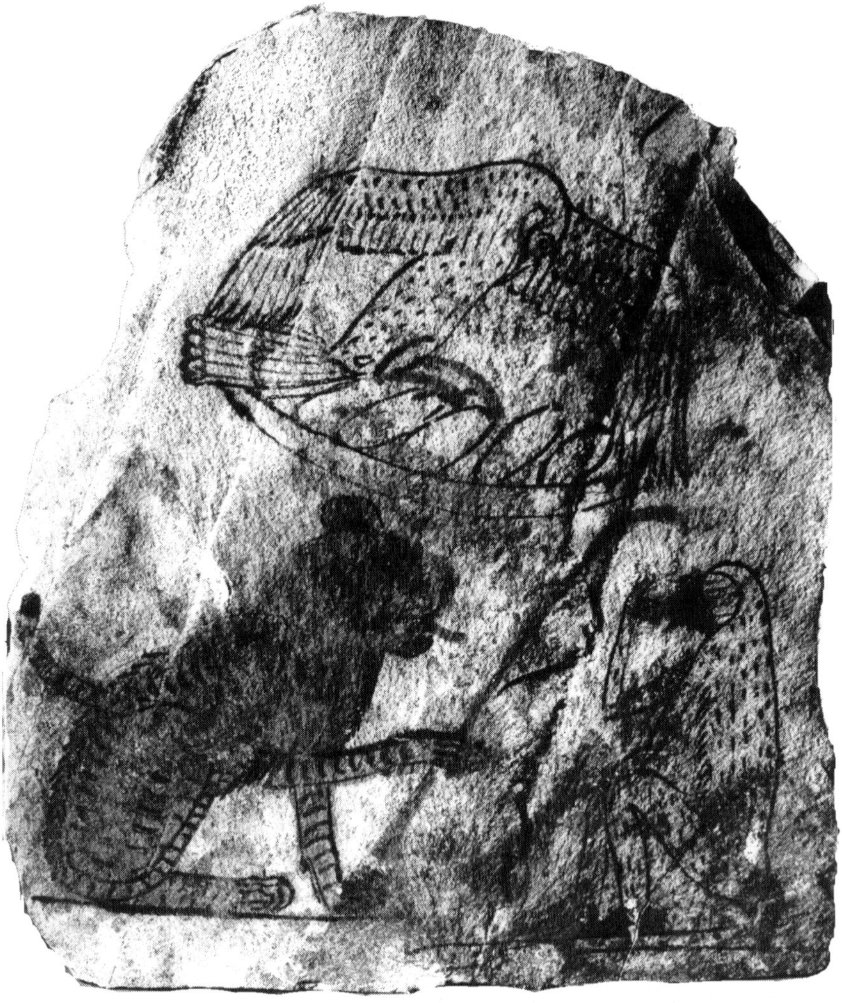

Fig. 113. Figured limestone ostracon picturing a seated baboon, representing the god Thoth, nibbling on something and conversing with a lioness, which carries a long stick, portraying the goddess Tefnut. Above them, a bird, likely to be a vulture, protects her clutch of eggs in a nest. This piece seems to offer firm evidence that some of the themes illustrated on figured ostraca reflect religious stories, since these three animal characters relate to an episode in The Myth of the Eye of the Sun. *The narrative of the legend relates how Tefnut runs away to Nubia, but is eventually persuaded back to Egypt by Thoth. From Deir el Medina. Ramesside Period.*

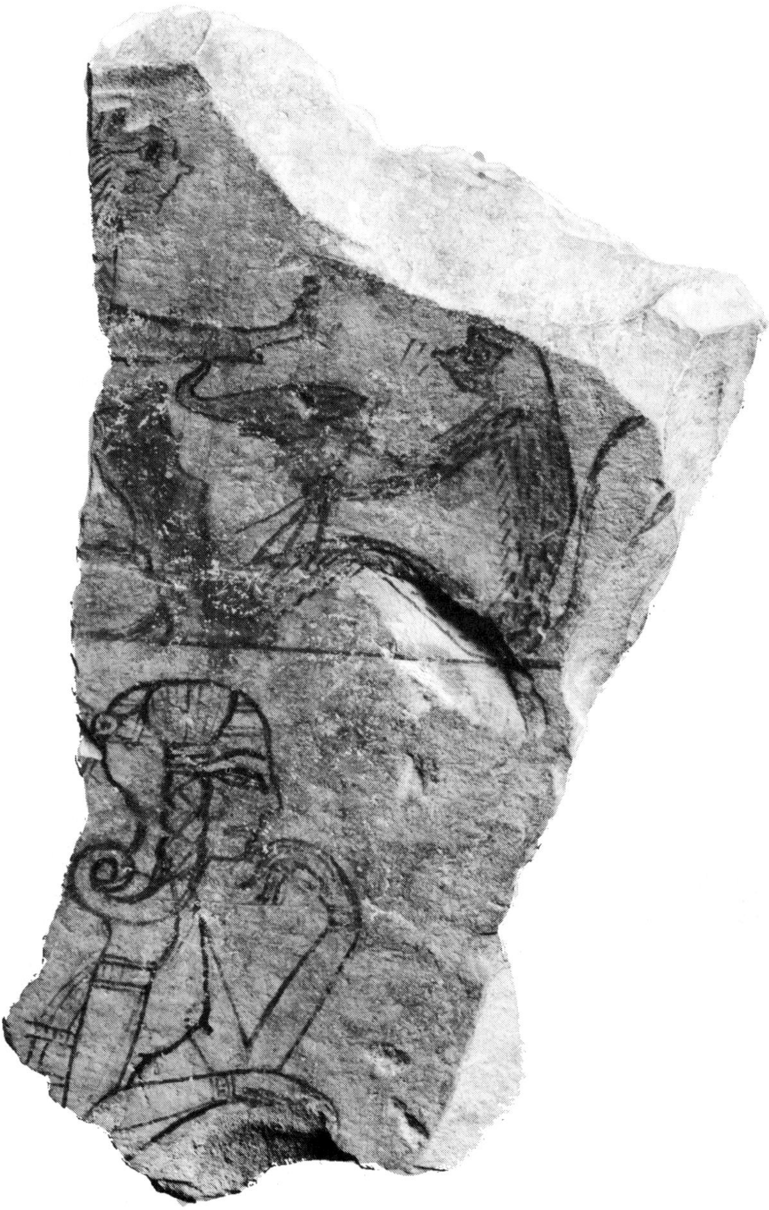

Fig. 114. Figured limestone ostracon with two apparently unrelated drawings. The upper motif consists of a seated baboon that appears to be holding a bundle of reeds in one hand, and in the other, a cucumber, which it is either offering to or taking from the other character, probably a lioness (damaged), whose arm is outstretched. This vignette seems to closely parallel an episode on another flake (see fig. 113). Below, there is a profile study of a girl sporting the youthful sidelock hairstyle. Probably from Deir el Medina. Ramesside Period.

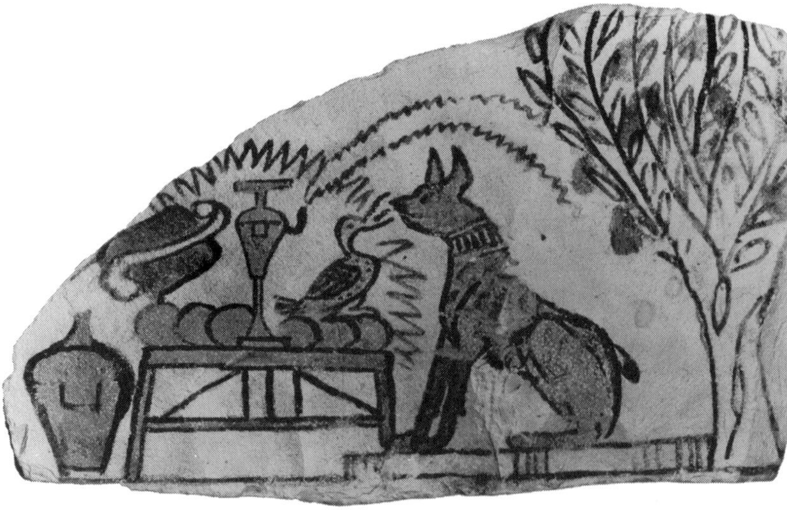

Fig. 115. Figured limestone ostracon with a vignette showing a cat, a form of the sun-god Re, sitting on a mat beneath the ished*-tree, the sacred tree of the sun-god at Heliopolis. In front of the cat there is a table of offerings, with a large* hes*-vase pouring a libation. On the table there is a chattering duck, an offering or does it depict the god Amen? The two appear to be conversing. This flake could possibly allude to a religious tale – or is it a parody? From Deir el Medina. Ramesside Period.*

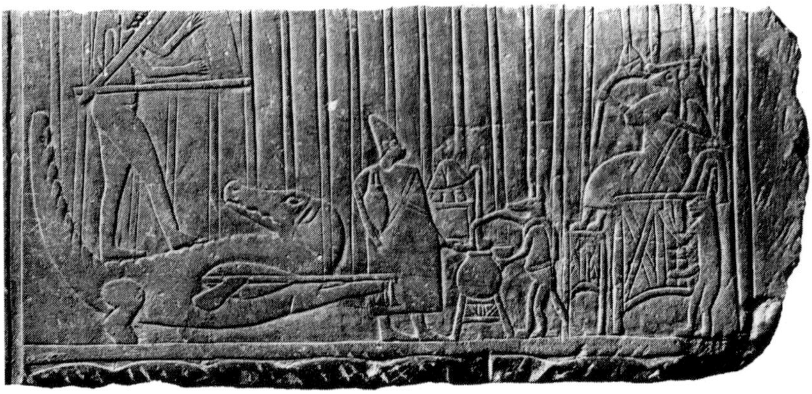

Fig. 116. Block of sandstone temple-relief illustrating a satirical banqueting scene, with animals burlesquing human roles, set against the backdrop of a papyrus thicket. A noblewoman mouse is sitting on a high chair or throne, her servants nearby. The entertainment is provided by a lute-playing crocodile and a harpist. The presence of this very unusual relief in a temple setting indicates that the scene must have had more than one layer of meaning attached to it. From Nag el Madamud. Dynasty XXV.

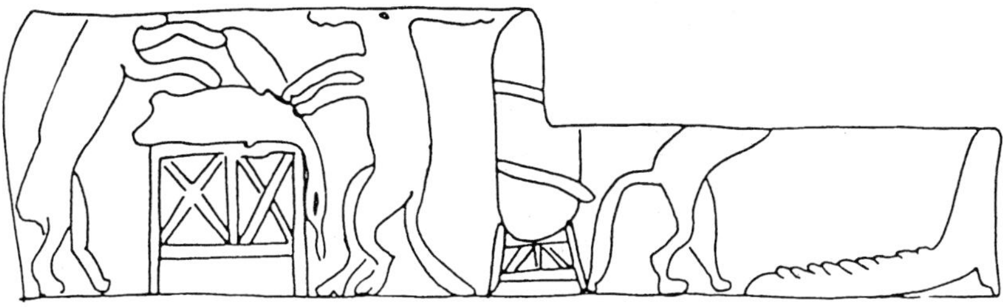

Fig. 117. Drawing of a much damaged scene on a fragment of wall-relief from a temple at Nag el Madamud, which is connected with the satirical scene on the preceding block (see fig. 116). It features animals engaged in the preparation of food for the great feast. Dynasty XXV.

cast of animal characters, long known from minor works on papyri and ostraca, enter into the monumental iconographic tradition, even if only fleetingly. The reliefs from Nag el Madamud would appear to lend further support to the view that some of the Ramesside Period satirical papyri and figured ostraca bear images that relate to the religious sphere. The assertion that episodes like this one may have found their way into holy temples surreptitiously seems overly cautious and unwarranted.[34]

While exceptional, animals acting in human capacities can occasionally be glimpsed in other religious contexts, and not without, I suspect, a touch of humour (figs. 118-121). The earliest example extends back to a representation of a fantastic flute-playing jackal carved on the so-called Two Dog Palette found at Kom el Ahmar (Hierakonpolis), dating from Dynasty "0" (Naqada III).[35] The final manifestations of this long artistic tradition can be seen more than three millennia later, after the Roman conquest of Egypt. A marvelous terracotta figurine from the Roman Period (First or Second Centuries CE) depicts a cat and a mouse squared up, fists raised, in a boxing match, with an eagle above them, serving as the referee (fig. 122).[36] Lastly, the old cat and mouse motif is revived once more in Egypt during the Coptic Period (Seventh or Eighth Century CE). A wall-painting executed in fresco from a room in the nuns' quarter at the monastery of St. Apa Apollo at Bawit, near Dairut in Middle Egypt, humorously captures what appears to be a well-equipped delegation of mice supplicating before a suspicious cat (fig. 123).[37] They carry a flag (of truce?) and offer gifts, which include a wine ewer and decanter. And for once, in this make-believe universe "peopled" with animals, a cat seems to have triumphed over a band of quick-witted mice, at least for the time being anyway. No doubt they are already planning their next move! This delightful little scene seems well in the tradition of animal burlesques going back to Ramesside Period times.

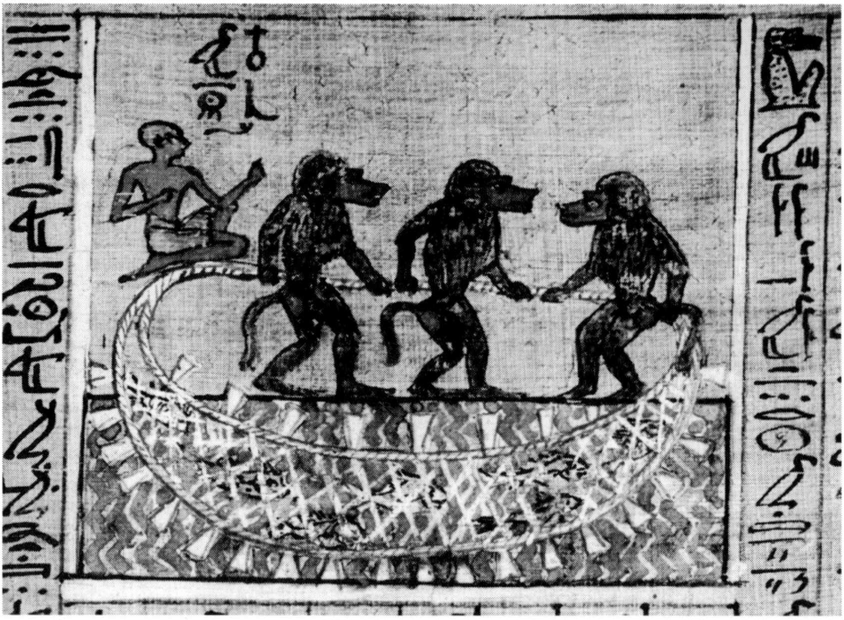

Fig. 118. Painted vignette from Chapter 153B of the papyrus Book of Going Forth by Day *prepared for Neferubenef. It shows three baboons fishing with a large seine net spread out between the sky and earth, from which the deceased owner had to be protected. Dynasty XVIII.*

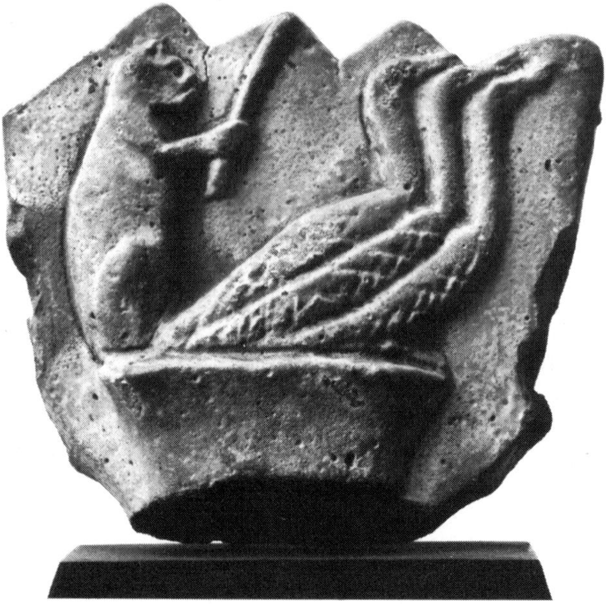

Fig. 119. Detail on the plumed headdress of a faience plaque of the dwarf-god Bes, showing a cat in a human-like pose, brandishing a stick to drive geese. Third Intermediate Period.

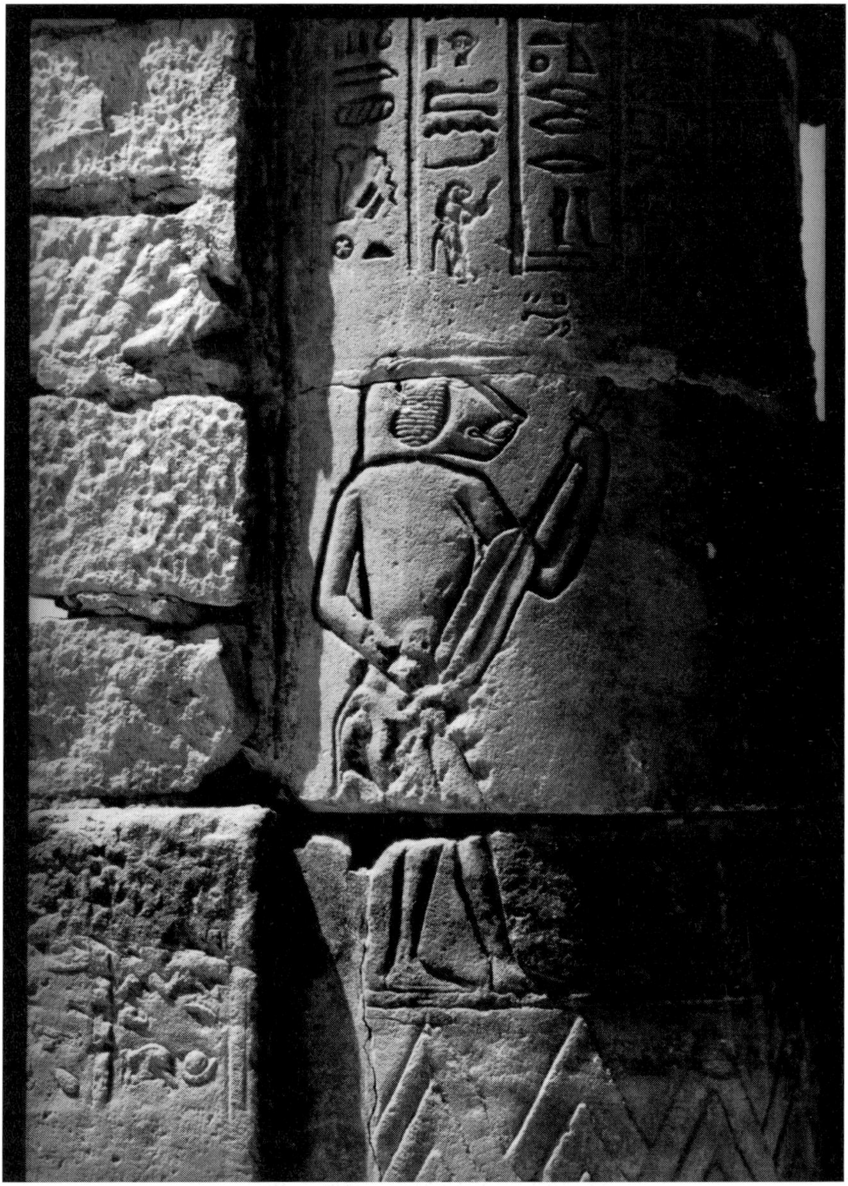

Fig. 120. Figure of a lute-playing baboon, perhaps representing the god Thoth, carved on a column at the entrance to the temple of the goddess Hathor on the island of Philae. The monkey is a member of a band of musicians, including the dwarf-god Bes, joyously celebrating the return of Hathor from Nubia, in her role as one of the many forms of the destructive "eye of Re". Ptolemaic Period.

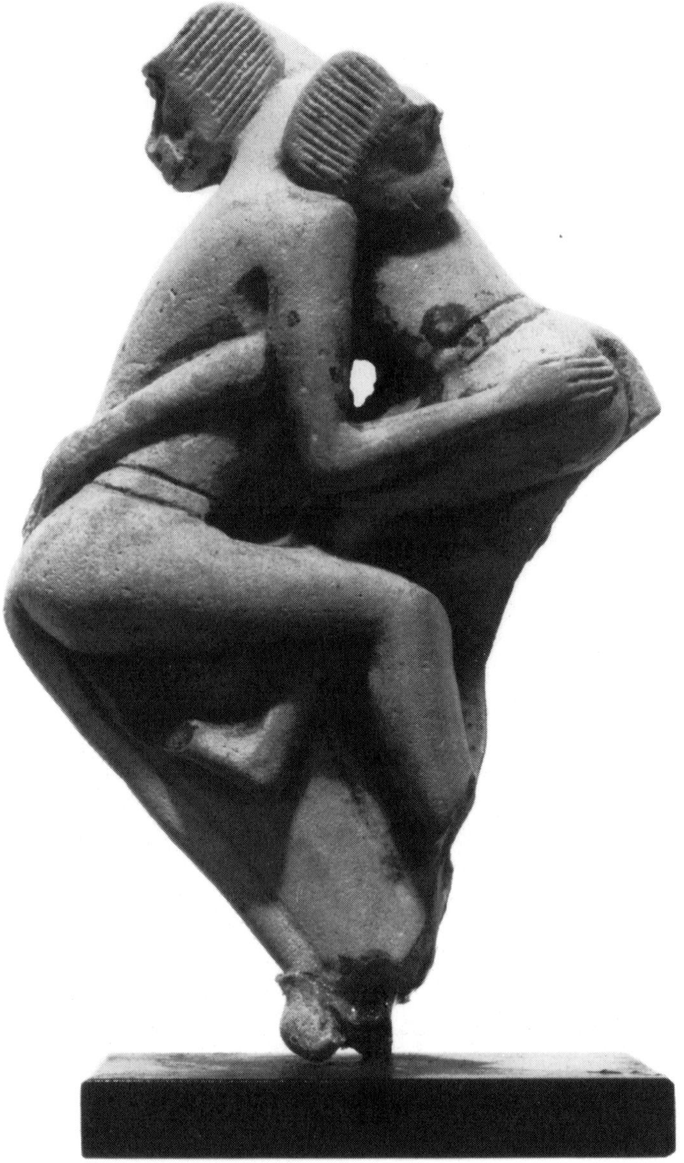

Fig. 121. Green faience statuette of a pair of monkeys, which have halters around their waists, engaged in what would appear to be a playful wrestling match. A more serious-minded analysis might compare their scuffle with the figurine capturing a fable-like boxing match (see fig. 122). Ptolemaic Period.

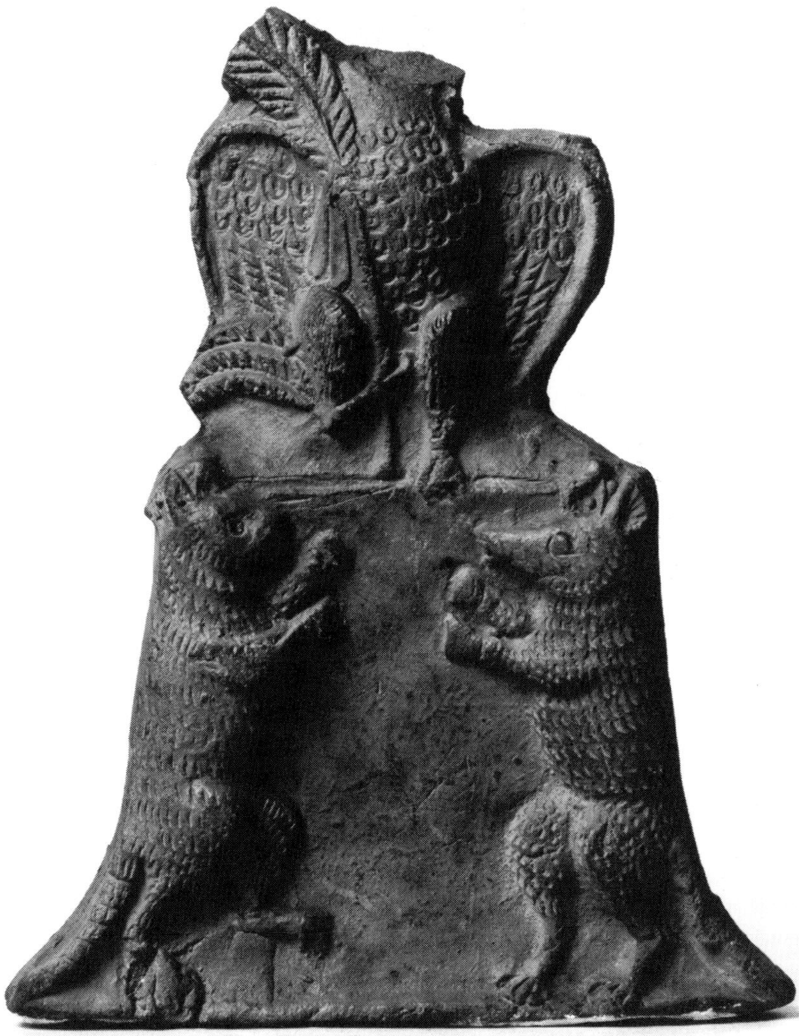

Fig. 122. This unusual terracotta figurine depicts a cat and a mouse, their fists raised in a boxing match, which is being refereed by an eagle (damaged) above them, grasping a palm frond, a trophy to be presented to the victor. This object may possibly refer to a mythological combat. Roman Period (First or Second Centuries CE).

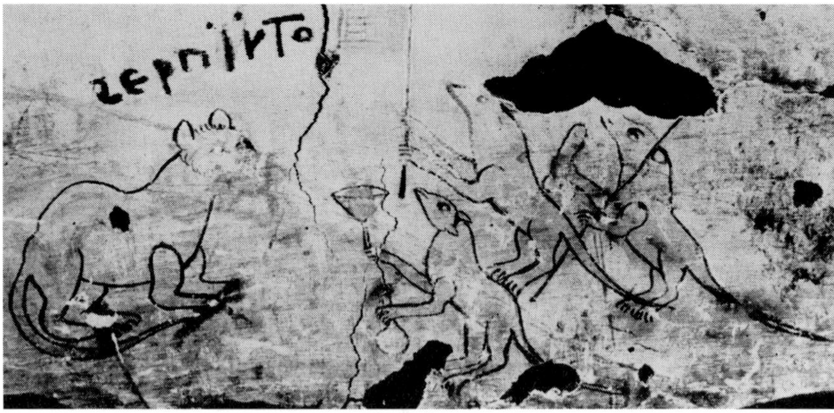

Fig. 123. A wall-painting executed in fresco that once decorated the monastery of St. Apa Apollo at Bawit, which humorously depicts the subservience of a delegation of mice before a cat. They carry a flag (of truce?) and offer gifts. The feline is named in an accompanying inscription: "the cat of Buto." Coptic Period (Seventh or Eighth Century CE).

Yet another group of figured ostraca is of a different variety. A relatively small number of flakes bear caricatures of actual people, drawings that seem to pointedly poke fun at fellow workers and others (fig. 124).[38] While we can only imagine the circumstances that prompted the joke observed on one figured ostracon, representing a caricature of a (funerary?) river journey, with a recumbent donkey substituted for the human passenger (a mummy?) in the vessel, its withering intent seems clear enough (fig. 125).[39] In a similar vein, there is a naughty student's drawing of a funky-looking baboon in the midst of a eulogy of his teacher on a Dynasty XX scribal manuscript. It seems to be very much in the spirit of a caricature against the master.[40] On another limestone flake, Pay and his wife, Meresger, must endure the brunt of sardonic humour (fig. 126). There is certainly something funny in the appearance of these contrasting images of husband and wife.[41] Pay, who is drinking beer from a jar through a long reed tube, is tall and thin, and wears a knee-length kilt, compared to the plumpness and nakedness of his (Nubian?) spouse, who is without her customary long wig, exposing a stubbly hairdo. She is the antithesis of the ancient Egyptian standard of physical feminine beauty. One is very tempted to see this drawing as a sort of cruel joke satirising them, executed by a waggish draughtsmen during the course of the arduous work on a tomb in the Valley of the Kings. It may well have brought a knowing grin to the faces of those familiar with this striking couple. Examples such as this one are a reminder that the Egyptians' sense of humour must not be judged by the politically correct sensibilities of modern scholarship – all is fair game for laughter.

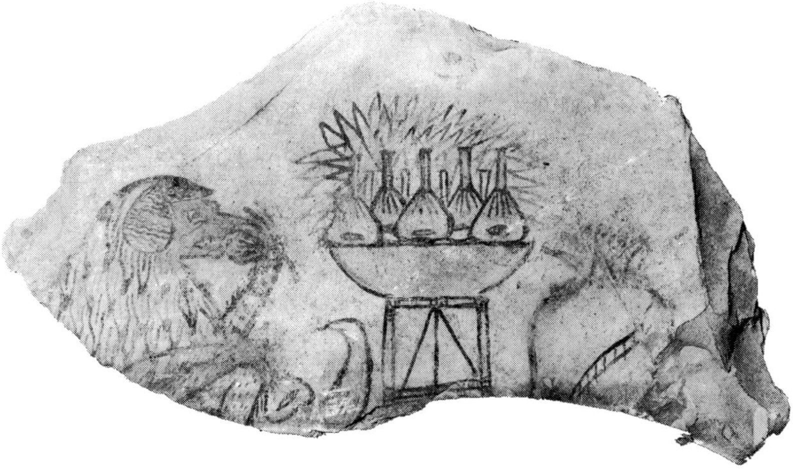

Fig. 124. Figured limestone ostracon portraying a baboon, in a human-like pose, munching on sycamore figs from a bowl standing on a table. Probably from Deir el Medina. Ramesside Period.

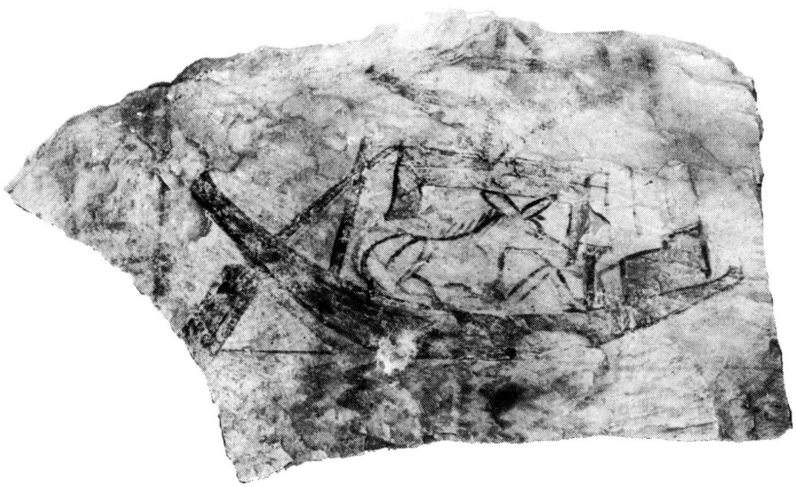

Fig. 125. Figured limestone ostracon showing a humorous caricature of a river voyage sketched in black and red ink, with a donkey lying beneath the boat's canopy, substituting for the human passenger. Probably from Deir el Medina. Ramesside Period.

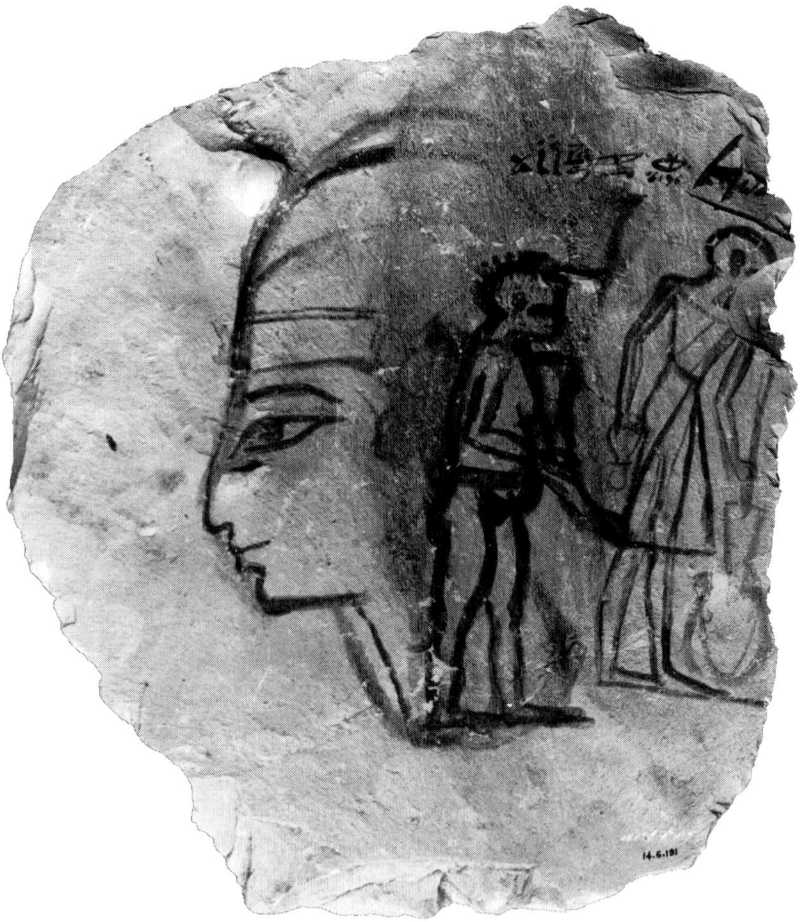

Fig. 126. Figured limestone ostracon bearing drawings which are both serious and humorous in nature. The earlier sketch is a trial portrait of a Ramesside king. This has been partially overlapped with sketches of two standing figures that have a comic quality to them. The couple is named in the brief inscription above them: "Pay and his wife, Meresger". Found in the Valley of the Kings. Ramesside Period.

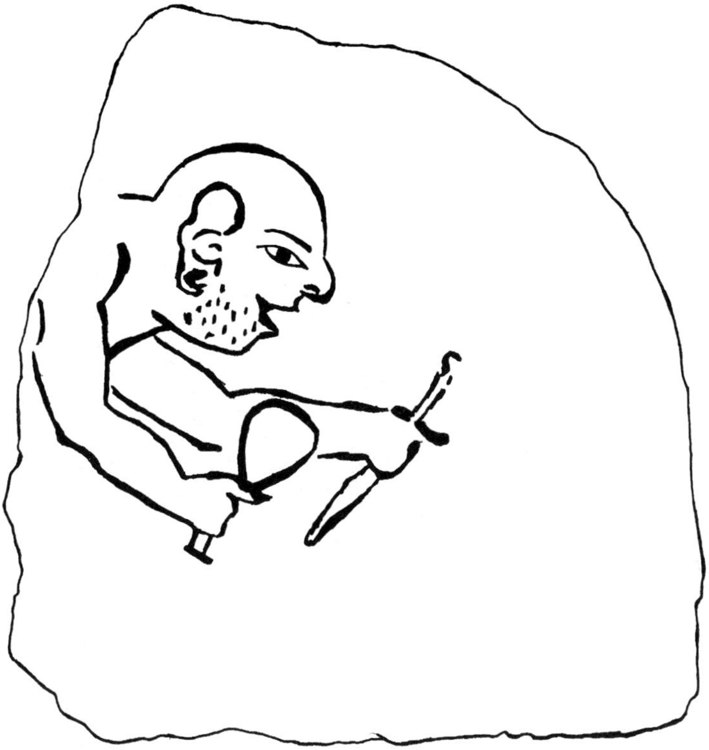

Fig. 127. This drawing of a figured limestone ostracon depicts the caricatured image of a bald and unshaven old stone-mason, who seems to be out of breath, on the job in the Theban necropolis, holding the tools of his occupation, the chisel and wooden mallet. He is characterised by an over-large ear and a prominent bulbous nose. This rapid ink sketch is obviously the product of a skilled draughtsman with a wry sense of humour. Probably from Deir el Medina. Ramesside Period.

Sometimes described as being one of the most clear-cut examples of visual humour from pharaonic Egypt, a figured limestone ostracon is decorated with a caricatured sketch of a burly, bald and unshaven old workman breaking up stone in the Theban necropolis (fig. 127).[42] This vivid drawing serves as a testimony to the power of Egyptian artisans to see traces of jocularity, even in the mundane moments of everyday life (fig. 128). Another unique limestone ostracon has been recognized to bear a copy from an actual monument (fig. 129). A later draughtsman of the Ramesside Period, who quite likely may have found her image amusing, has sketched a rather impressionistic likeness of the exotic and monstrously obese Queen of Punt. He was probably inspired to execute it after viewing her famous portrait on Queen Hatshepsut's mortuary temple at Deir el Bahri, carved two centuries earlier (fig. 54).[43]

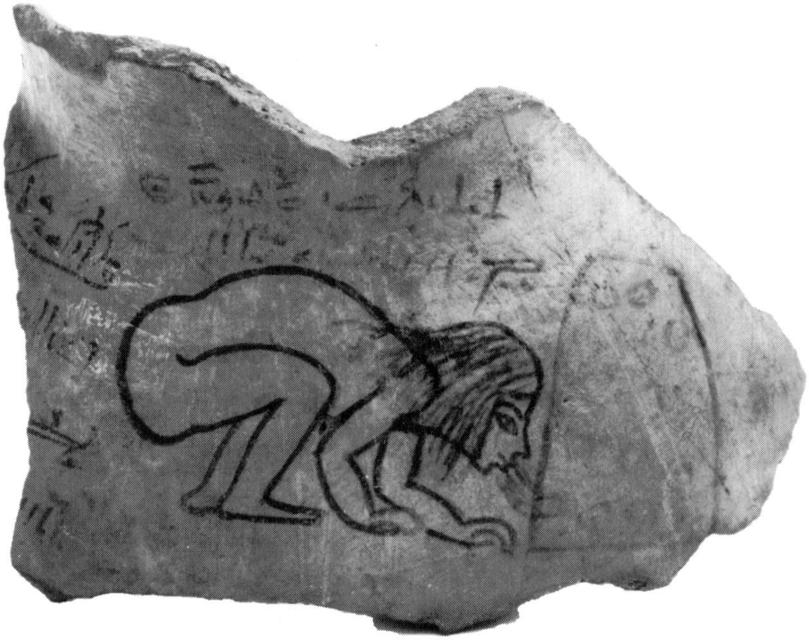

Fig. 128. Black ink sketch on a potsherd picturing a naked girl tending a hot baking oven. She is stooping down, blowing up the fire and, unusually, her breath is indicated. An inscription in hieratic above states that her "head is towards the chamber" and she is "blowing into the oven." This piece is an outstanding example of the quiet humour found in humble subjects on figured ostraca. Ramesside Period.

A few other figured ostraca appear to be of a more dangerous type, aimed at the royal circle itself. They smack of political satire. On one small ostracon, a woman, perhaps a queen, because she wears the royal uraeus-serpent on her brow, seems to be the butt of a joke. A ferocious creature, which could be a hyena or even a bear, is pictured directly above her image as if it were going to pounce on her (fig. 130). The juxtaposition of the two sketches does not seem to be coincidental, but of humorous intent.[44] It is only on ostraca that we see kings with unseemly stubble on their chins and shedding tears.[45] These may have been executed for comic impact, as sometimes suggested, but they are often described as being indications of his mourning. Mockery seems to be at the heart of a drawing on a limestone flake portraying a lion, the famed king of beasts and one of the most conspicuous symbols of Egyptian kingship, fleeing from a less powerful creature in pursuit, a lioness or leopard are possibilities, which is nipping at its left hind leg (fig. 131).[46] As it uncharacteristically runs away, it is glancing backward in fright or, perhaps, disbelief at the audacity of the (is it a queen?) aggressor. So there could be no possible way of mistaking the biting satire

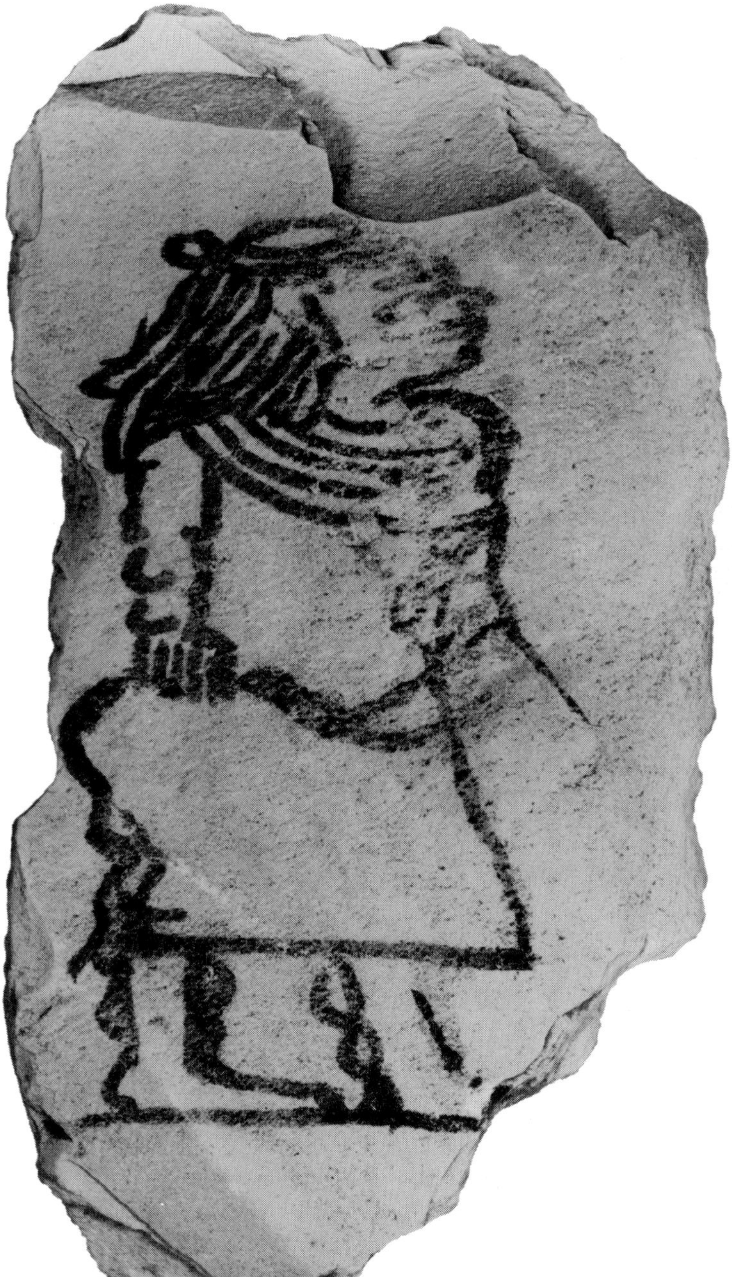

Fig. 129. On this figured limestone ostracon a draughtsman of the Ramesside Period, who appears to have found her amusing, has sketched an inaccurate, but an enlivened copy of the tremendously obese Queen of Punt (see fig. 54). From Deir el Medina.

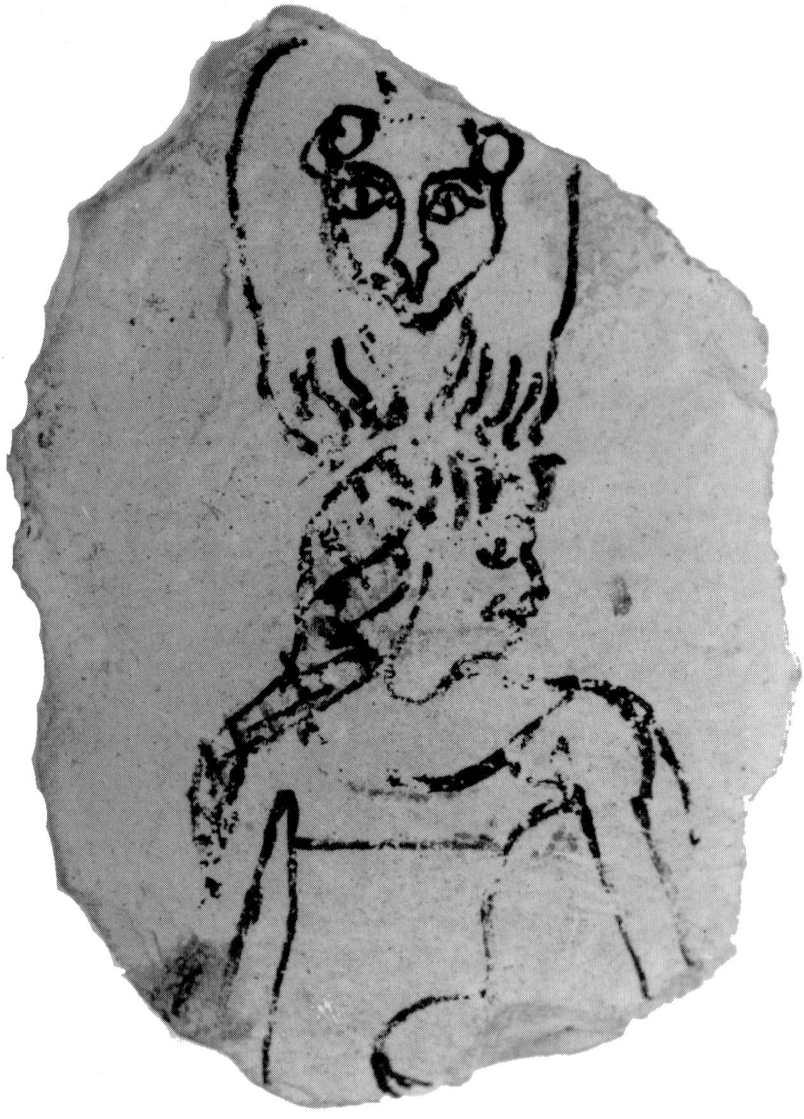

Fig. 130. A small figured limestone ostracon with depictions that do not seem to be the result of accidental juxtaposition, but of humorous intent. Here a royal woman, perhaps a queen, has been hastily sketched facing to the right, wearing a uraeus-serpent on her brow. Above, there is a menacing beast with round ears, possibly a hyena or a bear. It is rendered en face, *with its front legs extended, as if it were about to pounce on her. Probably from Deir el Medina. Ramesside Period.*

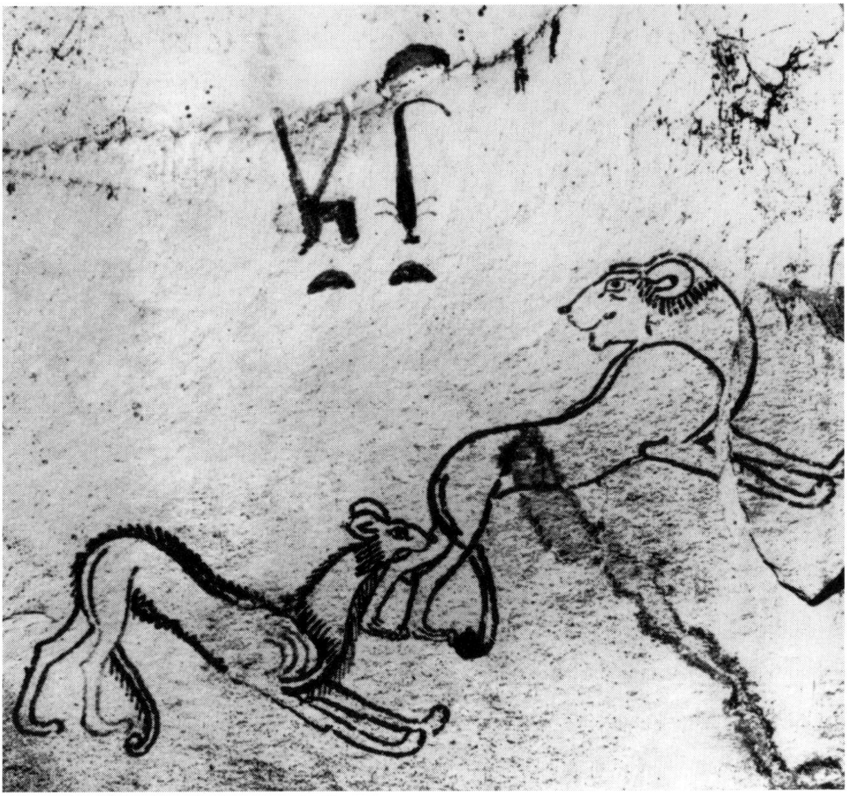

Fig. 131. Figured limestone ostracon with a drawing of royal derision. It shows a lion, the king of beasts and symbol of Egyptian kingship, fleeing from a less powerful creature in hot pursuit. A brief hieroglyphic legend identifies the lion as: "the King of Upper and Lower Egypt." Found in the tomb of Ramesses V and Ramesses VI (KV 9). Dynasty XX.

here, the draughtsman has included a laconic hieroglyphic legend above the pitiful lion, naming him as: "the King of Upper and Lower Egypt." Another limestone chip preserves a sadly damaged drawing of curious battle scenes sketched in red ink (fig. 132). In the upper register, a queen, or possibly the war-goddess Astarte, is standing in a horse-drawn chariot advancing to do combat against an oncoming opponent in another chariot, who is none other than an Egyptian pharaoh. The protagonists are showering each other with a hail of enormous arrows. Below, their respective forces continue the clash using bows and arrows. In the official iconographic repertoire, of course, the king is always portrayed utterly routing his enemies, who are never pictured on such an equal footing with him as conveyed in this drawing. Whichever view one supports, queen or goddess, there is likely to be an element of political caricature in this lively little composition.[47] With a good measure of spirited imagination, we might view

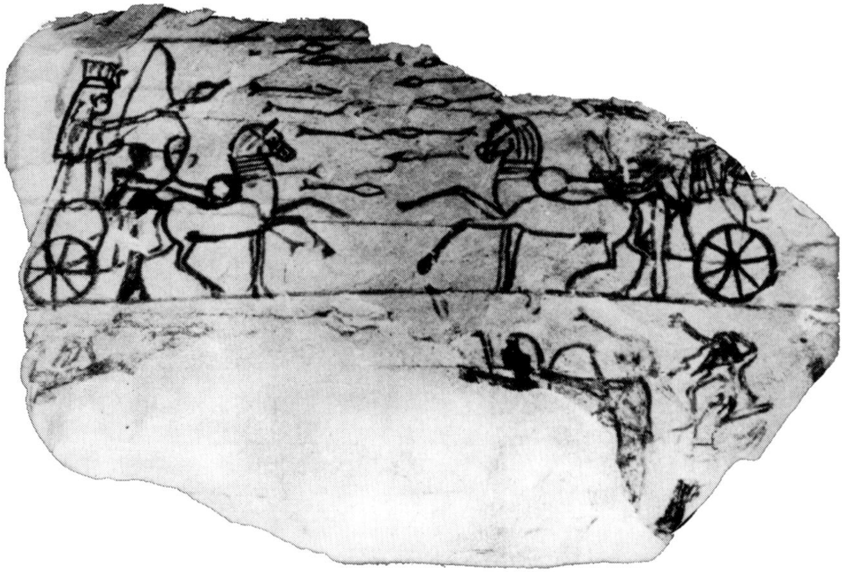

Fig. 132. Figured limestone ostracon bearing a damaged drawing of a unique battle scene. In the upper register, a queen, or perhaps it is the war-goddess Astarte, is standing in a horse drawn chariot engaged in face to face combat with an opponent in another chariot, who is no less an Egyptian king, and they are showering each other with arrows. Below, their respective forces continue the clash. While little can be said with certainty, there must be an element of parody in this spirited composition. Found in the tomb of Ramesses V and Ramesses VI (KV 9). Dynasty XX.

this little episode as a veiled reference to war of succession among members of the royal family or other palace conspiracy hatched in mid-Dynasty XX, a time of significant social turmoil and a weak central government. On the other hand, it is likely to be no more serious than the fanciful flight of a draughtsman with time on his hands or is, possibly, his illustration of a juicy gossip about a royal couple notoriously "at war" with each other! It is also of some considerable interest to note that the preceding pair of figured ostraca (figs. 131-132) can be specifically dated as coming from the reign of Ramesses VI. They were discovered, along with various other ostraca, in a rubbish-heap in his large tomb in the Valley of the Kings.[48] It is certainly ironic, but all too human, that while his sepulchre was under construction, the very men responsible for the work were not adverse to lampooning their monarch in these drawings. Then, to top off the insult, these daring jokes, tossed aside in the rubble after a good time was had by all, were left in the tomb to follow him into eternity. I only hope Ramesses VI took a keen sense of humour with him on his long voyage!

4 Some Humorous Sexual Situations

The entertaining mythological story, *The Contendings of Horus and Seth*, which dates from Dynasty XIX, centres around the struggle of the gods Horus and Seth for the succession to the throne of Osiris and the rule of Egypt.[1] The setting of this bawdy tale is a divine trial, with Horus and Seth as the litigants, and Re-Harakhty, the sun-god, serving as the presiding judge of the court. In the course of the proceedings, Re-Harakhty is insulted by Baba, a minor deity associated with Seth, who remarks to him that: "Your shrine is empty!" Having been deeply offended by this sarcastic quip, he goes off alone, bringing the trial to an abrupt standstill. After a long while, the sun-god's daughter Hathor, the goddess of love and sexual excitation, comes to him with the perfect remedy to cheer him up. She stands in front of him and exposes her naked body before his eyes.[2] Thereupon Re-Harakhty roared with laughter at her. With his good humour restored, he is able to return and the trial between the two gods can resume. In this comical literary tale, that has been called the supreme example of ancient Egyptian humour at its best, even the gods were not adverse to lewd antics and joking about sexual matters.[3] Through his outburst of divine laughter, the sun-god reveals a characteristic central to humanness. Moreover, this boisterousness originates from one of the oldest and most highly favoured comedic subjects among mere mortals.

Another slapstick sexual escapade featured in *The Contendings of Horus and Seth* is a homosexual episode, in which Seth attempts to seduce his rival, Horus. The latter, however, was able to avoid humiliation before the tribunal through the intervention of his clever mother, the goddess Isis; ultimately, it is Seth who ends up being disgraced. The laughs in this mythological farce come purely at the expense of the gods, who are plagued with all sorts of human foibles and weaknesses. A similar erotic encounter between them appears earlier on a very fragmentary late Dynasty XII papyrus from El Lahun, complete with Seth's memorable flirtatious observation to his arch-enemy: "How lovely your backside is!"[4] In the more complete New Kingdom version of the story, Seth said to Horus: "Come, let us have a feast day at my house." And Horus said to him: "I will, I will." Now when evening had come, a bed was prepared for them, and they lay down together. At night, Seth let his member become stiff and he inserted it between the thighs of Horus. And Horus placed his hands between his thighs and caught the semen of Seth. Then Horus rushed to tell his mother Isis: "Come, Isis my mother, come and see what Seth did to me."[5] Aghast at what had befallen her son, she immediately chopped off the hand of Horus that was holding Seth's semen and threw it into the water. (Through her powerful magic she provided him with a new one). She then caused Horus to become aroused and collected his semen in a container. Learning of Seth's appetite for cos lettuce, a plant thought to have aphrodisiac powers (its whitish milk sap recalling human semen), she scattered Horus's semen onto some of the leafy vegetable growing in Seth's garden. Isis's trick worked precisely according to plan, because when Seth ate the lettuce, he unknowingly became pregnant with the seed of his nephew, Horus. Moreover, Seth only became aware of his highly embarrassing condition, much to his utter dismay, upon the god Thoth ordering Horus's semen to come forth from his (Seth's) body at a crucial point of the juridical proceedings in which they were engaged. Thus he was outwitted by Isis and foolishly fell victim to his own mischievous doings, an outcome fittingly apt for a god of confusion.

Seth's predilection for sexual aggression is again depicted in a story in which he takes his pleasure with the Syrian war-goddess Anat, introduced as a woman: "who acts like a warrior, who dresses like a man." This incident may have appealed to audiences for its relatively crude amusement. Seth attacks this manly goddess while she is bathing in a river and is described as leaping upon her back (mounted) like a ram.[6]

Conspicuous instances of humour pertaining to the sexual sphere of people's lives, whether pictorial or textual, are extremely hard to come by in ancient Egypt. In their formal work on temples and tomb-chapels, probably for reasons of decorum or religious guidelines, Egyptian artisans were remarkably discreet about portraying explicit human sexual activity and sexuality, frequently relying on encoded imagery having certain erotic connotations, let alone doing so with an appreciable element of humour.[7] However, the gods' graphic sexual acts do occasionally occur in official iconography as, for instance, when Geb, the earth-god, is sometimes represented pleasuring in oral masturbation (fellatio) on himself, presumably as an act of self-fertilisation.[8] The fertility-god Min is portrayed unabashedly as a very ithyphallic man. In a scene on a birth-house at the late Ptolemaic Period temple of Hathor at Dendara, Isis, in the form of a hovering kite or falcon, is pictured being impregnated by the erect phallus of the deceased Osiris.[9] In literary works, examples like those already mentioned are exceptional. Some include the Middle Kingdom narrative titled *The Tale of King Neferkare and General Sasenet*, in which a monarch, possibly the historical Pepy II of Dynasty VI, is secretly involved in a homosexual affair with one of his generals.[10] A petitioner tries repeatedly to bring this impropriety to the attention of court members, but, when he attempts to speak, he is always amusingly drowned out: "by the singers' songs, the musicians' music, the acclaimers' acclamations and the whistlers' whistling."[11] Frustrated by his inability to be heard over the din, he leaves weeping and tearing out his hair. Finally, their nocturnal liaison is confirmed by the efforts of an amateur sleuth (Tjeti) who shadows the king. He watches the king throw a brick and kick the general's wall as a signal, so that a ladder is lowered for him to climb up to the house and spends some four hours there. The conclusion of this intrigue has not been preserved, but it seems to be disapproving of the behaviour of the pharaoh. An assault of this serious nature on the moral standing of an Egyptian king, even in a purely fictional piece of literature, might well have prompted howls of scurrilous laughter in antiquity.[12]

A couple of the light-hearted and lusty episodes recounted in another Middle Kingdom narrative, *The Tale of King Cheops' Court*, are not likely to have failed to bring smiles to the faces of an ancient audience. One of these involves the goings-on of an adulterous wife and her lover, and the savage revenge of her conjuring husband. The other is highly erotically charged. It features a crew of twenty half-naked sexy young women, wearing only see-through fish-net dresses, rowing King Snofru's pleasure boat:

> "Said his majesty, 'Indeed, I shall go boating! Let there be brought to me twenty oars of ebony plated with gold, their handles of sandalwood plated with electrum. Let there be brought to me twenty women with the shapeliest bodies, breasts, and braids, who have not yet given birth. Also let there be brought to me twenty nets and give these net to these women in place of their clothes!' All was done as his majesty commanded. 'They rowed up and down, and his majesty's heart was happy seeing them row…'"[13]

We note with some interest that in the decoration of a couple of Middle Kingdom rock-cut tomb-chapels of nomarchs, a number of titillatingly attired young females are represented performing otherwise exclusively male food-gathering occupations, fishing and fowling, which recalls the motif of the erotic rowers in the story.[14] The episodes in Dynasty XII tombs have been compared to the ladies of Marie Antoinette's court playing at being shepherdesses (a back-to-nature fantasy), but what we see has also been explained, probably correctly, as an element of the usurpation of royal prerogatives by these highly powerful provincial governors. Wherever the exact truth may lie, I think its fair to suppose that the deceased tomb-owners hoped that these hard-working young lovelies would provide them with a good deal more than merely their nutritional requirements in the netherworld.

There is also, arguably, detectable humour in the sarcastic descriptions of schoolboys devoting themselves to beer halls and women rather than their scribal studies mentioned in the instructional miscellany texts from the late New Kingdom. In one of these, the wayward student has raised the indignation of his teacher, who pointedly writes to him:

> "You follow the path of pleasure; you make friends with revellers. You have made your home in the brewery, as one who thirsts for beer. You sit in the parlour with an idler. You hold the writings in contempt. You visit the whore. Do not do these things! What are they for? Take note of it!"[15]

Finally, from wisdom (instructional) literature written in the demotic script, in *The Teaching of Ankhsheshonq*, dating to the Ptolemaic Period or possibly earlier, there are several unforgettable humorous maxims relating to aspects of human sexuality, even if some maybe judged indecorous. Here, we find such wry advice as: "Do not rejoice in your wife's beauty, her mind is set on her lover", "Man is even more eager to copulate than a donkey, his purse is what restrains him" and the prosaic "He who makes love to a woman of the street will have his purse cut open on its side."[16]

Traces of humour can also occasionally be detected in the rich sexual imagery and erotic *double entendres* of the deeply sensual love songs and romantic poetry dating from the late New Kingdom.[17] Use of the latter literary device, for example, is readily apparent in a metaphorical verse from a lyrical poem (Papyrus Harris 500) capturing the desire of young lovers: "Arousing is the foliage of her swamp." Elsewhere we read (Papyrus Chester Beatty I) the poet urging the youth to rush to his eager beloved and tells him: "Before you kiss your hand four times you will reach her grotto." In these cases, "swamp" and "grotto" are most likely euphemisms for vagina.[18] Such sly allusions of sexual pleasures to come may have excited knowing smiles.

It is usually only in unofficial sources, principally illustrations on papyri, figured ostraca and graffiti, that we can catch glimpses of ancient Egyptian erotic activities. Ignored and occasionally even censored by scholars of the past, this material has, in recent decades, been useful in attempting to better understand pharaonic sexual behaviours and attitudes. A number of these documents, nevertheless, were clearly satirical in intent, rather than being literal records of daily life practices. There is virtually no artistic evidence for anything that can remotely be labelled as licentious prior to the rise of the New Kingdom.[19] Such depictions become more common, especially as figurines, in the Late Dynastic and Graeco-Roman Periods; but there is still a reluctance to publish this somewhat indecent material, so that much of the corpus remains unknown (figs. 133 and 134). From Dynasty XVIII comes a sketch on a fragment of wood, said to be from a coffin, but this seems unlikely, portraying the seduction of a female lutenist sitting on a stool, by an obviously aroused, but still clad, male listener during her musical performance, the instrument just dangling from her hand (fig. 135).[20] Perhaps this over-eager fellow was carried away with desire by the air of her love song. While its precise significance, if any, beyond the obvious, may now be lost on the viewer, it would appear to be a forerunner of one of the burlesque interludes rendered on the celebrated satirical-erotic papyrus in Turin, where music-making and sexual intercourse go hand in hand, one apparently a prelude to the other (fig. 136).[21] Another noticeable instance of erotica from Dynasty XVIII, and again involving a musical theme, occurs on a fragment of painted leather, described as being either part of a wall-hanging, a canopy from a piece of furniture or perhaps even a scroll (fig. 137).[22] It features a unique and not easily explained vignette of a seated female harpist playing her instrument under an arching arbor, heavy with clusters of grapes. Directly in front of her there is a naked man, with a large erect phallus, that curiously protrudes from behind him, who is performing a humorous or erotic dance. As this piece was discovered at Deir el Bahri, it may have had some cultic associations with the goddess Hathor, who had a shrine there, and was used as a votive offering to her, but a comic reading of it also remains a distinct possibility. From the same dynasty comes a crude graffito which has generated considerable lively discussion among scholars. A hastily executed ink drawing, from an unfinished Middle Kingdom tomb above Queen Hatshepsut's mortuary temple at Deir el Bahri, shows a standing man having sexual intercourse from behind with a bending woman (fig. 138). This lewd graffito, though uninscribed, has been interpreted by several leading authorities as a sort of an early political cartoon, executed by an anonymous contemporary observer.[23] The woman is viewed as being none other than the female pharaoh herself, Hatshepsut, submitting sexually to the high ranking court official and her close favorite, the renowned Senenmut. His relationship with the queen has been the subject of much speculation. The motive for this assault, it is posited, may have been to boldly highlight the one way in which she could ever truly be kingly. If this is indeed the case, such a pasquinade of the reigning monarch, using sexual imagery as a weapon of ridicule, would make this graffito especially unique in ancient Egypt. While this casual scribble may have caused its maker and others to chuckle, we may confidently assume

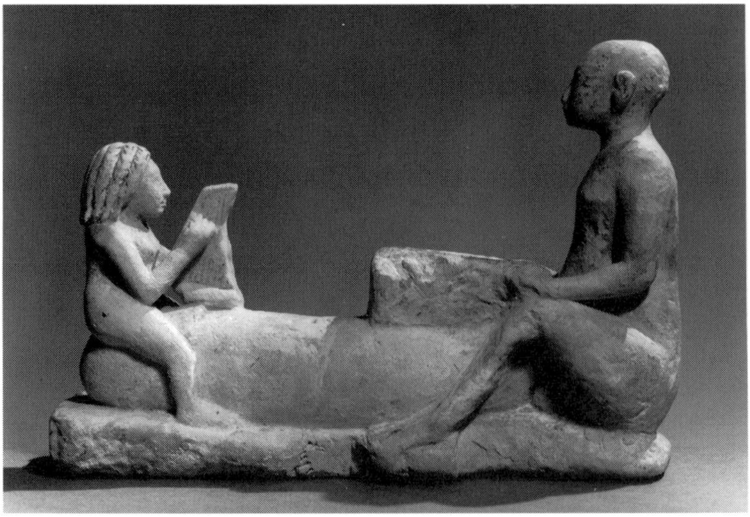

Fig. 133. A limestone erotic figurine of an ithyphallic nude male with a female harpist seated on the far end of his enormous phallus, on which there is also a block inscribed with unique markings that maybe musical notation. Objects such as this one were commonly produced during the Late Dynastic and Ptolemaic Periods. Ptolemaic Period.

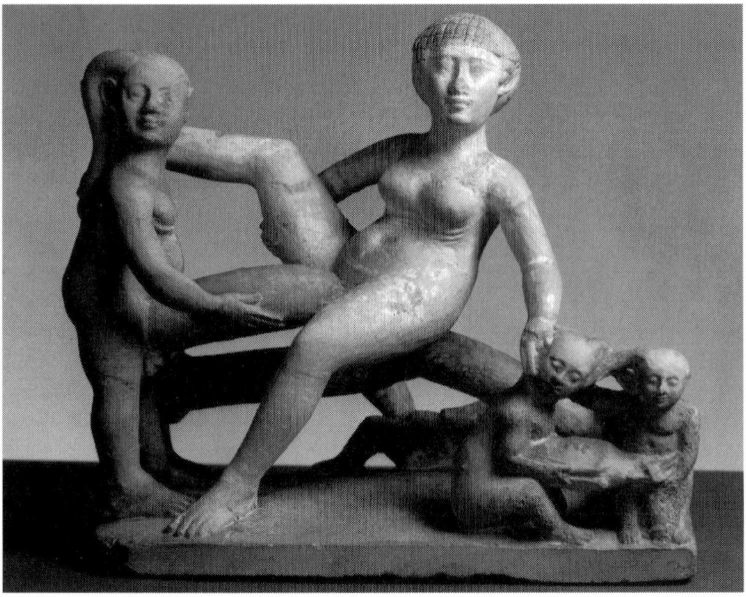

Fig. 134. A magnificent painted limestone erotic sculptural group of intertwined figures engaged in sexual activity. The central focus of the piece is a large nude female with six male attendants, each of whom sports a side-lock of hair. The tallest of these individuals, with a huge erect phallus, is copulating with the reclining woman, whose weight is, for the most part, borne by the serpentine phalluses of three other men. Reportedly from the vicinity of Alexandria. Ptolemaic Period.

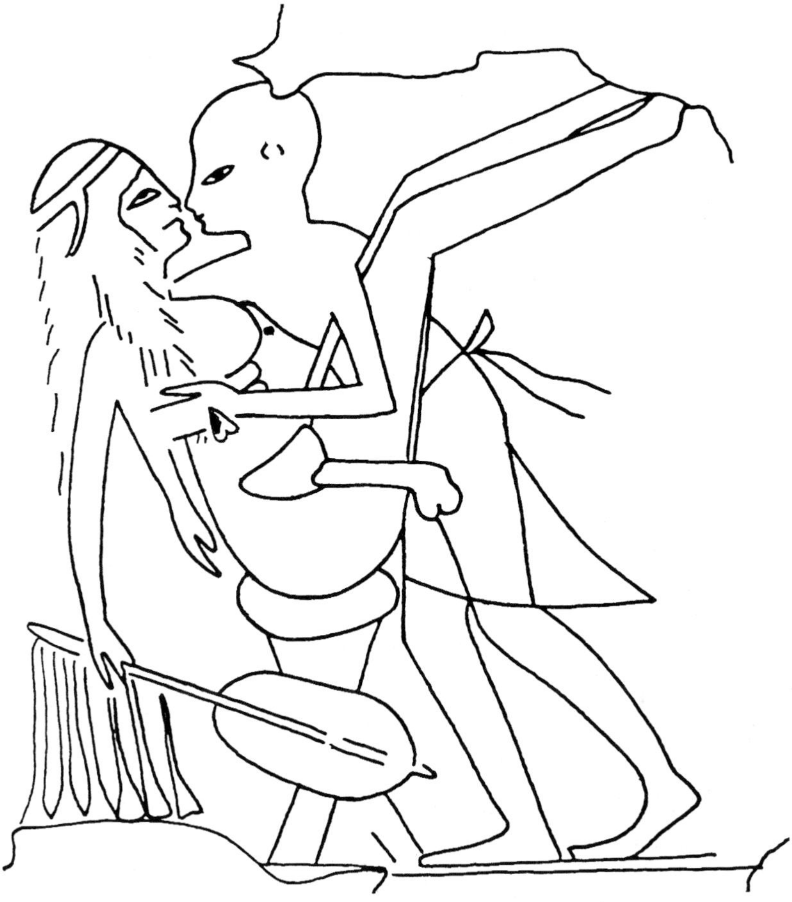

Fig. 135. Sketch on a fragment of wood, possibly from a coffin, portraying the seduction of a female lutenist by an obviously aroused male listener during the middle of her musical performance. Found in a Theban tomb-chapel, but now apparently lost. Dynasty XVIII.

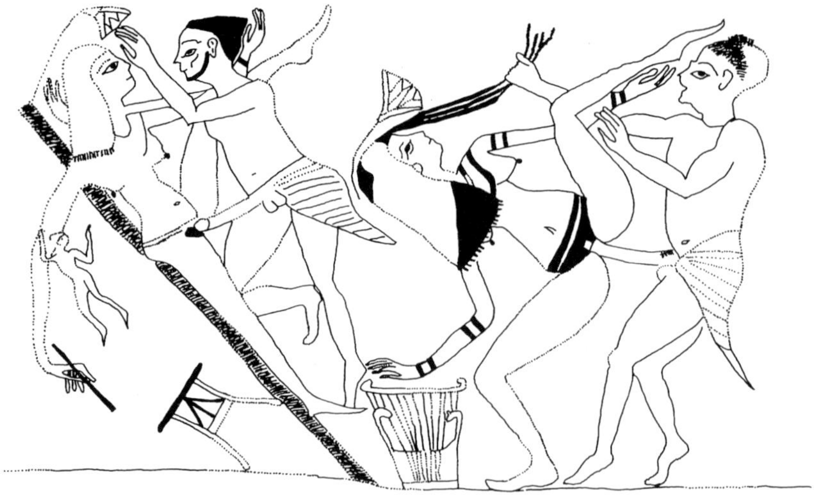

Fig. 136. Partially restored drawing of two ribald vignettes illustrating men and women making love in quasi-acrobatic positions on the satirical-erotic papyrus in the Turin Museum. At the left, a nude woman is reclining on a slanting board with one of her legs upraised, and is copulating with her partner in a face-to-face manner. To the left of them, a child appears to be running away. At the right, a standing nude woman with her legs spread widely apart, one is raised above the head of the man, and supporting her weight with a hand placed on a lyre, seems to be enjoying the company of her partner. This detail is another instance of the close association between eroticism and music. Probably from Deir el Medina. Ramesside Period.

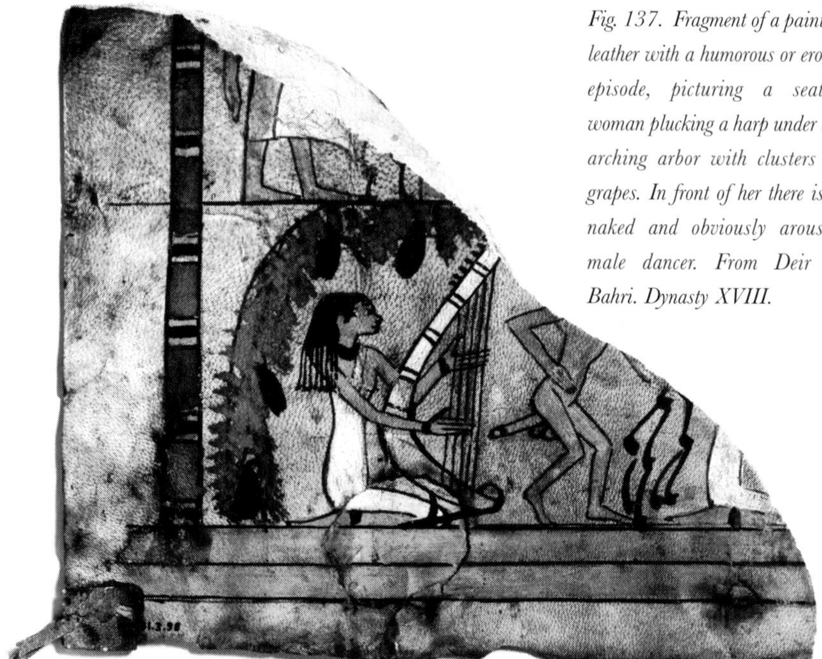

Fig. 137. Fragment of a painted leather with a humorous or erotic episode, picturing a seated woman plucking a harp under an arching arbor with clusters of grapes. In front of her there is a naked and obviously aroused male dancer. From Deir el Bahri. Dynasty XVIII.

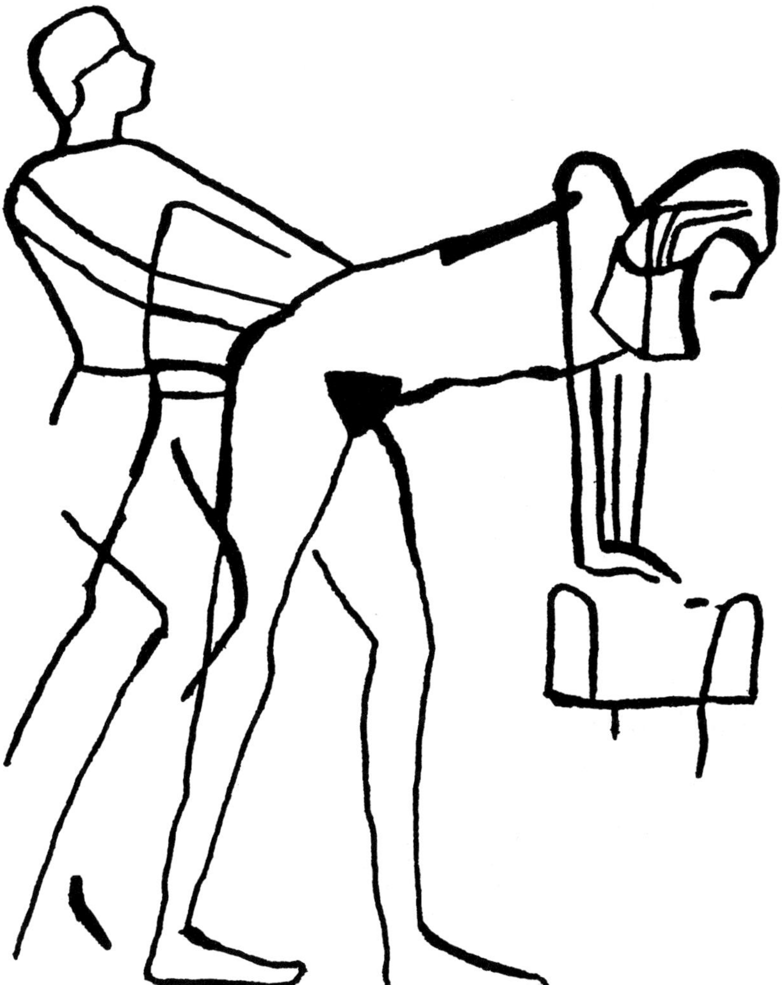

Fig. 138. Drawing of a hastily executed erotic ink graffito, from an unnumbered tomb above Queen Hatshepsut's mortuary temple at Deir el Bahri, of a standing man having sexual intercourse from behind with a naked woman. It has been interpreted as a political parody. She is viewed as representing Hatshepsut, submitting to her Chief Steward, Senenmut. Dynasty XVIII.

that no smile would have lit up the face of her majesty had she been aware of being immortalized in such an undignified pose (fig. 3).

As Queen Hatshepsut's "chief spokesman", Senenmut appears to have drawn his share of attention from political caricaturists. Another example, while not sexual in scope, is quite amusing and worthy of mention here. It comes from a figured limestone ostracon, found in the vicinity of his Theban tomb, and is now in The Metropolitan Museum of Art, New York. It shows two trial profiles of Senenmut in black ink. While on the reverse of the flake, there is a masterly drawing of a rare subject, a large rat.[24] There is no mistaking its disparaging message here. Many ordinary ancient Egyptians, we may well suppose, like people of all times everywhere, took delight in ridiculing those of higher station, especially prominent controversial public figures. These private gibes seem to attest to such a spirit being alive and well during the provocative reign of Queen Hatshepsut.

Attributable to artisans of the Ramesside Period are a selection of drawings on ostraca, seemingly of toss-away quality, of couples engaged in comic love-making.[25] These sketches often portray people, not necessarily always heterosexuals, in imaginative positions, who are nudged even closer together by interested onlookers, encouraging their sexual games (fig. 139). A fragmentary figured limestone ostracon with a black ink drawing may be a parody of a formal scene, represents a standing man penetrating a bending female(?) from the rear (fig. 140). The woman's head is turned back towards her partner. Part of her speech directed to him is written in the accompanying hieroglyphic caption: "Calm is the wish of my skin(?)!"[26]

Far and away the single most important piece of evidence for connecting eroticism with humour in ancient Egypt is the renowned painted satirical-erotic papyrus (Papyrus 55001) in the Museo Egizio, Turin, of late Ramesside Period date.[27] This fragmentary document, the only major one of its kind known so far, was acquired by the museum as far back as 1824, but was not published in its entirety until comparatively recently, presumably for reasons of propriety. In all likelihood, there must have been other papyri of this nature, but if so, they have not survived the ravages of time and man or have yet to be discovered. The work of a master draughtsman, this scroll is composed of two very distinctive sections (see Chapter 3).[28] The right side of the papyrus previously discussed, features a captivating series of fifteen fairy-tale drawings of birds and beasts behaving in quasi-human fashion (figs. 57 and 66-68). The left side, which is the larger section, comprises the so-called "erotic" portion, consisting of twelve vignettes of caricatured sexual encounters between rather seedy-looking middle-aged men, endowed with enormous erect phalli, and nubile young women (figs. 136 and 141-146). All the male figures wear

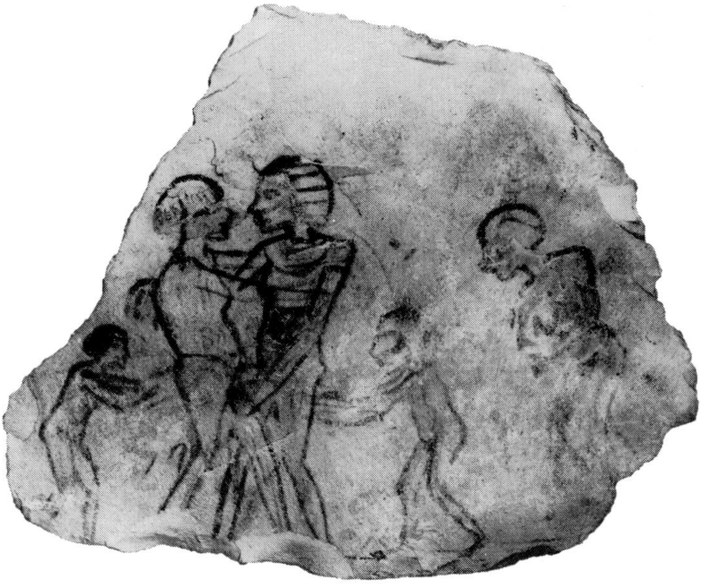

Fig. 139. Figured limestone ostracon with a racy erotic drawing of a couple standing in embrace. The woman, who is on the right, appears to be fondling the older man's genitals. On either side of them are onlookers, who seem to be encouraging their sexual foreplay. From Deir el Medina. Ramesside Period.

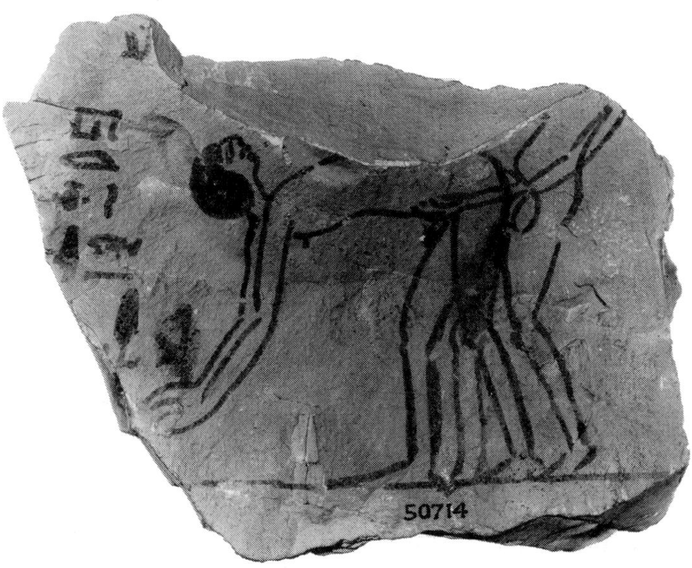

Fig. 140. A fragmentary figured limestone ostracon with an erotic black ink drawing of love-making. A man is depicted penetrating a bending woman(?) from the rear, her head turned back towards him. Probably from Deir el Medina. Ramesside Period.

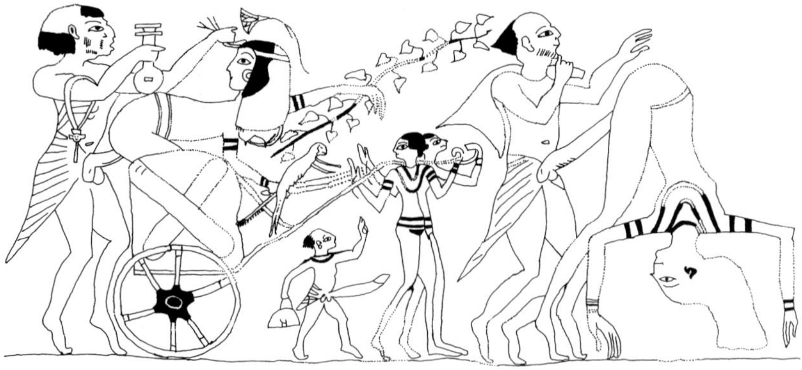

Figs. 141. Partially restored drawing of two vignettes of human couples engaging in burlesque sexual situations, as portrayed on the fragmentary satirical-erotic papyrus in the Turin Museum. At the left, a nude woman standing in a chariot drawn by two handmaidens, with a monkey assisting at the reins, receives her partner from behind. She is unhampered by clothes and coquettishly holds a long convolvulus vine. He is carrying a jar and a sistrum dangles from his arm. A dwarfish attendant with an over-sized phallus appears underneath the chariot, chasing the girls. At the right, there is another couple having sex, the woman bent over in an arched position. Probably from Deir el Medina. Ramesside Period.

short kilts, while their lovers are naked, except for being donned with jewelry and elaborate hairstyles or wigs. The adventures are punctuated with brief hieratic captions, expressing the protagonists' words of joy and delight; for example, a girl tells her ithyphallic partner:

> "I make your job a pleasant one. Do not fear. What would I do to you? You…day, you who knocks in, you who turn around! Look here, come round behind me. I contain your pleasure, your phallus is with me. You have not brought me…lovely, my bastard!"[29]

While we clearly do not fully understand the significance of the Turin papyrus, which has been the subject of many interpretations and observations, it is highly doubtful whether the obscene component ever served as a form of pornographic encouragement or was a pharaonic manual of sexual instruction. Although the couples' various sexual acts are explicit and imaginative, albeit gymnastically quite impossible, they are completely without passion and fail to either entice or arouse; rather, they have a strong comical effect. Their highly suggestive chit-chat aside, the men and women appear to be indifferent to one another. It is sex for the sake of sex, and a little rough at that. Taken as a whole, the intent of the Turin papyrus seems decidedly satirical in character and was not

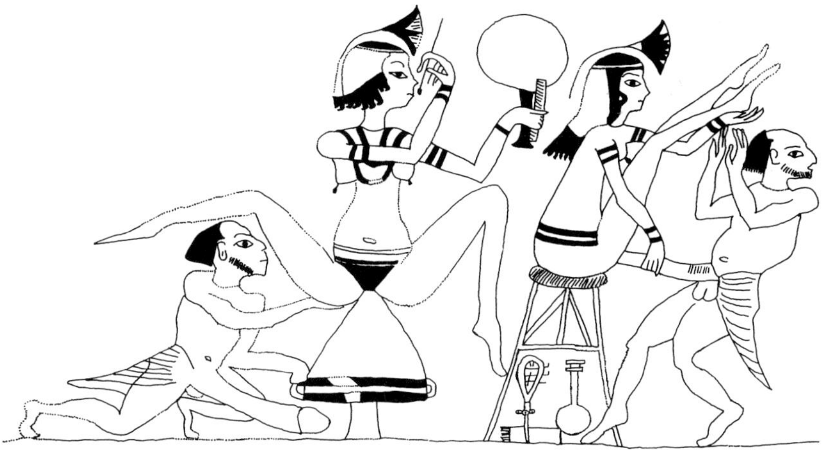

Figs. 142. Partially restored drawing of two vignettes depicting men and women having intercourse and performing other sexual capers on the satirical-erotic papyrus in the Turin Museum. At the left, a nude woman (a prostitute?) is shown applying lip colour and looking at herself in a mirror, her legs spread wide apart. Apparently as a means of achieving sexual pleasure, she is squatting, precariously balanced, on the bottom of an inverted jar. Her partner, displaying an enormous phallus, points his hand in the direction of her vulva. At the right, a woman sitting on a tall stool, her legs raised high, is copulating with a seemingly reluctant, unshaven and pot-bellied individual. An accompanying inscription in hieratic records part of her speech: "I make your job a pleasant one. Do not fear." Ramesside Period.

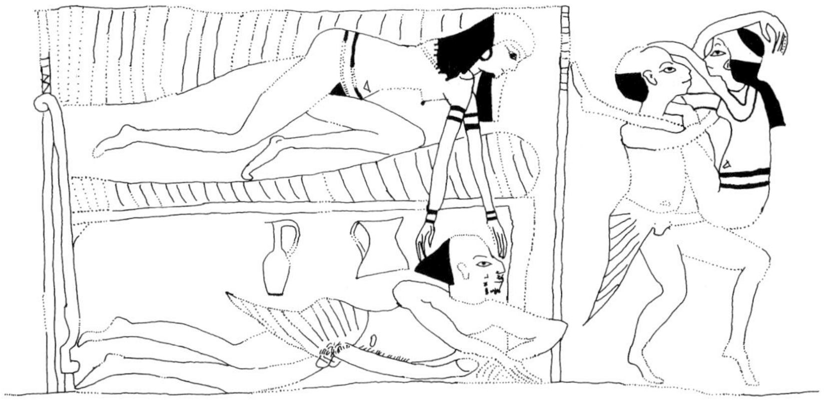

Figs. 143. Partially restored drawing of two vignettes picturing humorous sexual encounters on the satirical-erotic papyrus in the Turin Museum. At the left, a naked woman attempts to coax back into bed her exhausted or dead drunk partner, who is lying on the floor with a huge erect phallus. At the right, a couple has sex in a rather contorted position. Ramesside Period.

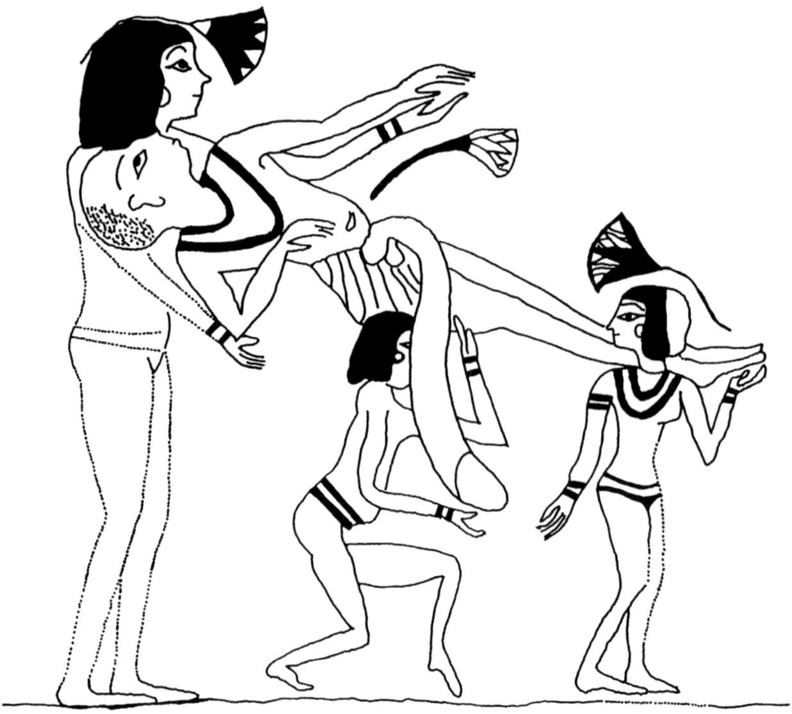

Figs. 144. Partially restored drawing of a risqué action vignette on the satirical-erotic papyrus in the Turin Museum. Here a nude woman, with the help of two handmaidens, is carrying away her thoroughly spent lover, his massive penis now limp. Ramesside Period.

didactic.[30] Its primary aim seems to have been to beguile and amuse, even if contemporary sensibilities may find the sexual fantasies coarse and woefully lacking in humorous sophistication.

It is not possible to specifically identify the amorous actors in the midst of these sexual escapades. It has been suggested that the erotic portion of the scroll is a satire aimed at the priestly-class, the sketches being said to show the debauchery of a priest of Amen and a singer of Hathor. This is speculative, however, and it seems far more likely that this orgy is not limited to only two participants. Another view, advanced by the Danish Egyptologist Lise Manniche, who has studied aspects of ancient Egyptian sexual life, is that the setting of these illustrations is in a brothel, one perhaps located in the artisans' village of Deir el Medina, the papyrus's likely provenance.[31] The action would thus take place between prostitutes and their clients. While this explanation certainly seems closer to the mark, it does not address the fanciful sexual intercourse in the back of a chariot, which is drawn by two handmaidens, who appear to be chased by a

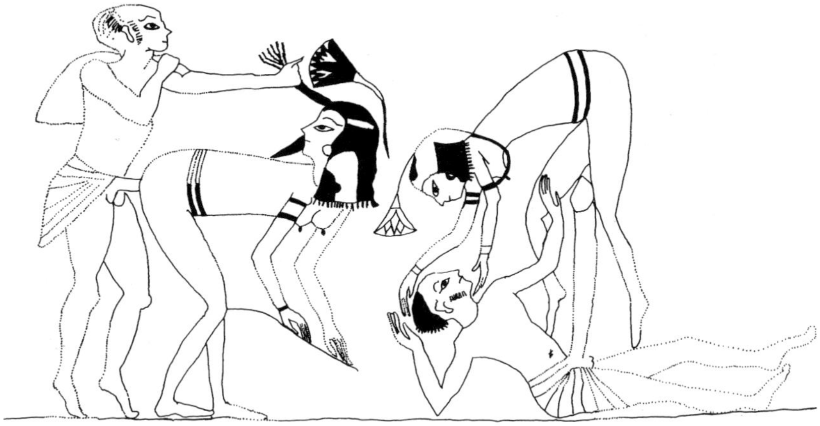

Fig. 145 Partially restored drawing of two vignettes of couples indulging in sexual intercourse on the satirical-erotic papyrus in the Turin Museum. At the left, a standing man, while grasping her hair, penetrates a naked woman from the rear, supporting her weight on a cushion. At the right, the position of the copulating pair, recalls that of an ithyphallic figure of the earth-god Geb beneath the sky-goddess Nut, known from scenes on later mythological papyri. Ramesside Period.

dwarfish attendant (fig. 141). On the other hand, bouts of excessive drinking and increased sexual activity were characteristic behaviours linked with the celebration of some religious festivals in ancient Egypt. Perhaps it is from this carnival atmosphere of revelry that the scroll takes its inspiration.[32] Several of the humorous depictions of coupling men and women are evidently parodies of conventional motifs in religious iconography.[33] The position of one copulating pair (fig. 145), and the direction of the man's larger-than-life-sized erect penis, is definitely reminiscent of that of an ithyphallic figure of the god Geb beneath his wife, the sky-goddess Nut, known from vignettes painted on mythological papyri and coffins.[34] The twelve erotic episodes on the scroll may be a reference to the same number of scenes of the hours of the night pictured in a mortuary book called the *Amduat* ("that which is in the Netherworld"). The episode that portrays a bed might allude to the myth of the god Osiris and his resurrection (fig. 143).[35] The couple reclining at an uncomfortable-looking 45 degree angle readily brings to mind a similarly positioned ithyphallic deity on a mound of sand illustrated on later mythological papyri (fig. 136).[36] A number of other religious elements have been noticed on the document as well. This includes the sistrum, a ceremonial rattle, shaken in religious and funerary rites, which is associated with two of the characters (figs. 141 and 142). Although its full meaning escapes our 21st-century gaze, the satirical-erotic papyrus in Turin is a breathtaking

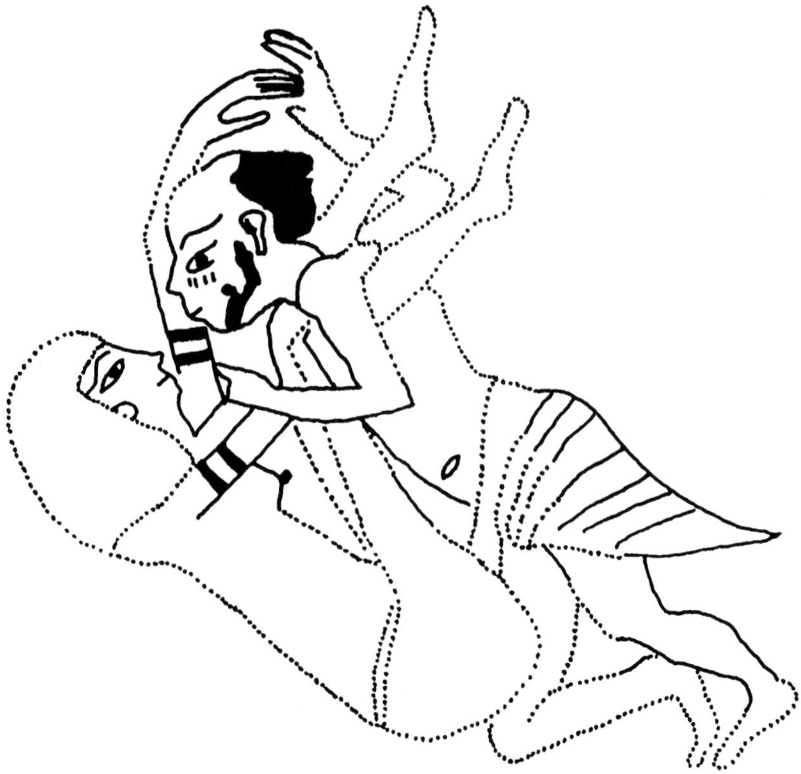

Fig. 146. Partially restored drawing of a very fragmentary vignette on the satirical-erotic papyrus in the Turin Museum. The characters shown here couple face-to-face, the woman lying on a cushion with her legs around the neck of her lover. Ramesside Period.

departure from the customary treatment in formal art, to a lesser degree in written texts, of dealing with human sexuality and eroticism delicately. It exhibits a view of the ancient Egyptian people which is vastly different from the conventional ones seen on temple and tomb-chapel walls.

There are innumerable erotic figurines, made of limestone, terracotta and faience, mostly dating from the Late Dynastic and Graeco-Roman Periods. The precise function of these artefacts has yet to be satisfactorily elucidated. This is partly due to the fact that the cultural context in which they were discovered has seldom been carefully recorded, and also by the inattention they have received in the Egyptological literature. Obscene objects are often found on settlement sites of these epochs. Others served as votive offerings for pilgrims visiting cult sites, and some have holes in them for suspension, apparently so they could be worn as amulets.[37] Many presumably relate to matters of personal sexuality and fertility, very possibly being men's potency charms or the like, while others could have had apostrophic powers to ward off evil. In any event, the ancient Egyptians would likely have viewed such images with a multiplicity of meanings at once, involving elements of religious beliefs, fertility, eroticism and even a healthy dose of humour.[38] The form of these figurines varies, but they usually have a decidedly phallocentric emphasis. Their iconography calls to mind the explicit drawings found on the papyrus in Turin. Always especially popular were portrayals of men with disproportionately large or serpentine phalli, which can even wrap around their heads. On one of these statuettes, now in the British Museum, London, the head of the man has been replaced with one of a large erect phallus, expressing clearly what he has on his mind![39] Examples of this category can be traced at least as far back as the late Ramesside Period at the village of Deir el Medina.[40] A notable limestone group, of Ptolemaic Period date, and a further instance of the connection between music-making and the sexual sphere, illustrates a naked ithyphallic man with a female harpist playing her instrument as she sits on the end of his gigantic erect phallus; one scholar describing it as a possible "erotic music lesson" (fig. 133).[41] Similarly, there are numerous statuettes featuring intertwined couples or groups of figures lustfully cavorting in various sexual acts in an array of provocative poses (fig. 134).[42] It is not entirely certain whether some of these pieces were straightforward erotica or votive in nature. While the *raison d'être* of these extraordinary objects was surely not to amuse, few could deny the overt comic quality inherent in a great many of them, an aspect of which their makers would have undoubtedly been keenly aware. Sexual intercourse, not surprisingly, was regarded by the ancient Egyptians as a natural and highly pleasurable activity, quite compatible with an ambience of humour, laughter and celebration. Already in *The Contendings of Horus and Seth*, when the goddess Hathor playfully stripped and exposed her genitals to her father Re-Harakhty in order to restore his good cheer, laughing and eroticism were linked in the Egyptian mind.[43]

The Greek traveller and historian Herodotus, who visited Egypt around 450 BCE, seems to have disseminated a few bawdy tales from Egypt to his Hellenic audience, assuming, of course, they are genuinely rooted in Egyptian culture.[44] These fanciful anecdotes appear to be really more in the nature of folk-tales, conveyed to him by his Egyptian informants. One he recounted deals with the wicked reputation of the famous King Cheops (Khufu) of Dynasty IV, builder of the Great Pyramid at Giza. According to the story, he is said to have prostituted his own daughter to help raise funds for its construction, while she required her many lovers to bring blocks of stone for her own monument:

> "And so evil a man was Cheops that for lack of money he made his own daughter to sit in a chamber and exact payment (how much, I know not; for they did not tell me this). She, they say, doing her father's bidding, was minded to leave some memorial of her own, and demanded of everyone who sought intercourse with her that he should give one stone to set in her work; and of these stones was built the pyramid that stands midmost of the three, over against the great pyramid; each side of it measures one hundred and fifty feet."[45]

In another of these tall tales, along somewhat similar lines as the preceding, a certain King Rhampsinitus, in order to find a cunning thief:

> "bade his daughter (such is the story, but I myself do not believe it) to sit in a certain room and receive alike all who came; before she had intercourse with any, she should compel him to tell her what was the cleverest trick and the greatest crime of his life."[46]

Whether legends as these were actually told to Herodotus during his Egyptian travels or were purely his own far-fetched concoctions is not certain, but it seems wholly conceivable that some minor official or guide might have imparted to him, an apparently gullible visitor, such amusing yarns of fantasy. His Greek audience could very well have found these barbarisms uproariously funny. Whatever the exact case may have been, they have come down to us as further instances of sexual situations used as a motif in Egyptian humour.

Epilogue

Few topics are as subjective or potentially elusive as humour. It is nearly inevitable in any study which attempts to examine wit and humour in another culture, let alone one so far removed in time from our own, where the jokes have been dead for more than thirty centuries, that something of the author's own sense of humour will be discernable in the interpretation of the material. It is also readily acknowledged, because of the significant cultural and linguistic differences which separate our times, that much of what the ancient Egyptians intended to raise a smile or produce a laugh has likely been missed or has otherwise, to some degree, been misconstrued. Nor has it proved possible to accurately gauge what the full impact humour had on its intended audiences in antiquity. These are just a few of the many difficulties I have encountered when investigating the subject at hand. Be that as it may, in this book, I have tried to discuss wit and humour as objectively as possible, cautiously suggesting an array of things that people in ancient Egypt may have found amusing.

The primary aim of the present work has been to convey to the informed general reader that, even from our 21st-century perspective, glimpses of what struck the ancient Egyptians as funny are recognisable. Humour is a universal phenomenon, and just like human beings the world over, people in ancient Egypt delighted in a good laugh and enjoyed making others laugh along with them. The extant pictorial and textual records seemingly provide an intriguing window onto their place in the "history of laughter". While in no way implying that the ancient Egyptians were frivolous, the evidence suggests they had a healthy and pervasive sense of humour, and recognised a broad range of different types, from high to low. They could chuckle at satire, parody, caricature, vulgarity, erotic indecencies, sardonic humour, farce, and general tomfoolery. In their literature, they utilized puns, metaphors, similes, and other sophisticated literary devices. The ancient Egyptians could poke fun at easy targets such as enemies and strange foreigners but also, and far more significantly, at their own gods and monarchs. The keen eye of talented artisans observed all sorts of humorous moments in the routine everyday life pursuits of the lower classes of society. Sometimes they included elements of this type of jocularity, in picture and in word, within the decorative programme of great tomb-chapels belonging to the wealthy and socially superior. In pharaonic Egypt, the images of various animals, especially beloved domestic pets, developed into a convenient vehicle for expressing a touch of comic relief within the constraints of established decorum and the strict conventions of artistic representation in scenes on tomb-chapel walls from early Old Kingdom onward. Zany representations of animals in human postures and occupations inhabiting an inverted world on the painted satirical papyri and figured limestone ostraca further attest to the pleasure they took in laughing. In sum, humour and sharpness of wit seem to have been highly prized in ancient Egypt. Is it only coincidental that these traits continue to be much admired in contemporary Egypt?

Increasingly, humour is being taken seriously and is recognised by many scholars as an important way in which a society expresses itself, and amply repays critical study. Coming to better understand the roles laughter played along the Nile in antiquity provides important insights into the character and humanness of the Egyptian people, helping to bridge the many centuries. It is a refreshing view from the crushing formality that seems to permeate much of the sources for the study of ancient Egypt. This legacy of wit and humour allows us all to further appreciate the brilliance of their remarkable and most fascinating civilisation just a little more.

The concluding words of this book will take us far afield from our subject of laughter in the days of the pharaohs to briefly touch upon a few aspects of the repeated use of things ancient Egyptian in contemporary popular humour, an exceedingly small niche in the sphere of "Egyptomania". To begin with, in the film world, there have been several Hollywood comedies that have had a pharaonic-related theme, the best known probably being the slapstick movie *Abbott and Costello Meet the Mummy* (1955), a screwball spoof on the classic horror of a vengeful mummy returning to life and carrying out an curse. More recently, there is the high-camp romp *Under Wraps* (1997), involving children who aid a revived Egyptian mummy in reuniting with his long lost love. On pure cinematic grounds, one could easy argue that these mummies ought to have stayed buried! There have also been numerous amusing short animated films which have had sequences in them utilising ancient Egypt as a setting. There were even lighthearted moments in the recent full-length animated feature *The Prince of Egypt* (1998). It is, however, in the scores of cartoons appearing in newspapers, magazines, books, and in other print media over the last one hundred years or so where the spirit of the world of the pharaohs has had an imaginative and creative impact (fig. 147). Various Egyptian adventures have been chronicled in such famous comic-strips as Flash Gordon, Tarzan, Tintin, Mickey Mouse, Donald Duck, Papyrus, Ramesses, and others. The mummy has also been the subject of extensive

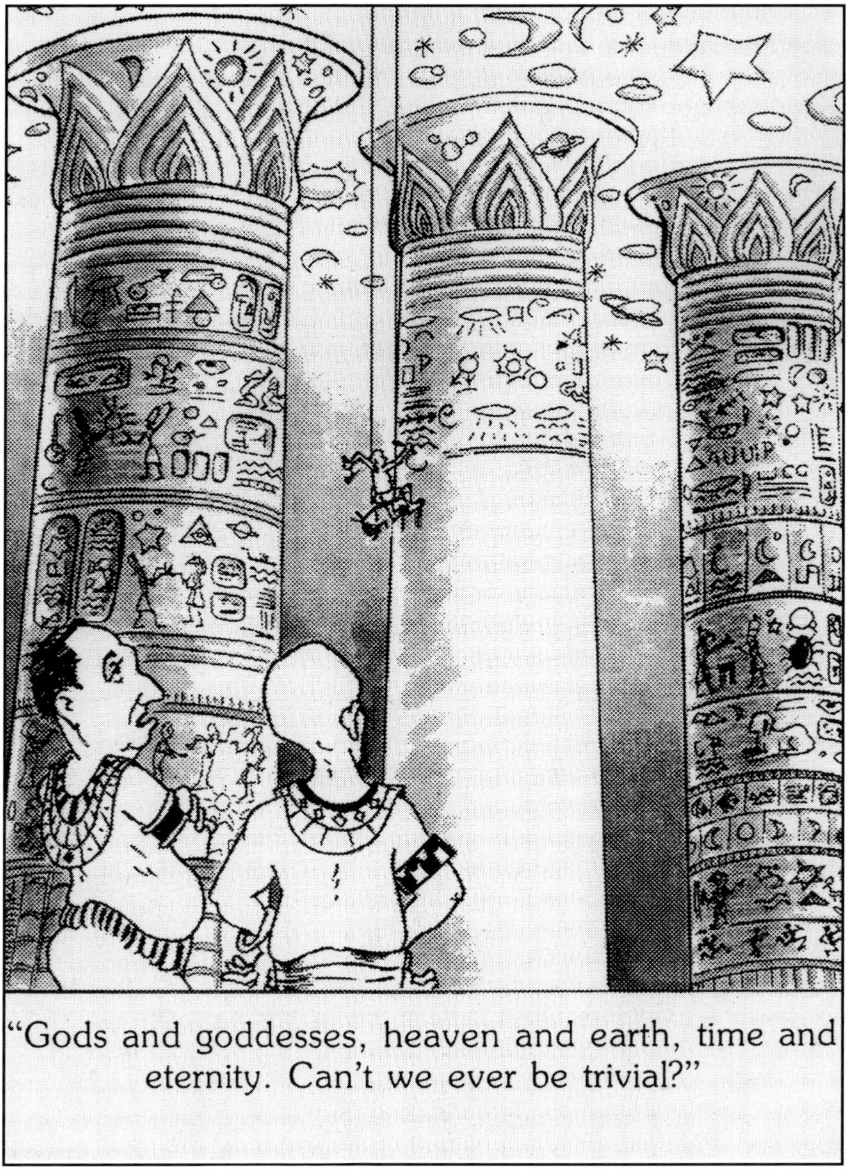

"Gods and goddesses, heaven and earth, time and eternity. Can't we ever be trivial?"

Fig. 147. A humorous cartoon set in ancient Egypt. From Pyramids and Puns *by Everett A. Blackman and Mark Bell.*

coverage in comic-books. Ancient Egypt in comics was the focus of an intriguing museum exhibition held in several French venues between 1998 and 2000 which was entitled, "Toutan 'BD' – L'Égypte dans la bande dessinée", with its informative accompanying catalogue, edited by Thierry Groensteen, of the same title. Humour, horror, mystery, and fantasy have been central motifs in many of these cleverly written and wittily illustrated cartoons. In the end, it is good to know that laughter is still linked with ancient Egyptian civilisation, even when a perceived "otherness" or a misunderstanding of their society makes them the butt of undeserved jokes. Nevertheless, I would like to imagine that ancient Egyptians in the blessed afterlife are joining us in smiling at some of them.

Notes

1 The Egyptian Wit: A Literary Sense of Humour

1. Wilson 1956, 146-153 and 265-267; Ward 1965, 103-116; van de Walle 1969, 3-5 and 7-15; Guglielmi 1979a; Guglielmi 1979b; Guglielmi 1980a; van de Walle 1980, 74-75; Assmann 1982; Brunner-Traut 1984b, 490; Guglielmi 1986; Guglielmi 1992; Meltzer 1992; Loprieno 2000.
2. van de Walle 1969, 9; Guglielmi 1979b, 81-82; Wente 1990, 173; Guglielmi 1992, 170-171 note 18; McDowell 1999, 31-32; Parkinson 1999a, 160.
3. Also McDowell 1999, 31 "a jokey letter."
4. Guglielmi 1979a, 199 note 70; Wente 1990, 149.
5. Wente 1990, 85; Parkinson 1991, 93.
6. Pritchard 1955, 475-479; Wente 1990, 98-100. For other examples in this literary genre, see McDowell 1999, 143-147.
7. Wilson 1956, 265-266; van de Walle 1969, 10 and 12-13; Guglielmi 1979b, 73 and 77; Brunner-Traut 1984b, 490; Guglielmi 1992, 167 and 171 note 21.
8. Brunner-Traut 1980, 339.
9. Wente 1990, 103.
10. Wente 1990, 110 note 14 states that this is possibly advice in love-making. For a discussion on the humorous erotic metaphors used in this episode of *The Satirical Letter*, see Guglielmi 1992, 167.
11. Wente 1990, 108.
12. Wente 1990, 109. See Guglielmi 1979b, 77.
13. Lichtheim 1973, 27. See Fischer 1987, 23.
14. Hayes 1942, 23 no. 78; Guglielmi 1992, 163.
15. Guglielmi 1992, 163.
16. CG 20506; Guglielmi 1979a, 188; Guglielmi 1979b, 79.
17. van de Walle 1969, 3-4 and 21 with note 77; Meltzer 1992, 326; Parkinson 1999a, 80-87.
18. van de Walle 1969, 16-17; Guglielmi 1984b; Meltzer 1992, 327.
19. Lichtheim 1973, 103-104. Also see Pritchard 1955, 414-418; Simpson 1973, 180-192; Parkinson 1997, 212-234.
20. Pritchard 1955, 18-22; Lichtheim 1973, 222-235; Simpson 1973, 57-74; Parkinson 1997, 21-53.
21. van de Walle 1969, 7; van de Walle 1980, 74.
22. Wilson 1956, 148-149; Meltzer 1992, 327; Parkinson 1997, 51 note 72.
23. Lichtheim 1973, 232.
24. Guglielmi 1992, 173 note 43. For further discussion of the humorous touches in *Sinuhe*, see Guglielmi 1979b, 73; Guglielmi 1986, 1290 notes 23 and 27; Guglielmi 1992, 166-167.
25. Lichtheim 1973, 233.
26. Lichtheim 1973, 215-222; Simpson 1973, 15-30; Parkinson 1997, 102-127.
27. Parkinson 1997, 113.
28. Wilson 1956, 149; Brunner-Traut 1980, 339; Meltzer 1992, 327.
29. Lichtheim 1973, 211-215; Simpson 1973, 50-56; Parkinson 1997, 89-101.
30. van de Walle 1969, 7-8; Meltzer 1992, 327; Foster 1995, 2465. For further discussion,

see Parkinson 1997, 101 note 30.

31. Pritchard 1955, 231-232; Simpson 1973, 77-80.
32. Pritchard 1955, 231; Meltzer 1992, 327 with references.
33. Pritchard 1955, 22-23; Simpson 1973, 81-84.
34. Guglielmi 1992, 159-160.
35. Pritchard 1955, 25-29; Simpson 1973, 142-155; Lichtheim 1976, 224-230.
36. Wilson 1956, 289-292; Guglielmi 1984b, 1170; Guglielmi 1992, 160 with references; Satzinger 1997. It has also been suggested that *The Report of Wenamun* is an imaginative and humorous literary reworking of an actual report, see Lichtheim 1976, 197.
37. Lichtheim 1976, 197 and 224.
38. Pritchard 1955, 12-14.
39. Wilson 1956, 267; van de Walle 1980, 75.
40. Pritchard 1955, 14-17; Simpson 1973, 108-126; Lichtheim 1976, 214-223.
41. Wilson 1956, 266-267; van de Walle 1969, 5 and 14-15; Guglielmi 1979b, 73-74 and 76; Brunner-Traut 1980, 339; van de Walle 1980, 75; Guglielmi 1984b, 1170; van Dijk 1994, 392.
42. Miosi 1979; Guglielmi 1986, 1288 with note 28.
43. Lichtheim 1976, 221.
44. Pritchard 1955, 15; Miosi 1979, 78; Guglielmi 1986, 1288 with note 28; Roberts 1995, 102.
45. Lichtheim 1976, 222.
46. Lichtheim 1980, 125-138.
47. van de Walle 1969, 14; Osing 1980, 181; Guglielmi 1984b, 1170 with note 38; Meltzer 1992, 327. For an English translation of *King Amasis and the Skipper*, see Maspero 1915, 280-284.
48. Herodotus (II, 174).
49. van de Walle 1969, 11-12; Lichtheim 1973, 184; Brunner-Traut 1980, 338-339; van de Walle 1980, 74; Brunner-Traut 1984b, 490; Guglielmi 1984b, 1170; Hoch 1991/1992, 88-89; Guglielmi 1992, 164-166; Meltzer 1992, 326.
50. Pritchard 1955, 432-434; Lichtheim 1973, 184-192; Simpson 1973, 329-336; Hoch 1991/1992, 89-100; Parkinson 1991, 72-76; Parkinson 1997, 273-283. *The Teaching of Khety* was the most widely-copied literary text at the village of Deir el Medina, making it a "best-seller." See McDowell 1999, 131-132.
51. Parkinson 1997, 275-276 and 278-279.
52. Caminos 1954; Lichtheim 1973, 167-175; Simpson 1973, 343-347.
53. Caminos 1954, 169.
54. Caminos 1954, 51.
55. Lichtheim 1980, 160; Brunner-Traut 1984b, 490; Guglielmi 1992, 160 and 172 note 34; Meltzer 1992, 327.
56. Lichtheim 1980, 159-184.

2 Smiling for Eternity: Humour in Tomb-chapel and Temple Decoration

1. James 1984, 100ff; Martin 1991; Schulz and Seidel 1998, 78-93, 118-131 and 248-269.
2. Ward 1968; van de Walle 1969, 6-7 and 16-17; Guglielmi 1973; Guglielmi 1979a; Guglielmi 1992.
3. Fischer 1959a, 250-254; Guglielmi 1979a, 184 with note 18; Houlihan 1996, 105-108 and 209-210. On the other hand, some authorities, seemingly unable to suspend all

seriousness, expressly deny the humorous intent behind these figures. They view them as imbued with deep symbolic meaning associated with the resurrection of the deceased.

4. Houlihan 1997.
5. Houlihan 1996, 96 fig. 71; Smith 1998, 42 fig. 73; *Egyptian Art* 1999, 200-201.
6. For more on the merry antics of pet monkeys in ancient Egypt, see Vandier d'Abbadie 1964; Vandier d'Abbadie 1965; Vandier d'Abbadie 1966. Playful images of monkeys continued to be produced in Egypt down to Graeco-Roman times. See Boutantin 1999.
7. Houlihan 1996, 106 note 19; *Egyptian Art* 1999, 405.
8. James 1984, 254-255 fig. 27.
9. Mekhitarian 1991; Malek 1993, 57-64.
10. Fischer 1977b, 175-176.
11. van de Walle 1969, 6-7; Guglielmi 1973; Guglielmi 1984a with all the principal references.
12. Guglielmi 1979a, 187-188 with note 31. In wisdom literature, there is praise for those who do not use coarse language. See Caminos 1954, 421 and 425; Lichtheim 1976, 174.
13. Montet 1925, 67-68; Guglielmi 1979a, 187 with note 32; Kadish 1979, 211 note 30. I am also grateful to Dr. Henry G. Fischer for his comments on the translation of this text. He wonders, however, whether the word in question isn't more like the French *emmerdeur.*
14. Montet 1925, 82 and 203-204; Parkinson 1995, 67.
15. Guglielmi 1979a, 187.
16. Guglielmi 1979a, 188.
17. Guglielmi 1979a, 188 with note 45.
18. Badawy 1965, 189-194; van de Walle 1969, 16; Guglielmi 1979a, 184-185; Brunner-Traut 1980, 338; Guglielmi 1984b, 1169-1170; Fischer 1987, 22-24; Guglielmi 1992, 158-159 and 160-161.
19. Dasen 1993, 114-118, 122-126, 148 and 156-157.
20. Davies 1905, 18; Guglielmi 1979a, 185; Brunner-Traut 1980, 338; Fischer 1987, 23; Dasen 1993, 147. For some apparently mocking nicknames dating from the reign of Amenhotpe III, see Millet 1988.
21. Lichtheim 1976, 160. See Guglielmi 1980a, 74; Guglielmi 1992, 159; Dasen 1993, 150.
22. Guglielmi 1977 with references.
23. Terrace and Fischer, 1970, 61; Guglielmi 1977, 243. These exclamations were studied by Montet 1925, 81-83.
24. Ward 1968, 31-32; Ward 1970, 185.
25. Pritchard 1955, 469; van de Walle 1969, 6; Manniche 1991, 20; Schulz and Seidel 1998, 89-90.
26. Ward 1977, who also comments on its humour; Parkinson 1991, 114-116.
27. This translation follows the suggestion made by Dr. Maarten J. Raven of the Rijksmuseum van Oudheden, Leiden. I am also grateful to him for his remarks on the humorous aspects of the stela. The reading of the text differs from what is usually proposed. See Ward 1977, 64; Parkinson 1991, 116. I would also like to thank Dr. R.B. Parkinson for his kind comments. He thinks Raven's view is very plausible but, on the whole, still prefers the earlier rendering.
28. Blackman 1915a, 17-19; Fischer 1959c, 249-251; Badawy 1965, 194-196; Guglielmi 1979a, 195-196. Also see the curious description of an Egyptian herdsman in

Kanawati 1983, 18. For more on emaciation amongst menial workers and the inhabitants of the Nile Valley margins, see *Egyptian Art* 1999, 360 and 390.

29. Guglielmi 1979a, 195-196.
30. van de Walle 1969, 16-17; Brunner-Traut 1980, 338; Silverman 1982, 277; Guglielmi 1984b, 1169-1170. For some examples and a brief discussion, see Fischer 1965, 175; Wildung 1996, 150-151 and 154; Page-Gasser and Wiese 1997, 140-141.
31. Blackman 1915b, 31; Guglielmi 1979a, 185-186; Morenz 1999, 261-262.
32. Blackman 1914, 29; Parkinson 1991, 82.
33 Blackman 1914, 26-27; Parkinson 1991, 81.
34. Davies 1920a, 15; Wreszinski 1923, pl. 221; Parkinson 1991, 82.
35. Davies 1920a, 15; Wreszinski 1923, pl. 221; Guglielmi 1979a, 190 with note 51; but following Parkinson 1991, 82.
36. Davies 1920a, 15-16; Wreszinski 1923, pl. 221; Guglielmi 1979a, 191; Parkinson 1991, 82.
37. Tylor and Griffith 1894, 14; Guglielmi 1979a, 188; James 1984, 123; Guglielmi 1992, 162.
38. Tylor and Griffith 1894, 14; Guglielmi 1979a, 195 with note 69; James 1984, 124. My interpretation of this vignette follows that of Guglielmi.
39. Tylor and Griffith 1894, 13; James 1984, 109.
40. Mekhitarian 1978, 72-95.
41. Smith 1998, 239-242 with references; Schulz and Seidel 1998, 282-283.
42. Wreszinski 1923, pl. 422; Schneider and Raven 1981, 96. I am grateful to Dr. Maarten J. Raven for his comments on the translation of this text.
43. Lichtheim 1976, 137.
44. Pinch 1995, 368-369.
45. Tylor and Griffith 1894, 25; Guglielmi 1979a, 186.
46. Säve-Söderbergh 1957, 18; Ward 1968, 31; van de Walle 1969, 7; Guglielmi 1979a, 189-190.
47. Humour may also come into play in another vignette in Intef's tomb-chapel relating to wine-making; see Guglielmi 1979a, 193-194.
48. Davies 1917, 237; Davies 1920b, 31-32. Dr. Waltraud Guglielmi has called this tomb one of the most humorous of the entire New Kingdom. See Guglielmi 1979a, 199 note 58; Guglielmi 1992, 172 note 30.
49. Needless to say, I do not agree with those who would view this scene as depicting various occupational injuries and their treatment. My interpretation follows Davies 1920b, 31-32; Davies 1927; Wilkinson and Hill 1983, 47-48; McDowell 1999, 214 fig. 26; among others.
50. Ipuy's tomb-chapel is fully published in Davies 1927. Also see Wreszinski 1923, pls. 363-370; Wilkinson and Hill 1983, 146-151; Smith 1998, 218-221. There could possibly be an element of religious parody in a scene depicting the opening of the mouth ceremony on a coffin in a carpenter's shop. See Guglielmi 1979a, 192-193; Guglielmi 1992, 162-163.
51. Wreszinski 1923, pl. 112; Guglielmi 1979a, 184.
52. See, for example, Wreszinski 1923; Davies 1927; Wilkinson and Hill 1983; Mekhitarian 1978.
53. Badawy 1965, 195-196; van de Walle 1969, 16; Terrace and Fischer 1970, 101-103; Fischer 1987, 24-25; Schulz and Seidel 1998, 184-188.
54. Wilson 1956, 176; Ward 1968, 31; Ward 1970, 185; Silverman 1982, 278; Meltzer 1992, 326.
55. Wilson 1956, 265 with note 62; Wenig 1969, 180 and pl. 24; Guglielmi 1979a, 200

note 74; Guglielmi 1992, 160.

56. Silverman 1982, 278. See, for example, Wilkinson and Hill 1983, 26-27, 104, 108, 125 and 127; Smith 1998, 147 fig. 255

57. Pritchard 1955, 477; Wilson 1956, 261; van de Walle 1969, 10 with note 36; Wente 1990, 108; Guglielmi 1992, 171 note 21.

3 Humorous Drawings on Papyri and Ostraca

1. Vandier d'Abbadie 1946, 68-80; Brunner-Traut 1955, 18-20; Curto 1965; Brunner-Traut 1975a, 798-800; Omlin 1973; Brunner-Traut 1984a, 2-6; Smith 1998, 222-223, 229-231.
2. Smith 1998, 230.
3. Bierbrier 1982; Romer 1984; Lesko 1994; McDowell 1999.
4. McDowell 1999, 4.
5. van de Walle 1969, 17-20; Assmann 1993, 35-39.
6. Brunner-Traut 1975a, 798-799; Brunner-Traut 1979, 14-15.
7. Frankfort and Pendlebury 1933, pl. 31; Brunner-Traut 1955, pls. 1-2; Fischer 1959a, 252 with note 52; Björkman 1971, 44-47; Samson 1972, 37-40; Silverman 1982, 280-281.
8. Frankfort and Pendlebury 1933, 99; Wilson 1956, 220 with note 24; Brunner-Traut 1984b, 489.
9. Brunton and Engelbach 1927, pl. 26; Vandier d'Abbadie 1946, 73 and 75.
10. Curto 1965, fig. 12; Omlin 1973, pl. 20(a); James 1985, 2-3 and 60-61.
11. Keimer 1941, 6 note 3. This damaged scene has also been previously described, presumably for euphemistic reasons, in terms of the lion being engaged in the rites of mummification on the creature lying down. See James 1985, 61; followed by Houlihan 1996, 216.
12. Parkinson 1999b.
13. With thanks to Dr. R.B. Parkinson for information concerning this portion of the papyrus, and for checking details on these fragments for me.
14. Curto 1965, fig. 13; Terrace and Fischer 1970, 150-151; Omlin 1973, pl. 20(b).
15. Brunner-Traut 1955, pl.3; Curto 1965, figs. 10-11; and fully in Omlin 1973. On its dating, see the remark of van Dijk 1994, 392 note 33.
16. See also Vandier d'Abbadie 1937, pl. 92; Omlin 1973, 23.
17. Omlin 1973, 31; Malek 1993, 119.
18. The most recent comprehensive survey of the subject is still Peterson 1973, which includes an extensive bibliography. For the principal literature on figure ostraca, also see Brunner-Traut 1975b, 811-813. To which the following references may now be added, Peck and Ross 1978; Brunner-Traut 1979; Page 1983; Gasse 1986.
19. Peterson 1973, 35.
20. Vandier d'Abbadie 1946, 119. Also see the appealing scenario outlined by Malek 1993, 114-116. The assertion that the illustrations of animals acting as human on papyri and ostraca were produced by schoolboys is unconvincing. See del Francia 1985.
21. Brunner-Traut 1979, 17-18.
22. The translation is that of the Oriental Institute Museum, The University of Chicago. Also see Brunner-Traut 1979, 17.
23. Keimer 1941, 3 no. 11; Vandier d'Abbadie 1946, 12-21, 74-76; Peterson 1973, 97-98; Brunner-Traut 1979, 50-51; Dulos 1981, 258-259; Strouhal 1988, 55-58; Bulté 1991,

87-88, 97-102; Houlihan 1997.

24. Houlihan 1991.
25. For a different view on this flake, see Peterson 1973, 81-83. He would link the motif on this figured ostracon to *The Myth of the Eye of the Sun*, but does so, admittedly, on a purely hypothetical basis.
26. Terrace and Fischer 1970, 152; Assmann 1993, 40-41; Smith 1998, 229. For the *The Admonitions of Ipuwer*, see Pritchard 1955, 441-444; Lichtheim 1973, 149-163; Parkinson 1991, 60-61 and 121-122; Parkinson 1997, 166-199.
27. Kessler 1988; Guglielmi 1992, 168-169; Assmann 1993, 44-46; Parkinson 1999a, 171.
28. Vandier d'Abbadie 1946, 79-80; Brunner-Traut 1977a; Brunner-Traut 1979, 14-17; Brunner-Traut 1984a.
29. Brunner-Traut 1979, 14-17; El-Shamy 1980.
30. Vycichl 1983; van Essche 1991, 76-77.
31. Brunner-Traut 1956, 91-92; van de Walle 1969, 19-20; Peterson 1973, 81-83; Assmann 1993, 43-44; Malek 1993, 117-118.
32. Smith 1984. For translations of the fables, see Williams 1956, 19-23; Lichtheim 1980, 156-159.
33. Vandier d'Abbadie 1946, 80 note 1; *Centenaire* 1981, 94-96; Brunner-Traut 1984a, 5; del Francia 1985, 35; Kessler 1988, 186-189; Bulté 1991, 93-94; Assmann 1993, 44-45.
34. Brunner-Traut 1979, 18.
35. Brunner-Traut 1979, 13 fig. 6; Brunner-Traut 1984a, fig. 36; Houlihan 1996, pl. 1.
36. Touny and Wenig 1969, 22-23; Brunner-Traut 1984a, 5-6; *Cleopatra's Egypt* 1988, 246-247; van Essche 1991, 70-71. One wonders whether this piece could in anyway be related to a Ptolemaic Period terracotta statuette recently uncovered at Tell Atrib, ancient Athribis, in the central Delta. This also shows anthropomorphised animals, portraying an armed frog fighting a mouse and each sporting an oversized phallus. See Mysliwiec 1996, 35. For more on whiffs of humour in animal terracottas of the Graeco-Roman Period see, for example, Guglielmi 1992, 169; Boutantin 1999.
37. Brunner-Traut 1984a, 6; del Francia 1985; van Essche 1991, 71-72.
38. Keimer 1941, pl. 5 no 16; Vandier d'Abbadie 1959, pls. 133-134; Badawy 1965, 196-197; Peterson 1973, nos. 18 and 73; Brunner-Traut 1980; Page 1983, no. 30.
39. Peck and Ross 1978, 148; Guglielmi 1992, 169.
40. Parkinson 1999a, 150 fig. 45.
41. Peck and Ross 1978, 106-107; Lilyquist *et al.* 1983/84, 43.
42. Peck and Ross 1978, 151. See also Brunner-Traut 1979, 40-41.
43. Badawy 1965, 195-196; Peck and Ross 1978, 115; Bierbrier 1982, 78-79; Fischer 1987, 24-25; Wildung 1996, 144-145.
44. Peterson 1973, 92, believes that they are not necessarily related.
45. Vandier d'Abbadie 1937, pls. 72-73; Vandier d'Abbadie 1946, 99-100; Vandier d'Abbadie 1959, pl. 142; Peck and Ross 1978, 104; Brunner-Traut 1979, 6 fig. 3; Dulos 1981, 262.
46. Davies 1917, 236 note 1; Forman and Kischkewitz 1972, no. 4; Peck and Ross 1978, 55 pl. 8; Guglielmi 1992, 168.
47. Davies 1917, 236 note 1; Forman and Kischkewitz 1972, no. 7; Peck and Ross 1978, 158-159; Romer 1984, 95-96; Guglielmi 1992, 173 note 46.
48. Daressy 1901; Peterson 1973, 11-12.

4 Some Humorous Sexual Situations

1. Pritchard 1955, 14-17; Simpson 1973, 108-126; Lichtheim 1976, 214-223.
2. Wilson 1956, 266; Guglielmi 1980b, 907; Manniche 1987, 53; Robins 1988, 69; Roberts 1995, 58-61; Montserrat 1996, 168.
3. Ward 1970, 185.
4. Manniche 1987, 57; Parkinson 1991, 120-121; Parkinson 1995, 70-74.
5. Lichtheim 1976, 219.
6. Manniche 1977, 22-23; Manniche 1987, 54; Roberts 1995, 98.
7. Manniche 1987, 36-51; Robins 1988; Robins 1996; O'Connor 1996. However, there is a unique Middle Kingdom hieroglyph representing a couple having sexual intercourse on a bed. See Manniche 1987, 35 fig. 21. On the other hand, the reproductive cycle of the animal world is commonly encountered in certain compositions on temple and tomb-chapel walls. See Houlihan 1996.
8. Omlin 1973, pl. 28(b); Manniche 1987, 31 fig. 18; Parkinson 1999a, 170 fig. 55. As an aside, we may note that the ancient Egyptians believed earthquakes to be the laughter of Geb. See Wilson 1956, 150; Guglielmi 1980a, 69 note 2.
9. Montserrat 1996, 49 fig. 6; Schulz and Seidel 1998, 310-311. For an earlier example of this scene, see Manniche 1987, 58 fig. 51.
10. Manniche 1987, 72-73; Parkinson 1991, 54-56; Parkinson 1995, 71-74; Parkinson 1997, 288-289.
11. Parkinson 1991, 55.
12. van de Walle 1969, 14; Brunner-Traut 1980, 339; van de Walle 1980, 74; Guglielmi 1984b, 1170 with note 38; van Dijk 1994, 391-393; Foster 1995, 2466; Parkinson 1995, 75.
13. Lichtheim 1973, 215-222; Simpson 1973, 15-30; Manniche 1987, 60-62 and 71-72; Parkinson 1997, 102-127. For more on these skimpy dresses, made of beaded netting, see *Egyptian Art* 1999, 306-307.
14. Fischer 1977a, 161-165. See especially Blackman and Apted 1953, 15 and 23 with pl. 11.
15. Lichtheim 1976, 171. See also Caminos 1954, 395-400.
16. Lichtheim 1980, 159-184; Manniche 1987, 97-99.
17. Pritchard 1955, 467-469; Simpson 1973, 296-306; Lichtheim 1976, 181-193; Manniche 1987, 74-95; Mathieu 1996, e.g., 173-174; DuQuesne 1998, 137-138; McDowell 1999, 152-157. Also see the humorous erotic metaphors used in a Dynasty XIX epistolary schoolboy exercise, *The Satirical Letter*, of Papyrus Anastasi I. See Guglielmi 1992, 167.
18. Fox 1981, 182.
19. Keimer 1941, 4-9; Keimer 1942, 26-27; Omlin 1973; Manniche 1977; Störk 1977; Manniche 1987. Also see the intriguing discussion of Egyptian sexual life in Meskell 1999, 95-106 especially.
20. Manniche 1977, 21 note 57 describes this fragment as coming from the Theban tomb of Puimre (TT 39). However, Manniche 1991, 110 fig. 66 states it is from that of Zeserkarasonb (TT 38).
21. Manniche 1991, 108-119.
22. Lilyquist *et al.* 1983/84, 31; Manniche 1991, 114; Goelet 1993, 21 and 30 note 12; Pinch 1993, 240-241.
23. Romer 1982, 157-160; Wente 1984; Guglielmi 1992, 168; Meltzer 1992, 326; van Dijk 1994, 392.
24. Arnold 1995, 58. For the profiles of Senenmut, see Peck and Ross 1978, 77.

25. Keimer 1941, 4-9; Keimer 1942, 26-27; Manniche 1987; Peck and Ross 1978, 151-153. Another has reportedly has come to light during recent excavations in the Valley of the Kings. See *KMT* 11 no. 1 (2000): 2 and 5.
26. Parkinson 1999a, 171.
27. Omlin 1973; Manniche 1987, 106-115; Kessler 1988.
28. Peck and Ross 1978, 94.
29. Manniche 1987, 109. See Omlin 1973, 67-68; Fox 1981, 182.
30. Davies 1917, 236; Omlin 1973, 72-76 who comments on erotic art as parody; Baines and Málek 1980, 206-208; van de Walle 1980, 76; Brunner-Traut 1984b, 490; Assmann 1993, 39; Goelet 1993, 28-29; Pinch 1993, 220; Pinch 1995, 375.
31. Manniche 1987, 107.
32. Kessler 1988, 189ff; Assmann 1993, 35-37 and 45-46; Roberts 1995, 10-16. The evidence from the Graeco-Roman Period in Egypt is discussed by Montserrat 1996, 163-179.
33. Omlin 1973, 32-36 and 62-63; Silverman 1982, 278; Assmann 1993, 36-37; Parkinson 1999b.
34. Omlin 1973, pl. 29; Manniche 1987, 52 fig. 43; Roberts 1995, 137 fig. 143.
35. Omlin 1973, 34-35 and 61.
36. Omlin 1973, 36 and 62-63 with pl. 21(a).
37. Parkinson 1999a, 173 with note 82. A number of these objects, mostly from the collections of British Museum, London, are illustrated in Manniche 1987.
38. Wilfong 1997, 72-74; Parkinson 1999a, 173.
39. Manniche 1987, 53 fig. 44.
40. Omlin 1973, pls. 30-31; Baines and Málek 1980, 208. For a possible related object from the village, see Pinch 1993, 235 and 241-243.
41. Manniche 1991, 14 and 114 with pl. 1.
42. Omlin 1973, pls. 30-31; Manniche 1987; Martin 1987; *Cleopatra's Egypt* 1988, 241-242; Mysliwiec 1996, 34-35; Montserrat 1996, pls. 24-25; Page-Gasser and Wiese 1997, 320-322. In addition, see Wâsif 1974, 327-328 with pls. 22-23, who interprets a find of a group of erotic statuettes, showing couples drinking together, musicians, and couples in various positions of coitus, as part of a sequence.
43. Guglielmi 1980b, 907.
44. van de Walle 1969, 14; van de Walle 1980, 74-75; Manniche 1987, 19-20; Meltzer 1992, 328.
45. Herodotus (II, 126).
46. Herodotus (II, 121).

Glossary

Abydos

Located on the western bank of the Nile in Upper Egypt, religious centre and holy place of pilgrimage for both the living and the dead as the traditional burial place of Osiris.

Amen

Chief deity of the city of Thebes and powerful state god of the New Kingdom in his identification with Re as Amen-Re, the King of the Gods.

Anat

Syro-Palestinian goddess of war.

Astarte

Syro-Palestinian goddess of war.

Aten

The disk of the sun and worshipped as the sole deity by the heretic pharaoh Akhenaten.

Avaris

The Hyksos capital, located in the eastern Nile Delta.

Ba

One of the major components of the human spirit that existed after death, often translated as "soul".

Beni Hasan

Located on the eastern bank of the Nile in Middle Egypt, necropolis with decorated rock-cut tombs of nomarchs of the Middle Kingdom.

Bes

Dwarf-god who served as a protector of pregnant women and the family.

Byblos

Principal Lebanese seaport on the Mediterranean Sea.

Book of Going Forth by Day

New Kingdom illustrated religious text. A collection of prayers and spells mostly written on papyrus and placed in burials to help guide the dead.

Cartouche

Oval-shaped magical symbol in which the name of the pharaoh was written from Dynasty IV onward.

Deir el Bahri

Located on the western bank of Thebes, site of Queen Hatshepsut's famed mortuary temple.

Deir el Medina

Located in the Theban necropolis, site of the artisans' village responsible for the construction and decoration of the royal tombs on the western bank of Thebes.

Demotic

Late form of highly cursive hieroglyphic writing, developed from hieratic. The normal everyday script from the Seventh century BCE onwards, mainly written on papyrus.

Dôm-palm

The fruits (or nuts) of this species of palm *Hyphaene thebaica* were enjoyed by both the living and dead in ancient Egypt, also being a favourite food of monkeys.

Eye of Re
: A daughter of the sun-god Re, a lioness-headed goddess, often identified with Tefnut or Hathor, who fled to Nubia in a rage, eventually returning to Egypt amid much rejoicing.

Elephantine
: City located in southern Upper Egypt, near the present-day city of Aswan.

El Kab
: City located on the eastern bank of the Nile in Upper Egypt, about halfway between Thebes and Elephantine.

Ennead
: A grouping of nine deities.

Faience
: Glazed ceramic, generally blue or green in colour. It was widely in Egypt, especially for amulets and jewellry.

Geb
: Earth-god, personified as male and married to the goddess Nut.

Giza
: Part of the necropolis for the city of Memphis, famous for the three pyramids of Dynasty IV. Near the city of Cairo.

Hathor
: Cow-goddess who served a variety of functions, but important as a goddess of women, of the sky, and associated with love, music and dancing. The daughter/wife of the sun-god Re.

Hieratic
: Cursive form of writing in ancient Egypt, based on hieroglyphs and mostly written on papyrus and ostraca.

Hittites
: Indo-European people who established an empire in northern Anatolia during the Seventeenth century BCE.

Horus
: Sky-god *par excellence* and represented in the form of a falcon, whose earthly manifestation was the reigning pharaoh.

Hyksos
: Name applied to several Western Asiatic groups that ruled Egypt from their capital at Avaris during the Second Intermediate Period.

Isis
: Wife of Osiris and mother of Horus, guardian of the dead.

Karnak
: Modern name for the precinct of the god Amen at Thebes.

Kom el Ahmar (Hierakonpolis)
: City located on the western bank of the Nile in Upper Egypt, about halfway between Thebes and Elephantine. It was the Predynastic capital of Upper Egypt.

l.p.h.
: Abbreviation of "live, prosper and be healthy!"

Luxor
: Temple located about a mile south of the temple of Karnak at Thebes. The site of the modern city of Luxor.

Mastaba
: Arabic word meaning bench, but in Egyptology used as a term for free-standing tombs with sloping sides primarily of the Early Dynastic Period and Old Kingdom.

Maat

Goddess, daughter of Re, personifying order, justice and truth.

Meir

Located on the western bank of the Nile in Middle Egypt, necropolis with decorated rock-cut tombs of nomarchs of the Old and Middle Kingdoms.

Memphis

City located southwest of present-day Cairo. Capital of Egypt during the Old Kingdom.

Min

An ithyphallic god of fertility.

Nag el Madamud

Religious centre located on the eastern bank of the Nile in Upper Egypt. The site is situated about three miles northeast of Karnak.

Necropolis

A large, important Egyptian cemetery associated with a city and used over a long period of time.

Nomarch

The chief official (governor) of an administrative province of Egypt.

Nubia

Area south of the first cataract, region through which African goods reached Egypt.

Nut

Goddess of the sky and wife of Geb.

Osiris

God of vegetation, but best known as king who ruled the netherworld and with whom the deceased person became associated.

Ostraca

Broken pieces of pottery and small, flat chips of limestone used for drawing and writing surfaces. Thousands of ostraca have been found from the New Kingdom.

Papyrus

Sheet of paper-like writing or drawing material made from the tall water-plant *Cyperus papyrus*. Also a scroll of the same material.

Philae

The island of Philae is located in southern Upper Egypt in the region of the first cataract.

Punt

Tropical African land yielding exotic products, probably located around Somalia.

Qadesh

City located strategically on the Orontes River in Syria.

Qubbet el Hawa

Located in southern Upper Egypt, part of the necropolis of the city of Elephantine.

Ramesseum

The mortuary temple of Ramesses II on the western bank of Thebes.

Re

The sun-god.

Re-Harakhty

God with the characteristics of Re and Horus, the rising "reborn" sun on the horizon.

Saqqara

Part of the necropolis for the city of Memphis.

Scarab

Sacred beetle *Scarabaeus sacer*, thought to possess powers of self-creation and rejuvenation. The image of the scarab was extremely popular as an amulet.

Seth

A god of confusion, represented as a fabulous creature and antithesis of Horus.

Sistrum

A ceremonial musical instrument resembling a rattle.

Stela

Upright slab of stone or wood with texts and reliefs or paintings, either commemorative in function or used in tombs.

Tefnut

Goddess of moisture and mother of Geb and Nut

Tell el Amarna

Located in Middle Egypt, site of the capital city founded by the heretic pharaoh Akhenaten for the worship of his god, the Aten.

Thebes

Great city located in Upper Egypt, site of the temples of Karnak and Luxor. At the site of modern Luxor.

Thoth

A lunar god, represented as an ibis or baboon and patron of the scribal profession.

Uraeus

Rearing cobra, a characteristic symbol of royalty.

Valley of the Kings

Located in the Theban necropolis, this ravine was selected for the rock-cut tombs of kings during the New Kingdom.

Valley of the Queens

Located in the Theban necropolis, this ravine was selected for the rock-cut tombs of queens and princes during the New Kingdom.

Bibliography

Arnold, D.

1995. "An Egyptian Bestiary." *Bulletin of The Metropolitan Museum of Art* (New York) 52 no.4 Spring: 1-64.

Assmann, J.

1982. "Parodie." *Lexikon der Ägyptologie*. Vol. 4. W. Helck, E. Otto and W. Westendorf (eds.). Wiesbaden. Cols. 911-912.

1993. "Literatur und Karneval im alten Ägypten." *Karnevaleske Phänomene in antiken und nachantiken Kulturen und Literaturen: Stätten und Formen der Kommunikation im Altertum I*. S. Döpp (ed.). Trier. Pp. 31-57.

Badawy, A.M.

1965. "Le grotesque: Invention égyptienne." *Gazette des beaux-arts* 66 no. 1161: 189-198.

Baines, J. and J. Málek.

1980. *Atlas of Ancient Egypt*. Oxford.

Bierbrier, M.

1982. *The Tomb-Builders of the Pharaohs*. London.

Björkman, G.

1971. *A Selection of the Objects in the Smith Collection of Egyptian Antiquities at the Linköping Museum, Sweden*. Stockholm.

Blackman, A.M.

1914. *The Rock Tombs of Meir*. Vol. 1. London.

1915a. *The Rock Tombs of Meir*. Vol. 2. London.

1915b. *The Rock Tombs of Meir*. Vol. 3. London.

Blackman, A.M. and M.A. Apted.

1953. *The Rock Tombs of Meir*. Vol. 6. London.

Blackman, E. A. and M. Bell.

1988. *Pyramids and Puns: The 1st Book of Egyptian Humor*. Chicago.

Boutantin, C.

1999. "Une figurine caricaturale du Musée du Caire." *Chronique d'Égypte* 74: 161-170.

Brunner-Traut, E.

1955. "Ägyptische Tiermärchen." *Zeitschrift für ägyptische Sprache und Altertumskunde* 80: 12-32.

1956. *Die altägyptischen Scherbenbilder (Bildostraka) der Deutschen Museen und Sammlungen*. Wiesbaden.

1975a. "Bildgeschichte." *Lexikon der Ägyptologie*. Vol. 1. W. Helck, E. Otto and W. Westendorf (eds.). Wiesbaden. Cols. 798-800.

1975b. "Bildostraka." *Lexikon der Ägyptologie*. Vol. 1. W. Helck, E. Otto and W. Westendorf (eds.). Wiesbaden. Cols. 811-813.

1977a. "Fabel." *Lexikon der Ägyptologie*. Vol. 2. W. Helck, E. Otto and W. Westendorf (eds.). Wiesbaden. Cols. 68-74.

1977b. *Tiergeschichten aus dem Pharaonenland*. Mainz.

1979. *Egyptian Artists' Sketches: Figured Ostraka from the Gayer-Anderson Collection in the Fitzwilliam Museum, Cambridge*. Istanbul.

1980. "Karikatur." *Lexikon der Ägyptologie*. Vol. 3. W. Helck, E. Otto and W. Westendorf (eds.). Wiesbaden. Cols. 337-339.

1984a. *Altägyptische Tiergeschichte und Fabel: Gestalt und Strahlkraft*. 7th edn. Darmstadt.

1984b. "Satire." *Lexikon der Ägyptologie*. Vol. 5. W. Helck, E. Otto and W. Westendorf (eds.). Wiesbaden. Cols. 489-491.

Brunton, G. and R. Engelbach.

1927. *Gurob*. London.

Bulté, J.

1991. *Talismans égyptiens d'heureuse maternité: "Faïence" bleu-vert à pois foncés*. Paris.

Caminos, R.A.

1954. *Late-Egyptian Miscellanies*. London.

Capart, J.

1937. *Makit: une histoire de souris au temps des pharaons*. Brussels.

1939. "Humor en wijsheid in het oude Egypte." *Radiobode* (Amsterdam) Kerstnummer: 21-25.

Centenaire de l'Institut Français d'Archéologie Orientale: Musée du Caire 8 Janvier - 8 Février 1981.

1981. (Exhibition catalogue). Cairo and Paris.

Cleopatra's Egypt: Age of the Ptolemies.

1988. (Exhibition catalogue). Brooklyn.

Curto, S.

1965. *La satira nell' antico Egitto*. Turin.

Daressy, G.

1901. *Ostraca (Catalogue général des antiquités égyptiennes du musée du Caire, I)*. Cairo.

Davies, N. de Garis.

1905. *The Rock Tombs of El Amarna*. Vol. 2. London.

1917. "Egyptian Drawings on Limestone Flakes." *Journal of Egyptian Archaeology* 4: 234-240.

1920a. *The Tomb of Antefoker, Vizier of Sesostris I, and of His Wife, Senet (No. 60)*. London.

1920b. "The Work of the Tyus Memorial Fund." *The Egyptian Expedition 1916-1919: Part 2 of the Bulletin of The Metropolitan Museum of Art* (New York) 15 July: 24-33.

1927. *Two Ramesside Tombs at Thebes*. New York.

1933a. "The Work of the Graphic Branch of the Expedition." *The Egyptian Expedition 1931-1932: Part 2 of the Bulletin of The Metropolitan Museum of Art* (New York) 28 April: 23-29.

1933b. *The Tomb of Nefer-hotep at Thebes*. New York.

Dasen, V.

1993. *Dwarfs in Ancient Egypt and Greece*. Oxford.

del Francia, L.

1985. "Scènes d'animaux personnifiés dans l'Égypte pharaonique et copte. À propos d'une peinture de Baouit." *Acts of the Second International Congress of Coptic Study*. T. Orlandi and F. Wisse (eds.). Rome. Pp. 31-57.

Dulos, C.

1981. "Ostraca." *Un siècle de fouilles françaises en Égypte 1880-1980: À l'occasion du centenaire de l'école du Caire (IFAO)*. (Exhibition catalogue). Paris and Cairo. Pp. 256-263.

DuQuesne, T.

1998. Review of Mathieu 1996. *Discussions in Egyptology* 42: 135-140.

Egyptian Art in the Age of the Pyramids.

1999. (Exhibition catalogue). New York.

El-Shamy, H.M.

1980. *Folktales of Egypt*. Chicago and London.

Fischer, H.G.

1959a. "A Scribe of the Army in a Saqqara Mastaba of the Early Fifth Dynasty." *Journal of Near Eastern Studies* 18 no. 4: 233-272.

1959b. "A Foreman of Stoneworkers and His Family." *Bulletin of The Metropolitan Museum of Art* (New York) 17 no.6: 145-153.

1959c. "An Example of Memphite Influence in a Theban Stela of the Eleventh Dynasty." *Artibus Asiae* 22: 240-252.

1965. "Anatomy in Egyptian Art." *Apollo* 82: 169-175.

1977a. "Some Iconographic and Literary Comparisons." *Fragen an die altägyptische Literatur: Studien zum Gedenken an Eberhard Otto.* J. Assmann, *et al.* (eds.). Wiesbaden. Pp. 155-170.

1977b. "More Ancient Egyptian Names of Dogs and Other Animals." *Metropolitan Museum Journal* 12: 173-178.

1987. "The Ancient Egyptian Attitude Towards the Monstrous." *Monsters and Demons in the Ancient and Medieval Worlds: Papers Presented in Honor of Edith Porada.* A.E. Farkas, *et al.* (eds.). Mainz. Pp. 13-26.

Forman, W. and H. Kischkewitz.

1972. *Egyptian Drawings.* London and New York.

Foster, B.R.

1995. "Humor and Wit in the Ancient Near East." *Civilizations of the Ancient Near East.* Vol. 4. J.M. Sasson (ed.). New York and London. Pp. 2459-2469.

Fox, M.V.

1981. "'Love' in the Love Songs." *Journal of Egyptian Archaeology* 67: 181-182.

Frankfort, H. and J. Pendlebury.

1933. *The City of Akhenaten.* Vol. 2. London.

Gasse, A.

1986. *Catalogue des ostraca figurés de Deir el-Médineh (Nos. 3100-3372).* Fasc. 5. Cairo.

Goelet, O.

1993. "Nudity in Ancient Egypt." *Source: Notes in the History of Art* 12 no. 2: 20-31.

Groensteen, T. (ed.).

1998. *L'Égypte dans la bande dessinée.* (Exhibition catalogue). Angoulême.

Guglielmi, G.

1973. *Reden, Rufe und Lieder auf altägyptischen Darstellungen der Landwirtschaft, Viehzucht, des Fisch- und Vogelfangs vom Mittleren Reich bis zur Spätzeit.* Bonn.

1977. "Fischerstechen." *Lexikon der Ägyptologie.* Vol. 2. W. Helck, E. Otto and W. Westendorf (eds.). Wiesbaden. Cols. 242-243.

1979a. "Humor in Wort und Bild auf altägyptischen Grabdarstellungen." *Wort und Bild: Symposion des Fachbereichs Altertums- und Kulturwissenschaften zum 500jährigen Jubiläum der Eberhard-Karls-Universität Tübingen 1977.* H. Brunner, *et al.* (eds.). Munich. Pp. 181-200.

1979b. "Probleme bei der Anwendung der Begriffe 'Komik', 'Ironie' und 'Humor' auf die altägyptische Literatur." *Göttinger Miszellen* 36: 69-85.

1980a. "Lachen und Weinen in Ethik, Kult und Mythos der Ägypter." *Chronique d'Égypte* 55: 69-86.

1980b. "Lachen." *Lexikon der Ägyptologie.* Vol. 3. W. Helck, E. Otto and W. Westendorf (eds.). Wiesbaden. Cols. 907-908.

1984a. "Reden und Rufe." *Lexikon der Ägyptologie.* Vol. 5. W. Helck, E. Otto and W. Westendorf (eds.). Wiesbaden. Cols. 193-195.

1984b. "Spott." *Lexikon der Ägyptologie.* Vol. 5. W. Helck, E. Otto and W. Westendorf (eds.). Wiesbaden. Cols. 1169-1173.

1986. "Wortspiel." *Lexikon der Ägyptologie.* Vol. 6. W. Helck, E. Otto and W. Westendorf (eds.). Wiesbaden. Cols. 1287-1291.

1992. "Das Lachen der Götter und Menschen am Nil: Die religiöse und alltagsweltliche

Bedeutung des Lachens im alten Ägypten." *Vom Lachen: Einem Phänomen auf der Spur.* T. Vogel (ed.). Tübingen. Pp. 154-173.

Hassan, S.

1936. *Excavations at Gîza 2: 1930-1931.* Cairo.

Hayes, W.C.

1942. *Ostraka and Name Stones from the Tomb of Sen-mut (No. 71) at Thebes.* New York.

Hoch, J.E.

1991/1992. "The Teaching of Dua-Kheti: A New Look at the Satire of Trades." *The Journal of the Society for the Study of Egyptian Antiquities* 21/22: 88-100.

Houlihan, P.F.

1986. *The Birds of Ancient Egypt.* Warminster. (New edition 1988: Cairo).

1991. "A Figured Ostracon with a Humorous Scene of Judgment." *Muse: Annual of the Museum of Art and Archaeology, University of Missouri – Columbia* 25: 30-35.

1996. *The Animal World of the Pharaohs.* London and New York.

1997. "Harvesters or Monkey Business?" *Göttinger Miszellen* 157: 31-47.

2001. "Birds, Beasts, and Bugs in Egyptian Art and Hieroglyphs." *A History of the Animal World in the Ancient Near East.* B. J. Collins (ed.). Leiden. (Forthcoming).

James, T.G.H.

1984. *Pharaoh's People: Scenes from Life in Imperial Egypt.* London.

1985. *Egyptian Painting and Drawing in the British Museum.* London.

Jasnow, R.

2000. "'And Pharaoh Laughed...' Meditations on Humor in Demotic Texts." Paper delivered at the "Eighth International Congress of Egyptologists", Cairo, 28 March - 3 April 2000. *Abstracts of Papers.* Pp. 91-92.

Kadish, G.E.

1979. "The Scatophagous Egyptian." *The Journal of the Society for the Study of Egyptian Antiquities* 9 no. 4: 203-217.

Kanawati, N.

1983. *The Rock Tombs of El-Hawawish.* Vol. 4. Sydney.

Keimer, L.

1941. "Sur un certain nombre d'ostraca figurés, de plaquette sculptées, etc., provenant de la nécropole thébaine et encore inédits." *Études d'égyptologie.* Fasc. 3. Cairo. Pp. 1-25.

1942. "Notes additionelles et corrections adjointes au fascicule III." *Études d'égyptologie.* Fasc. 4. Cairo. Pp. 26-29.

Kessler, D.

1988. "Der Satirisch-erotische Papyrus Turin 55001 und das 'Verbringen des Schönen Tages'." *Studien zur altägyptischen Kultur* 15: 171-196.

Lepsius, K. R.

1842. *Auswahl der wichtigsten Urkunden des ægyptischen Alterthums.* Leipzig.

Lesko, L.H. (ed.).

1994. *Pharaoh's Workers: The Villagers of Deir el Medina.* Ithaca and London.

Lexová, I.

1935. *Ancient Egyptian Dances.* Prague.

Lichtheim, M.

1973. *Ancient Egyptian Literature. Volume 1: The Old and Middle Kingdoms.* Berkeley and London.

1976. *Ancient Egyptian Literature. Volume 2: The New Kingdom.* Berkeley and London.

1980. *Ancient Egyptian Literature. Volume 3: The Late Period.* Berkeley and London.

Lilyquist, C., *et al.*

1983/84. "Egyptian Art." *Bulletin of The Metropolitan Museum of Art* (New York) 41 no.3 Winter: 1-56.

Loprieno, A.

2000. "Puns and Word Play in Ancient Egyptian." *Puns and Pundits: Word Play in the Hebrew Bible and Ancient Near Eastern Literature.* S.B. Noegel (ed.). Bethesda, MD. Pp. 3-20

Malek, J.

1993. *The Cat in Ancient Egypt.* London.

Manniche, L.

1977. "Some Aspects of Ancient Egyptian Sexual Life." *Acta Orientalia* 38: 11-23.

1987. *Sexual Life in Ancient Egypt.* London and New York.

1991. *Music and Musicians in Ancient Egypt.* London.

Mariette-Bey, A.

1877. *Deir-el-Bahari.* Leipzig.

Martin, G.T.

1987. "'Erotic' Figurines: The Cairo Museum Material." *Göttinger Miszellen* 96: 71-84.

1991. "Funerary but not Funereal: Reflections on Egyptian Art of the Late Eighteenth Dynasty." *Minerva* 2 no. 2: 28-34.

Maspero, G.

1915. *Popular Stories of Ancient Egypt.* London.

Maspero, J.

1931. *Fouilles exécutées à Baouît.* Fasc. 1. Cairo.

Mathieu, B.

1996. *La poésie amoureuse de l'Égypte ancienne.* Cairo.

McDowell, A.G.

1999. *Village Life in Ancient Egypt: Laundry Lists and Love Songs.* Oxford and New York.

Mekhitarian, A.

1978. *Egyptian Painting.* 2nd edn. New York and Geneva.

1991. "Le chat dans les tombes thébaines privées." *Les divins chats d'Égypte: Un air subtil, un dangereux parfum.* L. Delvaux and E. Warmenbol (eds.). Louvain. Pp. 23-30.

Meltzer, E.S.

1992. "Humor and Wit: Ancient Egypt." *The Anchor Bible Dictionary.* Vol. 3. D.N. Freedman (ed.). New York and London. Pp. 326-328.

Meskell, L.

1999. *Archaeologies of Social Life: Age, Sex, Class* et cetera *in Ancient Egypt.* Oxford and Malden.

Millet, N.B.

1988. "Some Canopic Inscriptions of the Reign of Amenhotep III." *Göttinger Miszellen* 104: 91-93.

Miosi, F.T.

1979. "Horus as a Trickster." *The Journal of the Society for the Study of Egyptian Antiquities* 9 no. 2: 75-78.

Montet, P.

1925. *Scènes de la vie privée dans les tombeaux égyptiens de l'Ancien Empire.* Strasbourg.

Montserrat, D.

1996. *Sex and Society in Græco-Roman Egypt.* London and New York.

Morenz, L.D.

1999. "Humor." *Studien zur altägyptischen Kultur* 27: 261-269.

Moussa, A.M. and H. Altenmüller.

1971. *The Tomb of Nefer and Ka-hay*. Mainz.

Mysliwiec, K.

1996. "In the Ptolemaic Workshops of Athribis." *Egyptian Archaeology* 9: 34-36.

O'Connor, D.

1996. "Sexuality, Statuary and the Afterlife; Scenes in the Tomb-chapel of Pepyankh (Heny the Black). An Interpretive Essay." *Studies in Honor of William Kelly Simpson*. Vol. 2. P. Der Manuelian (ed.). Boston. Pp. 621-633.

Omlin, J.A.

1973. *Der Papyrus 55001 und seine Satirisch-erotischen Zeichnungen und Inschriften*. Turin.

Osing, J.

1980. "Ironie." *Lexikon der Ägyptologie*. Vol. 3. W. Helck, E. Otto and W. Westendorf (eds.). Wiesbaden. Col. 181.

Page, A.

1983. *Ancient Egyptian Figured Ostraca in the Petrie Collection*. Warminster.

Page-Gasser, M. and A.B. Wiese.

1997. *Ägypten-Augenblicke der Ewigkeit: Unbekannte Schätze aus Schweizer Privatbesitz*. (Exhibition catalogue). Mainz.

Paget, R.F.E. and A.A. Pirie.

1898. *The Tomb of Ptah-hetep*. London.

Parkinson, R.B.

1991. *Voices from Ancient Egypt: An Anthology of Middle Kingdom Writings*. London.

1995. "'Homosexual' Desire and Middle Kingdom Literature." *Journal of Egyptian Archaeology* 81: 57-76.

1997. *The Tale of Sinuhe and other Ancient Egyptian Poems, 1940-1640 BC*. Oxford.

1999a. *Cracking Codes: The Rosetta Stone and Decipherment*. (Exhibition catalogue). London.

1999b. "Laughter in the Tomb: Identifying Humour in Ancient Egypt." Paper delivered at the colloquium "Humour in World Art", Warburg Institute, London, 26-27 February 1999.

Peck, W.H. and J.G. Ross.

1978. *Drawings from Ancient Egypt*. London.

Peterson, B.E.J.

1973. "Zeichnungen aus einer Totenstadt: Bildostraka aus Theben-West, ihre Fundplätze, Themata und Zweckbereiche mitsamt einem Katalog der Gayer-Anderson-Sammlung in Stockholm." *Medelhavsmuseet Bulletin* 7-8: 1-141.

Pinch, G.

1993. *Votive Offerings to Hathor*. Oxford.

1995. "Private Life in Ancient Egypt." *Civilizations of the Ancient Near East*. Vol. 1. J.M. Sasson (ed.). New York and London. Pp. 363-381.

Pritchard, J.B. (ed.).

1955. *Ancient Near Eastern Texts Relating to the Old Testament*. 2nd edn. Princeton.

Roberts, A.

1995. *Hathor Rising: The Serpent Power of Ancient Egypt*. Totnes, Devon.

Robins, G.

1988. "Ancient Egyptian Sexuality." *Discussions in Egyptology* 11: 61-72.

1996. "Dress, Undress, and the Representation of Fertility and Potency in New Kingdom Egyptian Art." *Sexuality in Ancient Art*. N.B. Kampen (ed.). Cambridge. Pp. 27-40.

Romer, J.

1982. *Romer's Egypt: A New Light on the Civilization of Ancient Egypt*. London.

1984. *Ancient Lives: Daily Life in Egypt of the Pharaohs*. London.

Saleh, 'Abdel-'Aziz.
1964. "Humorous Representations in Ancient Egyptian Art." *Al-Migallah* 88 April: 33-42 (in Arabic).
Samson, J.
1972. *Amarna: City of Akhenaten and Nefertiti.* London.
Satzinger, H.
1997. "How Good was Tjeker-Ba'l's Egyptian? Mockery at Foreign Diction in the Report of Wenamun." *Lingua Aegyptia* 5: 171-176.
Säve-Söderbergh, T.
1957. *Four Eighteenth Dynasty Tombs.* Oxford.
Schäfer, H.
1916. "Ägyptische Zeichnungen auf Scherben." *Jahrbuch der Königlich preussischen Kunstsammlungen* 37: 23-51.
Schibli, H.S.
1983. "Fragments of a Weasel and Mouse War." *Zeitschrift für Papyrologie und Epigraphik* 53: 1-26.
Schneider, H.D. and M.J. Raven.
1981. *De Egyptische Oudheid.* The Hague.
Schulz, R. and M. Seidel (eds.).
1998. *Egypt: The World of the Pharaohs.* Cologne.
Scott, N.E.
1962. "A Stela and an Ostracon: Two Acquisitions from Deir el Medineh." *Bulletin of The Metropolitan Museum of Art* (New York) 21 no.4: 149-153.
Silverman, D.P.
1982. "Wit and Humor." *Egypt's Golden Age: The Art of Living in the New Kingdom 1558-1085 B.C. Catalogue of the Exhibition.* Boston. Pp. 277-281.
Simpson, W.K. (ed.).
1973. *The Literature of Ancient Egypt: An Anthology of Stories, Instructions, and Poetry.* New edition. New Haven and London.
Singer, C., *et al.* (eds.).
1954. *A History of Technology.* Vol. 1. Oxford.
Smith, M.J.
1984. "Sonnenauge, Demotischer Mythos vom." *Lexikon der Ägyptologie.* Vol. 5. W. Helck, E. Otto and W. Westendorf (eds.). Wiesbaden. Cols. 1082-1087.
Smith, W.S.
1998. *The Art and Architecture of Ancient Egypt.* 3rd edn., revised by W.K. Simpson. New Haven and London.
Störk, L.
1977. "Erotik." *Lexikon der Ägyptologie.* Vol. 2. W. Helck, E. Otto and W. Westendorf (eds.). Wiesbaden. Cols. 4-11.
Strouhal, E.
1988. "Three Figured Ostraka from the Ancient Egyptian Collection of the Náprstek Museum." *Annals of the Náprstek Museum* 15: 47-65.
A Table of Offerings: 17 Years of Acquisitions of Egyptian and Ancient Near Eastern Art by William Kelly Simpson for the Museum of Fine Arts, Boston. 1987. Boston.
Terrace, E.L.B. and H.G. Fischer.
1970. *Treasures of the Cairo Museum: From Predynastic to Roman Times.* (Exhibition catalogue). London.

Touny, A.D. and S. Wenig.
1969. *Sport in Ancient Egypt.* Cairo and Leipzig.
Trokay, M.
1992. "Les représentations d'animaux figurés en attitudes humaines du Proche-Orient ancien et de l'Égypte pharaonique." *L'Atelier de l'orfèvre: Mélanges offerts à Ph. Derchain.* M. Broze and P. Talon (eds.). Louvain. Pp. 157-168.
Tylor, J.J. and F. Ll. Griffith.
1894. *The Tomb of Paheri at El Kab.* London.
van de Walle, B.
1969. *L'Humour dans la littérature et dans l'art de l'ancienne Égypte.* Leiden.
1980. "Humor." *Lexikon der Ägyptologie.* Vol. 3. W. Helck, E. Otto and W. Westendorf (eds.). Wiesbaden. Cols. 73-77.
van Dijk, J.
1994. "The Nocturnal Wanderings of King Neferkare'." *Hommages à Jean Leclant.* Vol. 4. C. Berger, *et al.* (eds.). Cairo. Pp. 387-393.
van Essche, E.
1991. "Le chat dans les fables et les contes: La guerre entre chats et souris, le monde retourné." *Les divins chats d'Égypte: Un air subtil, un dangereux parfum.* L. Delvaux and E. Warmenbol (eds.). Louvain. Pp. 69-83.
Vandier d'Abbadie, J.
1936. *Catalogue des ostraca figurés de Deir el-Médineh (Nos. 2001 à 2255).* Fasc. 1. Cairo.
1937. *Catalogue des ostraca figurés de Deir el-Médineh Nos. 2256 à 2722).* Fasc. 2. Cairo.
1940/41. "Deux nouveaux ostraca figurés." *Annales du Service des Antiquités de l'Égypte* 40: 467-488.
1946. *Catalogue des ostraca figurés de Deir el-Médineh.* Fasc. 3. Cairo.
1959. *Catalogue des ostraca figurés de Deir el-Médineh (Nos. 2734à 3053).* Fasc. 4. Cairo.
1960. "Deux sujets originaux sur ostraca figurés." *Revue d'égyptologie* 12: 83-88.
1964. "Les singes familiers dans l'ancienne Égypte (peintures et bas-reliefs) I. L'Ancien Empire." *Revue d'égyptologie* 16: 146-177.
1965. "Les singes familiers dans l'ancienne Égypte (peintures et bas-reliefs) II. Le Moyen Empire." *Revue d'égyptologie* 17: 177-188.
1966. "Les singes familiers dans l'ancienne Égypte (peintures et bas-reliefs) III. Le Nouvel Empire." *Revue d'égyptologie* 18: 143-201.
Vycichl, W.
1983. "Histoires des chats et de souris: Un problème de la littérature égyptienne." *Bulletin de la société d'égyptologie de Genève* 8: 101-108.
Ward, W.A.
1965. *The Spirit of Ancient Egypt.* Beirut.
1968. "Humor from the Tombs." *Aramco World Magazine* 19 no. 3: 30-33.
1970. Review of van de Walle 1969. *Bibliotheca Orientalis* 27: 185.
1977. "Neferhotep and His Friends: A Glimpse at the Lives of Ordinary Men." *Journal of Egyptian Archaeology* 63: 63-66.
Wâsif, F.M.
1974. "Soundings on the Borders of Ancient Sais." *Oriens Antiquus* 13 no. 4: 327-328.
Wente, E.F.
1984. "Some Graffiti from the Reign of Hatshepsut." *Journal of Near Eastern Studies* 43 no.1: 47-54.
1990. *Letters from Ancient Egypt.* E. S. Meltzer (ed.). Atlanta.
Werbrouck, M.
1932. "Ostraca à figures." *Bulletin des musées royaux d'art et d'histoire* (Brussels) 4: 106-109.

1934. "Ostraca à figures." *Bulletin des musées royaux d'art et d'histoire* (Brussels) 6: 138-140.

1939. "Ostraca à figures." *Bulletin des musées royaux d'art et d'histoire* (Brussels) 11: 41-45.

1953. "Ostraca à figures." *Bulletin des musées royaux d'art et d'histoire* (Brussels) 25: 93-111.

Wilber, D. N.

1960. "The Off-beat in Egyptian Art." *Archaeology Magazine* 13 no. 4: 259-266.

Wild, H.

1953. *Le tombeau de Ti.* Fasc. 2. Cairo.

Wildung, D. (ed.).

1996. *Sudan: Antike Königreiche am Nil.* (Exhibition catalogue). Munich.

Wilfong, T.G.

1997. *Women and Gender in Ancient Egypt: From Prehistory to Late Antiquity.* (Exhibition catalogue). Ann Arbor.

Williams, R.J.

1956. "The Fable in the Ancient Near East." *A Stubborn Faith: Papers Presented to Honor W.A. Irwin.* E.C. Hobbs (ed.). Dallas. Pp. 3-26.

Wilkinson, C.K. and M. Hill.

1983. *Egyptian Wall Paintings: The Metropolitan Museum of Art's Collection of Facsimiles.* New York.

Wilson, J.A.

1956. *The Culture of Ancient Egypt.* Chicago and London.

de Wit, C.

1966. "Ostraca." *Illustrations pour l'éternité: Peintures et dessins égyptiens provenant des collections nationales de Belgique et des Pays-Bas.* (Exhibition catalogue). Brussels. Pp. 27-36.

Wreszinski, W.

1923. *Atlas zur altägyptischen Kulturgeschichte.* Vol. 1. Leipzig.

1927. *Bericht über die photographische Expedition von Kairo bis Wadi Halfa zwecks Abschluß der Materialsammlung für meinen Atlas zur altägyptischen Kulturgeschichte.* Halle.

1935. *Atlas zur altägyptischen Kulturgeschichte.* Vol. 2. Leipzig.

1936. *Atlas zur altägyptischen Kulturgeschichte.* Vol. 3. Leipzig.

Würfel, R.

1952-1953. "Die ägyptische Fabel in Bildkunst und Literatur." *Wissenschaftliche Zeitschrift der Universität Leipzig* 3: 63-77, 153-160.

Index

Page numbers in *italic type* refer to the illustrations

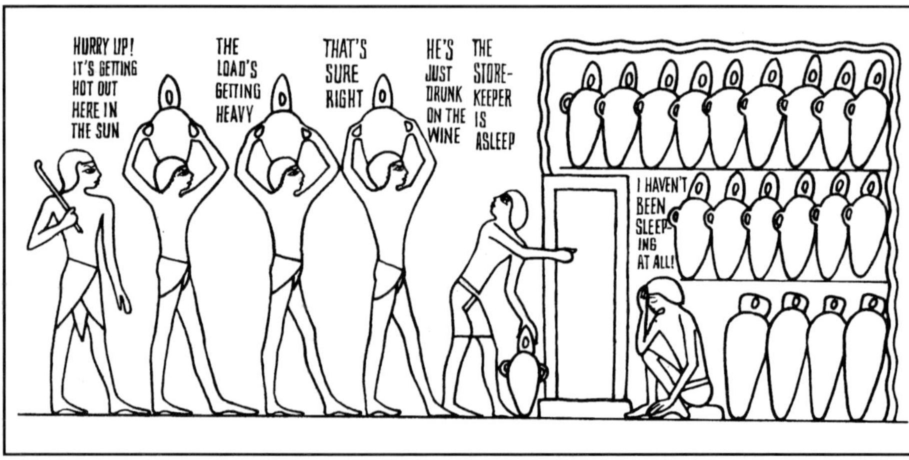
HURRY UP! IT'S GETTING HOT OUT HERE IN THE SUN
THE LOAD'S GETTING HEAVY
THAT'S SURE RIGHT
HE'S JUST DRUNK ON THE WINE
THE STORE-KEEPER IS ASLEEP
I HAVEN'T BEEN SLEEP-ING AT ALL!